PORTUGUESE

in 10 minutes a day®

by Kristine K. Kershul, M.A., University of California, Santa Barbara

Consultant: Rosana do Rio Broom

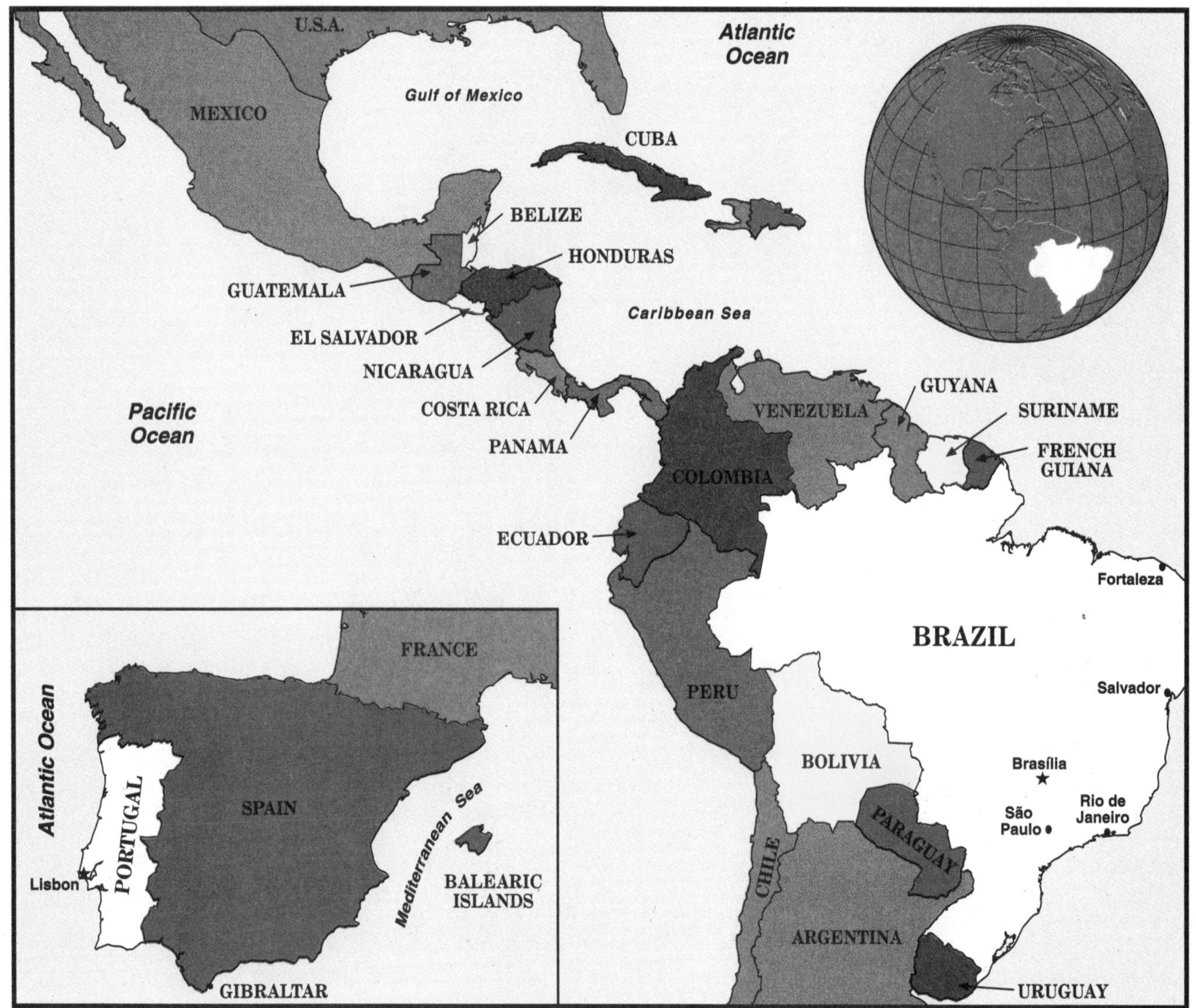

Bilingual Books, Inc.
1719 West Nickerson Street, Seattle, WA 98119
Tel: (206) 284-4211 Fax: (206) 284-3660
www.10minutesaday.com

ISBN-13: 978-0-944502-37-2 ISBN-10: 0-944502-37-7 Third printing, November 2005

Can you say this?

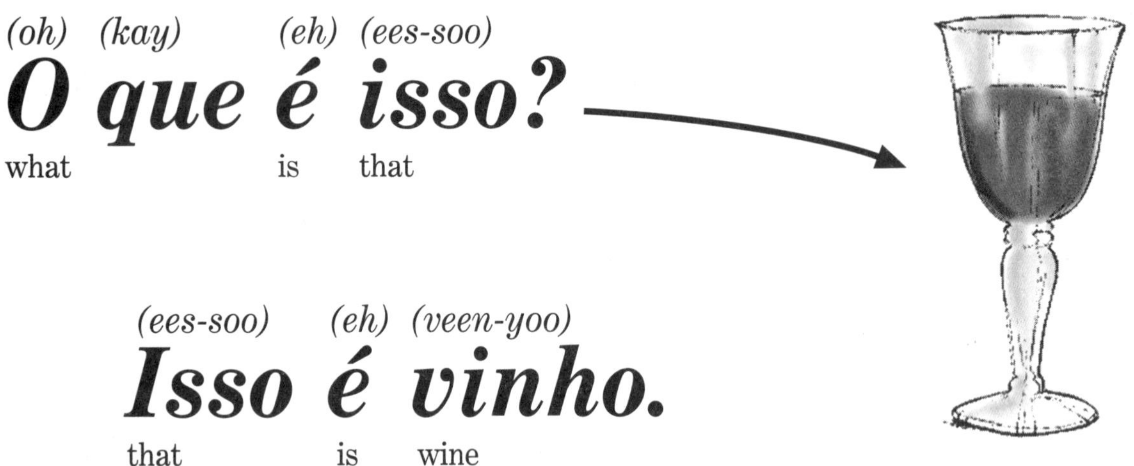
(oh) (kay) (eh) (ees-soo)
O que é isso?
what is that
(ees-soo) (eh) (veen-yoo)
Isso é vinho.
that is wine

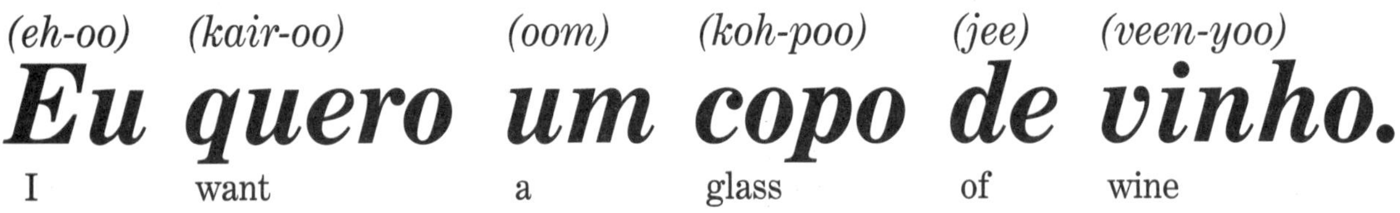
(eh-oo) (kair-oo) (oom) (koh-poo) (jee) (veen-yoo)
Eu quero um copo de vinho.
I want a glass of wine

If you can say this, you can learn to speak Portuguese. You will be able to easily order wine, lunch, theater tickets, pastry, or anything else you wish. You simply ask **"O que é isso?"** *(oh) (kay) (eh) (ees-soo)* and, upon learning what it is, you can order it with **"Eu quero isso"** *(eh-oo) (kair-oo) (ees-soo)*. Sounds easy, doesn't it?

The purpose of this book is to give you an **immediate** speaking ability in Portuguese. Portuguese is spoken not only in Portugal and Brazil, but in Angola, Mozambique and other countries as well. Using the acclaimed *"10 minutes a day®"* methodology, you will acquire a large working vocabulary that will suit your needs, and you will acquire it almost automatically. To aid you, this book offers a unique and easy system of pronunciation above each word which walks you through learning Portuguese.

If you are planning a trip or moving to where Portuguese is spoken, you will be leaps ahead of everyone if you take just a few minutes a day to learn the easy key words that this book offers. Start with Step 1 and don't skip around. Each day work as far as you can comfortably go in those 10 minutes. Don't overdo it. Some days you might want to just review. If you forget a word, you can always look it up in the glossary. Spend your first 10 minutes studying the map on the previous page. And yes, have fun learning your new language.

As you work through the Steps, always use the special features which only this series offers. You have sticky labels and flash cards, free words, puzzles, and quizzes. When you have completed the book, cut out the menu guide and take it along on your trip.

O Alfabeto — 1

(oh) (ahl-fah-beh-too)
O Alfabeto
the alphabet

Throughout this book you will find an easy pronunciation guide above all new words. Refer to this Step whenever you need help, but remember, spend no longer than *10 minutes a day®*.

Many letters in Portuguese are pronounced just as they are in English, at least part of the time!

(b)	*(d)*	*(f)*	*(g)*	*(l)*	*(m)*	*(n)*	*(p)*	*(r)*	*(s)*	*(t)*	*(v)*	*(x)*	*(z)*
b	**d**	**f**	**g**	**l**	**m**	**n**	**p**	**r**	**s**	**t**	**v**	**x**	**z**

Here is a guide to help you learn the sounds of the Portuguese letters which are pronounced somewhat differently. Practice these sounds with the examples given which are mostly first names.

Portuguese letter	English sound	Examples	*Write it here*
a	ah	**Ana** *(ah-nah)*	
ai	eye/i/y	**Jaime** *(zhy-mee)*	
au	*(as in how)* ow	**Paulo** *(pow-loo)*	
(before e and i) **c**	s	**Alice** *(ah-lee-see)*	
(before a, o, u) **c**	k	**Catarina** *(kah-tah-ree-nah)*	Catarina, Catarina
ç	s	**Iguaçu** *(ee-gwah-soo)* waterfall on Brazilian-Argentinian border	
ch	sh	**Chuí** *(shoo-ee)* town on Brazilian-Uruguayan border	
(before e and i) **d**	*(as in jeep)* j	**Diana** *(jee-ah-nah)*	
e	*(as in let)* eh	**Elena** *(eh-leh-nah)*	
(at word end) **e**	ee	**Simone** *(see-moh-nee)*	
ei	*(as in day)* ay	**Reinaldo** *(hay-nahl-doo)*	
er	air	**Fernando** *(fair-nahn-doo)*	
eu	eh-oo	**Eugênio** *(eh-oo-zheh-nee-oo)*	
(before e and i) **g**	zh	**Gina** *(zhee-nah)*	
h	silent	**Haroldo** *(ah-rohl-doo)*	
i	ee	**Cíntia** *(seen-chee-ah)*	
j	zh	**José** *(zhoh-zeh)*	
lh	l-y	**ilha** *(eel-yah)* island	

Letter	Sound	Example	Write it here
nh	*(as in canyon)* n-y	**senhor** *(sehn-yor)* Mr.	
o	oh / oo	**Orlando** *(or-lahn-doo)*	
oi	oy	**oi!** *(oy)* hi	
ou	oh	**Ouro Preto** *(oh-roo)(preh-too)* town, World Cultural Heritage Site	
(before e and i) **qu**	k	**parque** *(par-kay)* park	
(before a and o) **qu**	kw	**quatro** *(kwah-troo)* four	
(initially) **r**	h	**Rosana** *(hoh-zah-nah)*	Rosana, Rosana
rr	r-h	**terra** *(tair-hah)* land	
(between vowels) **s**	z	**Isabel** *(ee-zah-bel)*	
(at word end) **s**	s/sh	**Carlos** *(kar-loosh)*	
(before e and i) **t**	ch	**Vicente** *(vee-sehn-chee)*	
u	oo	**Úrsula** *(oor-soo-lah)*	
(initially and after ai, e, ei, ou, n) **x**	sh	**Alexandre** *(ah-leh-shahn-dree)*	
(at syllable end) **z**	s/sh	**Beatriz** *(beh-ah-trees)*	

Note: In addition to the sounds above, Portuguese has many nasal sounds. Whenever you see a tilde (˜) over a vowel, think nasal!

ã	ahn	**irmã** *(eer-mahn)* sister	
		amanhã *(ah-mahn-yahn)* tomorrow	
ão	*("ow" as in how plus "n")* own	**João** *(zhoh-own)*	
		São Paulo *(sown)(pow-loo)*	
õe	oyn	**cartões** *(kar-toynsh)* cards	
		direções *(jee-reh-soynsh)* directions	

If you were able to pronounce **direções** without hesitating, give yourself a giant pat on the back!

Accents such as ˆ (**ê**) and ´ (**é**) are used to indicate stress, either in the word or even in a sentence. See **Cíntia, Úrsula, Eugênio,** and **José** above.

Sometimes the phonetics may seem to contradict your pronunciation guide. Don't panic! The easiest and best possible phonetics have been chosen for each individual word. Pronounce the phonetics just as you see them. Don't over-analyze them. Speak with a Portuguese accent and, above all, enjoy yourself!

Key Question Words

When you arrive in *(brah-zeel)* **Brasil**, *(por-too-gahl)* **Portugal** or another Portuguese-speaking country, the very first thing you will need to do is ask questions — "Where *(ohn-jee)* (**onde**) [where] is the bus stop?" "*(ohn-jee)* **Onde** [where] can I exchange money?" "*(ohn-jee)* **Onde** [where] is the lavatory?" "*(ohn-jee)* **Onde** is a restaurant?" "*(ohn-jee)* **Onde** do I catch a taxi?" "**Onde** is a good hotel?" "**Onde** is my luggage?" — and the list will go on and on for the entire length of your visit. In Portuguese, there are SEVEN KEY QUESTION WORDS to learn. For example, the seven key question words will help you find out exactly what you are ordering in a restaurant before you order it — and not after the surprise (or shock!) arrives. Notice that only one letter is different in the Portuguese words for "when" and "how much." Don't confuse them! Take a few minutes to practice saying the seven key question words listed below. Then cover the Portuguese with your hand and fill in each of the blanks with the matching Portuguese *(pah-lah-vrah)* **palavra** [word].

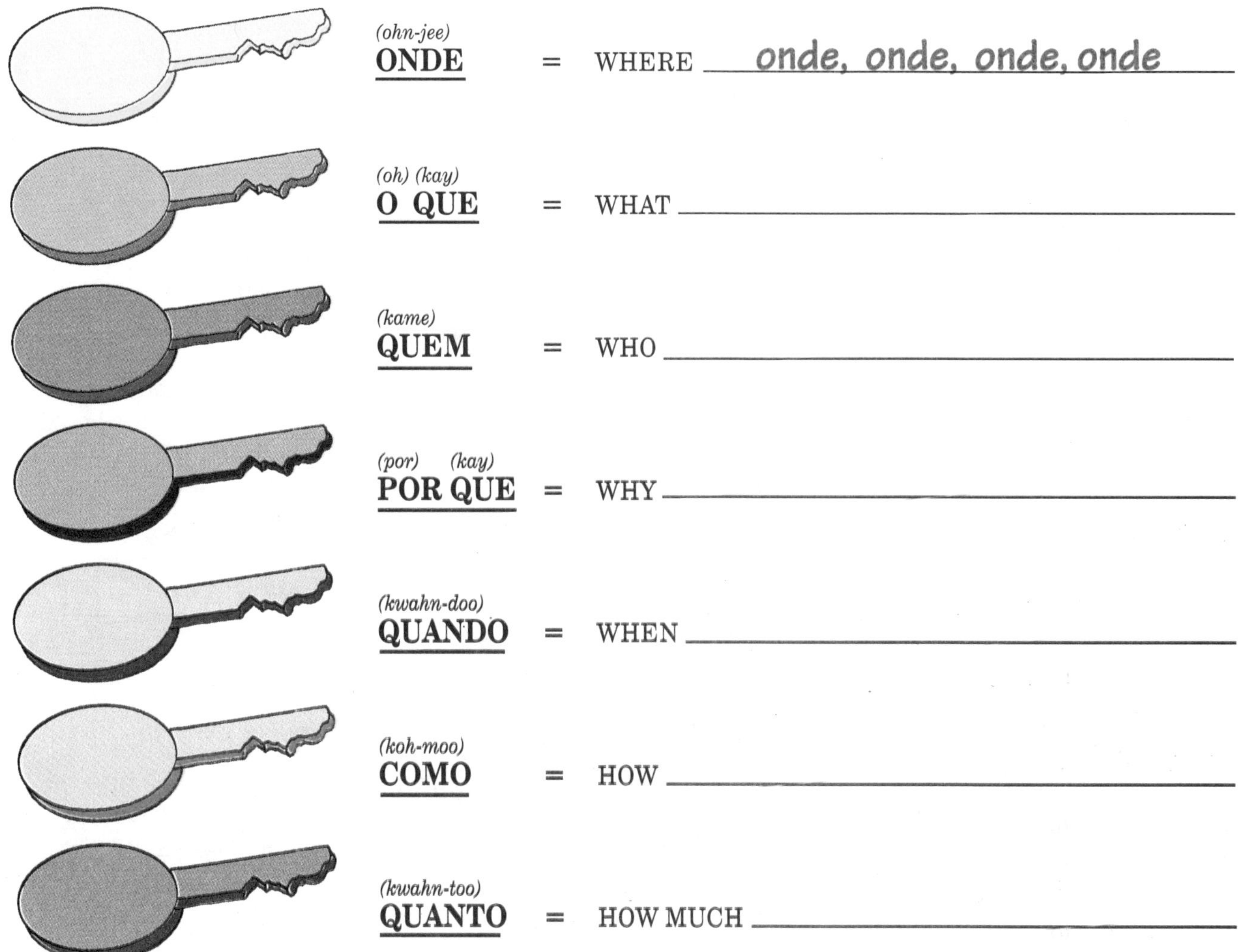

(ohn-jee) **ONDE** = WHERE onde, onde, onde, onde

(oh) (kay) **O QUE** = WHAT ____________

(kame) **QUEM** = WHO ____________

(por) (kay) **POR QUE** = WHY ____________

(kwahn-doo) **QUANDO** = WHEN ____________

(koh-moo) **COMO** = HOW ____________

(kwahn-too) **QUANTO** = HOW MUCH ____________

Now test yourself to see if you really can keep these *(pah-lah-vrahs)* **palavras** (words) straight in your mind. Draw lines between the Portuguese *(eh)* **e** (and) English equivalents below.

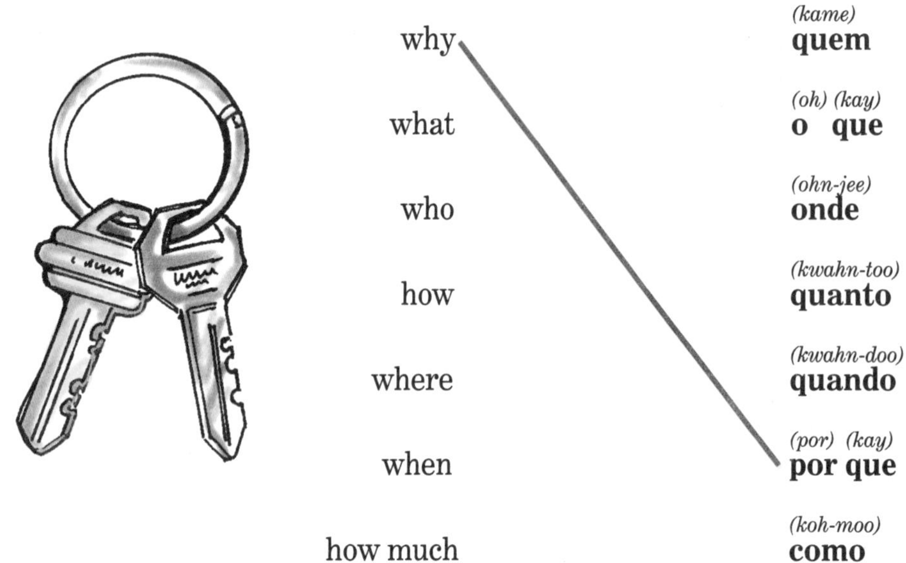

why	*(kame)* **quem**
what	*(oh) (kay)* **o que**
who	*(ohn-jee)* **onde**
how	*(kwahn-too)* **quanto**
where	*(kwahn-doo)* **quando**
when	*(por) (kay)* **por que**
how much	*(koh-moo)* **como**

Examine the following questions containing these *(pah-lah-vrahs)* **palavras**. Practice the sentences out loud *(eh)* **e** (and) then practice by copying the Portuguese in the blanks underneath each question.

(oh) (kay) (eh) (ees-soo)
O que é isso?
What is that

O que é isso?

(koh-moo) (es-tah) (ah) (sah-lah-dah)
Como está a salada?
How is the salad

(kame) (eh)
Quem é?
Who is it

(kwahn-doo) (vame) (oh) (trame)
Quando vem o trem?
When comes the train

(kwahn-too) (koos-tah) (ees-soo)
Quanto custa isso?
How much costs that

(ohn-jee) (es-tah) (oh) (teh-leh-foh-nee)
Onde está o telefone?
Where is the telephone

(ohn-jee) **"Onde"** will be your most used question *(pah-lah-vrah)* **palavra.** Say each of the following Portuguese sentences aloud. Then write out each sentence without looking at the example. If you don't succeed on the first try, don't give up. Just practice each sentence until you are able to do it easily. Remember **"<u>ei</u>"** is pronounced like "ay" in "day" *(eh)* **e** (and) **"<u>ai</u>"** is pronounced "eye."

(ohn-jee) (eh) (oh) (bahn-yay-roo)
Onde é o banheiro?
Where is the restroom

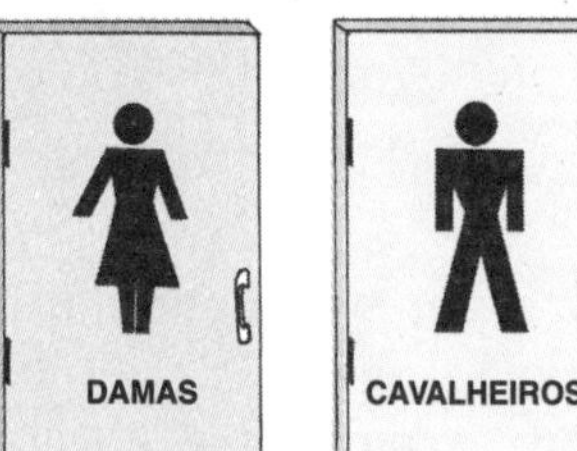

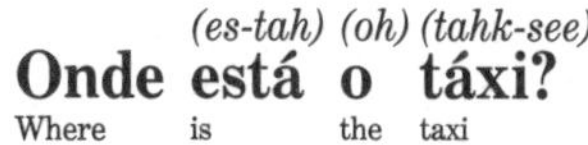

(es-tah) (oh) (tahk-see)
Onde está o táxi?
Where is the taxi

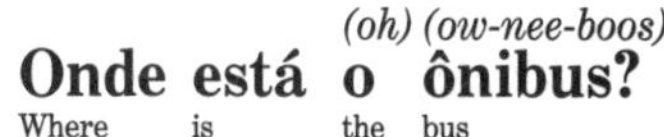

(oh) (ow-nee-boos)
Onde está o ônibus?
Where is the bus

____

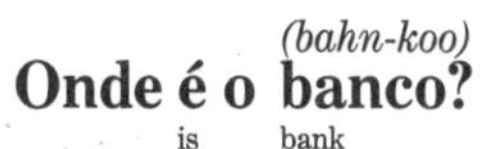

____

(eh) (oh) (hehs-tow-rahn-chee)
Onde é o restaurante?
is restaurant

(bahn-koo)
Onde é o banco?
is bank

(oh-tel)
Onde é o hotel?
hotel

_______________ _______________ _______________

Sim (seem) (yes), you can see similarities between **inglês** (een-glaysh) (English) and **português** (por-too-gaysh) (Portuguese) if you look closely. You will be amazed at the number of **palavras** (pah-lah-vrahs) (words) which are identical (or almost identical) in both languages. Of course, they do not always sound the same when spoken by a Portuguese-speaker, but the similarities will certainly surprise you **e** (eh) make your work here easier. Listed below are five "free" **palavras** beginning with " **a** (ah) " to help you get started. Be sure to say each **palavra** aloud **e** (eh) then write out the Portuguese **palavra** in the blank to the right. Remember whenever you see "ow" in the phonetics, it is like the "ow" in "how" or "cow."

☑ **abril** *(ah-breel)*	April		abril, abril, abril, abril, abril
☐ **absoluto** *(ahb-soh-loo-too)*	absolute		____________
☐ **absurdo** *(ahb-soor-doo)*	absurd	**a**	____________
☐ **o acidente** *(ah-see-dehn-chee)*	accident		____________
☐ **agosto** *(ah-gohs-too)*	August		____________

Free **palavras** like these will appear at the bottom of the following pages in a yellow color band. They are easy — enjoy them! Remember, in Portuguese, the letter **"h"** **é** (eh) (is) silent.

3 Odds 'n Ends

(por-too-gaysh) **Português** (Portuguese) has multiple **palavras** (words) for "the" and "a," but they are very easy. If the Portuguese word ends in "**a**" (feminine) it *usually* will have the article "**a**" *(ah)* (the) or "**uma**." *(oo-mah)* (a) If the word ends in "**o**" (masculine) it *usually* will have the article "**o**" *(oh)* (the) or "**um**." *(oom)* (a) Of course there are exceptions!

(oh) (meh-nee-noo)
o menino — the boy

(ohs) (meh-nee-noosh)
os meninos — the boys

(ah) (meh-nee-nah)
a menina — the girl

(ahs) (meh-nee-nahs)
as meninas — the girls

(trame)
o trem — the train

(trains)
os trens — the trains

(oo-mah) (pah-lah-vrah)
uma palavra — a word

(oo-mahs) (pah-lah-vrahs)
umas palavras — some words

(oo-mah) (ah-meh-ree-kah-nah)
uma americana — an American (female)

(oo-mahs) (ah-meh-ree-kah-nahs)
umas americanas — some Americans (female)

(oom) (ah-meh-ree-kah-noo)
um americano — an American (male)

(oons) (ah-meh-ree-kah-noosh)
uns americanos — some Americans (male or mixed)

At first this might appear difficult, but only because it is different from **inglês** *(een-glaysh)* (English). Just remember you will be understood whether you say "**a palavra**" or "**o palavra**." Soon you will automatically select the right article without even thinking about it.

In Step 2 you were introduced to the Seven Key QuestionWords. These seven words are the basics, the most essential building blocks for learning Portuguese. Throughout this book you will come across keys asking you to fill in the missing question word. Use this opportunity not only to fill in the blank on that key, but to review all your question words. Play with the new sounds, speak slowly and have fun.

- ❒ **a agricultura** *(ah-gree-kool-too-rah)* .... agriculture
- ❒ **a álgebra** *(ahl-zhee-brah)* .... algebra
- ❒ **a América** *(ah-meh-ree-kah)* .... America
- ❒ **o animal** *(ah-nee-mahl)* .... animal
- ❒ **anual** *(ah-noo-ahl)* .... annual

a ______

Look Around You 4

Before you proceed with this Step, situate yourself comfortably in your living room. Now look around you. Can you name the things that you see in this **sala** *(sah-lah)* (living room) in Portuguese? You can probably guess **o telefone** *(teh-leh-foh-nee)* (telephone) and maybe even **o sofá.** *(soh-fah)* (sofa) Let's learn the rest of them. After practicing these **palavras** out loud, write them in the blanks below.

o abajur *(oh) (ah-bah-zhoor)* — the lamp ____________

o sofá *(soh-fah)* — sofa ____________

a cadeira *(ah) (kah-day-rah)* — the chair ____________

o tapete *(tah-peh-chee)* — carpet ____________

a mesa *(ah) (meh-zah)* — the table a mesa, a mesa

a porta *(por-tah)* — door ____________

o relógio *(heh-loh-zhee-oo)* — clock/watch ____________

a cortina *(kor-chee-nah)* — curtain ____________

o telefone *(teh-leh-foh-nee)* — telephone ____________

a janela *(ah) (zhah-neh-lah)* — the window ____________

o quadro *(kwah-droo)* — picture ____________

You will notice that the correct form of o or a is given **com** *(kohm)* (with) each noun. This tells you whether the noun is masculine (**o**) or feminine (**a**). Now open your **livro** *(lee-vroo)* (book) to the sticky labels on page 17 and later on page 35. Peel off the first 11 labels **e** *(eh)* proceed around **a sala,** *(sah-lah)* (living room) labeling these items in your home. This will help to increase your Portuguese **palavra** (word) power easily. Don't forget to say each **palavra** as you attach the label.

Now ask yourself, **"Onde está o abajur?"** *(ohn-jee) (ah-bah-zhoor)* (is) **e** point at it while you answer, **"O abajur está ali."** *(ah-bah-zhoor) (ah-lee)* (lamp, is, there) Continue on down the list above until you feel comfortable with these new **palavras.**

- ❒ **a aplicação** *(ah-plee-kah-sown)* .... application ____________
- ❒ **a/o artista** *(ar-chees-tah)* .... artist ____________
- ❒ **a atenção** *(ah-tehn-sown)* .... attention **a** ____________
- ❒ **ativo** *(ah-chee-voo)* .... active ____________
- ❒ **o ato** *(ah-too)* .... act (of a play) ____________

(kah-zah)
a casa = the house

(ah) (kah-zah) (ah-lee)
A casa está ali.
the house is there

(es-kree-toh-ree-oo)
o escritório
the office

(bahn-yay-roo)
o banheiro
bathroom

(koh-zeen-yah)
a cozinha
the kitchen

(kwahr-too)
o quarto
bedroom

(sah-lah) (deh) (zhahn-tar)
a sala de jantar
dining room

(sah-lah)
a sala
living room

(gah-rah-zhame)
a garagem
garage

(poh-rown)
o porão
basement

While learning these new **palavras,** let's not forget:

(oh) (kar-hoo)
o carro
the car

____

(ah) (moh-toh-see-kleh-tah)
a motocicleta
the motorcycle

____

(bee-see-kleh-tah)
a bicicleta
bicycle

____

- ❒ **o balão** *(bah-lown)*........................ balloon
- ❒ **o balcão** *(bahl-kown)*..................... balcony
- ❒ **o banco** *(bahn-koo)* .... bank
- ❒ **básico** *(bah-zee-koo)*....................... basic
- ❒ **o bife** *(bee-fee)*............................. beefsteak

b

____
____
____
____
____

(gah-too)
o gato
cat

(zhar-deem)
o jardim
garden

o jardim, o jardim

(ahs) (floh-reesh)
as flores
flowers

(kah-shor-hoo) (kown)
o cachorro / o cão
dog / dog

(ah) (ky-shah) (doh) (kor-hay-oo)
a caixa do correio
mailbox

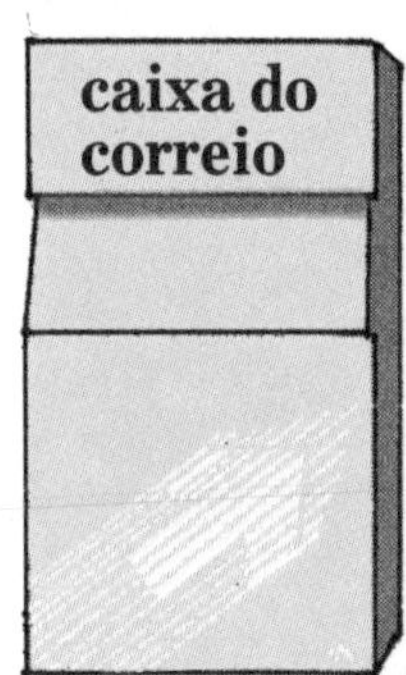

(ah) (kor-hehs-pohn-dane-see-ah)
a correspondência
mail

Peel off the next set of labels **e** wander through your **casa** *(kah-sah)* learning these new **palavras.** It will be somewhat difficult to label **o gato** *(gah-too)* [cat], **as flores** *(floh-reesh)* [flowers] **ou** *(oh)* [or] **o cachorro** *(kah-shor-hoo)* [dog], but be creative. Practice by asking yourself, **"Onde está o carro?"** *(kar-hoo)* [car] and reply, **"O carro está ali."** *(ah-lee)* [there]

Onde está a casa?
is

❒ **a calma** *(kahl-mah)*	calm		______
❒ **a capacidade** *(kah-pah-see-dah-jee)*	capacity		______
❒ **a capela** *(kah-peh-lah)*	chapel	**c**	______
❒ **a capital** *(kah-pee-tahl)*	capital		______
❒ **o caramelo** *(kah-rah-meh-loo)*	caramel		______

5 Um, dois, três!

(oom) (doysh) (traysh)
one two three

Consider for a minute how important numbers are. How could you tell someone your phone number, your address **ou** (oh) (or) your hotel room if you had no numbers? And think of how difficult it would be if you could not understand the time, the price of an apple **ou** (oh) the correct bus to take. When practicing **os** (ohs) **números** (noo-meh-roosh) (numbers) below, notice the similarities which have been underlined for you between **oito** (oy-too) (eight) and **dezoito,** (deh-zoy-too) (eighteen) **nove** (noh-vee) (nine) and **dezenove,** (deh-zeh-noh-vee) (nineteen) and so on.

0	*(zeh-roo)* **zero**	________	10	*(dehsh)* **dez**	________
1	*(oom)* **um**	________	11	*(ohn-zee)* **onze**	________
2	*(doysh)* **dois**	________	12	*(doh-zee)* **doze**	________
3	*(traysh)* **três**	________	13	*(treh-zee)* **treze**	________
4	*(kwah-troo)* **quatro**	________	14	*(kwah-tor-zee) (kah-tor-zee)* **quatorze / catorze**	________
5	*(seen-koo)* **cinco**	________	15	*(keen-zee)* **quinze**	________
6	*(saysh)* **seis**	________	16	*(deh-zehs-saysh)* **dezesseis**	________
7	*(seh-chee)* **sete**	sete, sete, sete, sete	17	*(deh-zehs-seh-chee)* **dezessete**	________
8	*(oy-too)* **oito**	________	18	*(deh-zoy-too)* **dezoito**	________
9	*(noh-vee)* **nove**	________	19	*(deh-zeh-noh-vee)* **dezenove**	________
10	*(dehsh)* **dez**	________	20	*(veen-chee)* **vinte**	________

- ☑ **o carro** *(kar-hoo)* .... car — o carro, o carro, o carro, o carro
- ☐ **a causa** *(kow-zah)* .... cause
- ☐ **o centro** *(sehn-troo)* .... center
- ☐ **o cheque** *(sheck-ee)* .... check
- ☐ **o chocolate** *(shoh-koh-lah-chee)* .... chocolate

C

Use these *(noo-meh-roosh)* **números** (numbers) on a daily basis. Count to yourself *(ehm)* **em** (in) *(por-too-gaysh)* **português** (Portuguese) when you brush your teeth, exercise *(oh)* **ou** commute to work. Fill in the blanks below according to **os** *(noo-meh-roosh)* **números** (numbers) given in parentheses. Now is also a good time to learn these two very important phrases.

(eh-oo) (kair-oo)
eu quero ______________________
I want

(noys) (kair-eh-moosh)
nós queremos ______________________
we want

(eh-oo) (kair-oo) **Eu quero** ________ (1) *(kar-town) (pohs-tahl)* **cartão postal.** (I want ... postcard) *(kwahn-toosh)* **Quantos?** (how many) ________ (1)

Eu quero ________ (7) *(seh-loosh)* **selos.** (stamps) **Quantos?** ________ (7)

Eu quero oito (8) *(seh-loosh)* **selos.** (stamps) **Quantos?** ________ (8)

Eu quero ________ (5) **selos.** **Quantos?** cinco (5)

(noys) (kair-eh-moosh) **Nós queremos** ________ (9) *(kar-toynsh) (pohs-tiesh)* **cartões postais.** (we want ... postcards) **Quantos?** ________ (9)

Nós queremos ________ (10) *(kar-toynsh) (pohs-tiesh)* **cartões postais.** (we ... postcards) **Quantos?** ________ (10)

(eh-oo) (kair-oo) **Eu quero** ________ (1) *(een-grehs-soo)* **ingresso.** (ticket) **Quantos?** ________ (1)

(kair-eh-moosh) **Nós queremos** ________ (4) *(een-grehs-soos)* **ingressos.** (we ... tickets) **Quantos?** ________ (4)

Nós queremos ________ (11) *(een-grehs-soos)* **ingressos.** **Quantos?** ________ (11)

Eu quero ________ (3) *(shee-kah-rahs) (deh) (shah)* **xícaras de chá.** (cups of tea) *(kwahn-tahs)* **Quantas?** ________ (3)

Nós queremos ________ (4) *(koh-poosh) (jee) (ah-gwah)* **copos de água.** (glasses of water) ________ (how many) ________ (4)

❒ **científico** *(see-ehn-chee-fee-koo)*	scientific		________
❒ **o cinema** *(see-neh-mah)*	cinema		________
❒ **clássico** *(klahs-see-koo)*	classical, classic	**c**	________
❒ **o closet** *(kloh-zet)*	closet		________
❒ **cômico** *(koh-mee-koo)*	comical		________

Now see if you can translate the following thoughts into **português** (Portuguese). The answers are provided upside down at the bottom of the *(pah-zhee-nah)* **página** (page).

1. I want seven postcards.

____

2. I want nine stamps.

____

3. We want four cups of tea.

____

4. We want three tickets.

____

Review **os números** 1 through 20. Write out your telephone number, fax number, **e** cellular number. Then write out a friend's telephone number and a relative's telephone number.

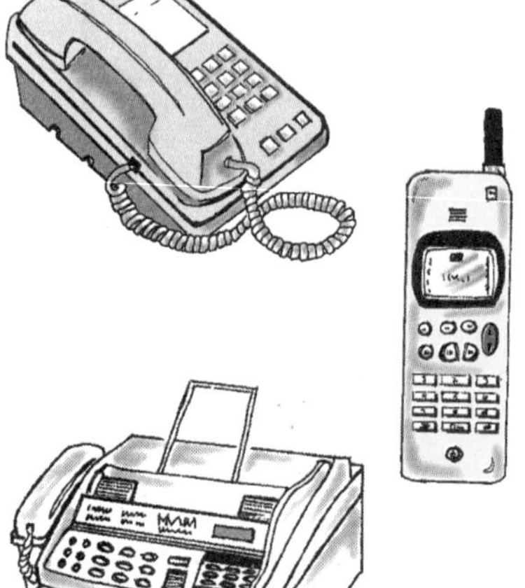

(8 0 0) 4 8 8 — 5 0 6 8

oito zero zero ______________________________

(___ ___ ___) ___ ___ ___ — ___ ___ ___ ___

____

(___ ___ ___) ___ ___ ___ — ___ ___ ___ ___

____

ANSWERS

1. **Eu quero sete cartões postais.**
2. **Eu quero nove selos.**
3. **Nós queremos quatro xícaras de chá.**
4. **Nós queremos três ingressos.**

(ahs) (koh-reesh) As Cores — colors 6

(ahs) **As** *(koh-reesh)* **cores** (colors) *(sown)* **são** (are) the same **no** (in) *(brah-zeel)* **Brasil** as they are *(nohs)* **nos** (in the) *(es-tah-doosh) (oo-nee-doosh)* **Estados Unidos** (United States) — they just have different *(noh-meesh)* **nomes** (names). You can easily recognize *(vee-oh-leh-tah)* **violeta** as violet and **púrpura** as purple. So when you are invited to someone's *(kah-zah)* **casa** (house) *(eh)* **e** you want to bring flowers, you will be able to order the color you want. Let's learn the basic *(koh-reesh)* **cores.** Once you've learned *(ahs)* **as cores,** quiz yourself. What color are your shoes? Your eyes? Your hair? Your house? Your car? What is your favorite color?

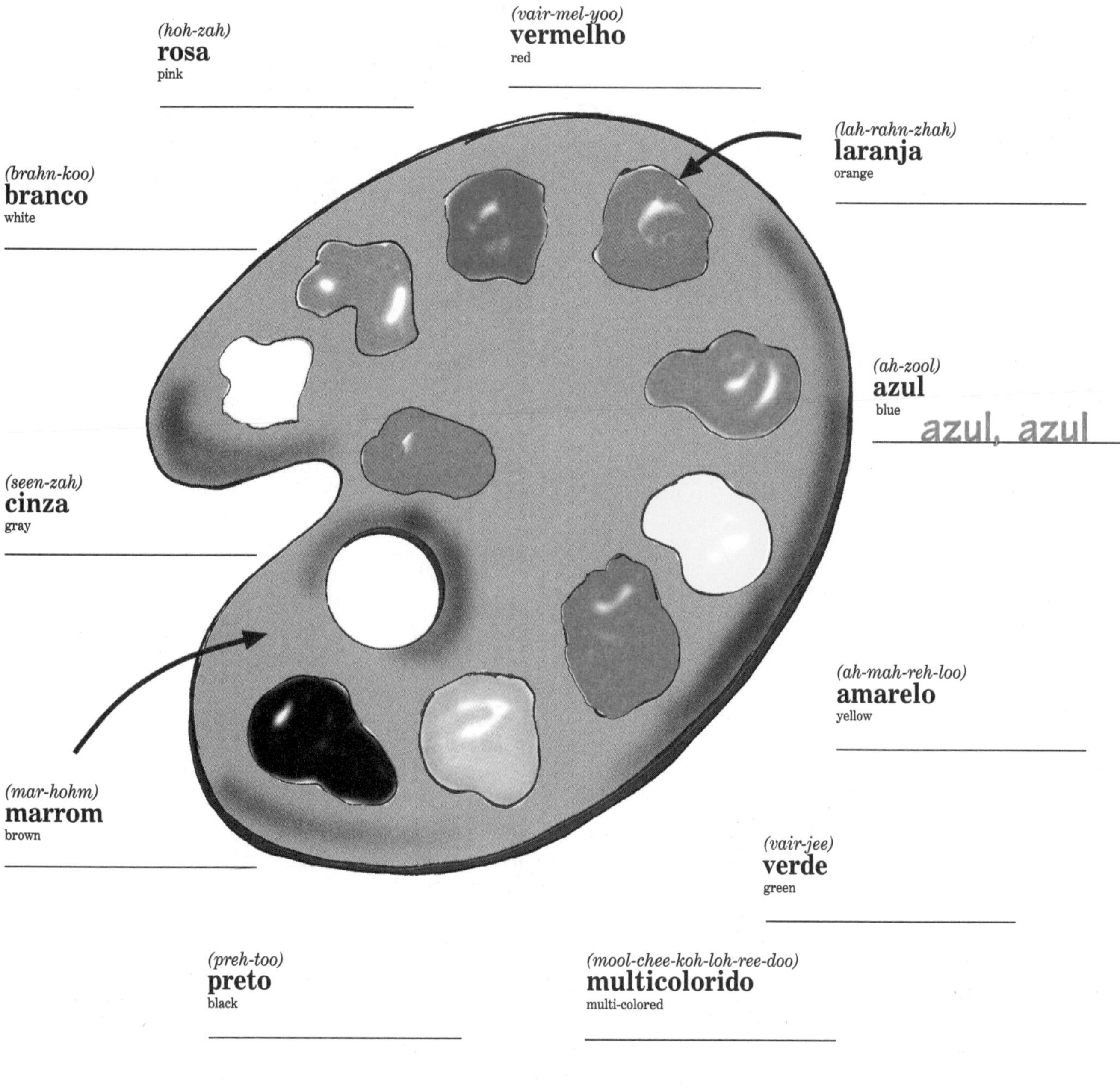

- ❒ **a companhia** *(kohm-pahn-yee-ah)* . . . . company
- ❒ **a conversação** *(kohn-vair-sah-sown)* . . . . conversation
- ❒ **correto** *(kor-heh-too)* . . . . correct
- ❒ **o creme** *(kreh-mee)* . . . . cream
- ❒ **a cultura** *(kool-too-rah)* . . . . culture

c

Peel off the next group of labels **e** *(eh)* proceed to label these **cores** *(koh-reesh)* in your **casa** *(kah-zah)* (house). Identify the two **ou** *(oh)* three dominant colors in the flags below.

______ Argentina

______ Guinea - Bissau

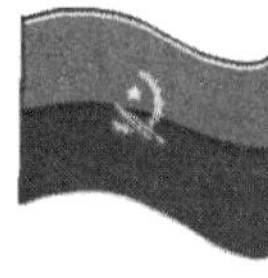
vermelho, preto
Angola

______ Mexico

______ Brazil

______ Mozambique

______ Canada

______ Portugal

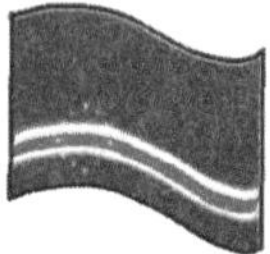
______ Cape Verde Islands

______ São Tomé and Príncipe

______ Chile

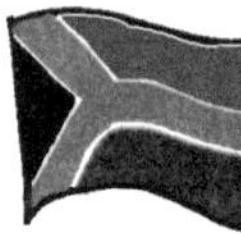
______ South Africa

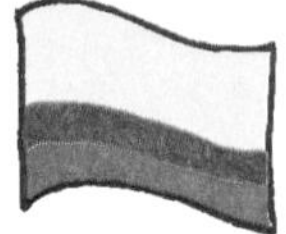
______ Colombia

______ Spain

______ Ecuador

______ United Kingdom

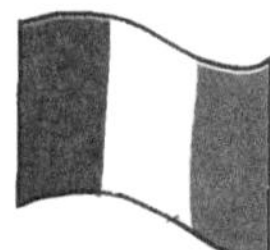
______ France

______ United States

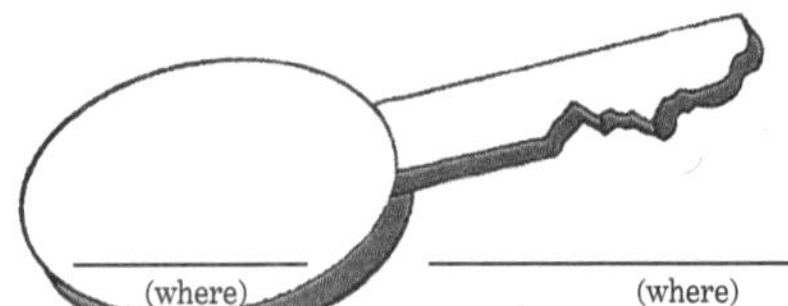

______ (where) **está o táxi?** *(oh) (tahk-see)*

______ (what) ______ (what) **é isso?** *(eh) (ees-soo)* (is that)

- ❒ **a decisão** *(deh-see-sown)* .... decision
- ❒ **a declaração** *(deh-klah-rah-sown)* .... declaration
- ❒ **o desconforto** *(dehs-kohn-for-too)* .... discomfort
- ❒ **a diferença** *(jee-feh-rehn-sah)* .... difference
- ❒ **a direção** *(jee-reh-sown)* .... direction

d

(oh) (jeen-yay-roo) O Dinheiro — money

Before starting this Step, go back and review Step 5. It is important that you can count to **vinte** *(veen-chee)* (twenty) without looking at **o livro** *(lee-vroo)* (book). Let's learn the larger **números** *(noo-meh-roosh)* now. After practicing aloud **os números portugueses** *(noo-meh-roosh) (por-too-gay-zeesh)* 10 through 11,000 below, write these **números** *(noo-meh-roosh)* in the blanks provided. Again, notice the similarities between **números** such as **seis** *(saysh)* (6), **dezesseis** *(deh-zehs-saysh)* (16), **sessenta** *(sehs-sehn-tah)* (60), **e seis mil** *(eh) (saysh) (meel)* (6,000).

10	*(dehsh)* **dez** ________	1.000	*(meel)* **mil** ________
20	*(veen-chee)* **vinte** ________	2.000	*(doysh)(meel)* **dois mil** ________
30	*(treen-tah)* **trinta** ________	3.000	*(traysh)* **três mil** ________
40	*(kwah-rehn-tah)* **quarenta** quarenta, quarenta	4.000	*(kwah-troo)* **quatro mil** ________
50	*(seen-kwehn-tah)* **cinqüenta** ________	5.000	*(seen-koo)* **cinco mil** ________
60	*(sehs-sehn-tah)* **sessenta** ________	6.000	*(saysh)* **seis mil** ________
70	*(seh-tehn-tah)* **setenta** ________	7.000	*(seh-chee)* **sete mil** ________
80	*(oy-tehn-tah)* **oitenta** ________	8.000	*(oy-too)* **oito mil** ________
90	*(noh-vehn-tah)* **noventa** ________	9.000	*(noh-vee)* **nove mil** ________
100	*(same)* **cem** ________	10.000	*(dehsh)* **dez mil** ________
500	*(keen-yehn-toosh)* **quinhentos** ________	10.500	**dez mil e quinhentos** *(eh) (keen-yehn-toosh)* ________
1.000	*(meel)* **mil** ________	11.000	*(ohn-zee)* **onze mil** ________

Aqui *(ah-key)* (here) are **duas** *(doo-ahs)* important phrases to go with all these **números.** Say them out loud over and over and then write them out twice as many times.

(eh-oo)(tehn-yoo) **eu tenho** (I have) ________________________________

(noys) (teh-moosh) **nós temos** (we have) ________________________________

- ❒ **discreto** *(jees-kreh-too)*. . . . . discreet ________
- ❒ **a distância** *(jees-tahn-see-ah)*. . . . . distance ________
- ❒ **a divisão** *(jee-vee-sown)* . . . . division ________
- ❒ **o documento** *(doh-koo-mehn-too)* . . . . document ________
- ❒ **o doutor** *(doh-tor)* . . . . doctor (title) ________

d

The unit of currency **no** (in) **Brasil** *(brah-zeel)* **é** *(eh)* (is) **o real,** *(heh-ahl)* abbreviated **"R$."** Let's learn the various kinds of **moedas** *(moh-eh-dahs)* (coins) **e notas.** *(noh-tahs)* (bills) Always be sure to practice each **palavra** out loud. You might want to exchange some money **agora** *(ah-goh-rah)* (now) so that you can familiarize yourself **com** *(kohm)* (with) **as** *(ahs)* **várias** *(vah-ree-ahs)* (various) **notas** *(noh-tahs)* **e moedas.** *(moh-eh-dahs)*

no Brasil		em Portugal	
um real *(heh-ahl)*		**cinco euros** *(seen-koo) (eh-oo-roosh)*	
cinco reais *(heh-eyes)*		**dez euros** *(dehsh)*	
dez reais *(heh-eyes)*		**vinte euros** *(veen-chee)*	
cinqüenta reais *(seen-kwehn-tah)* / **cem reais** *(same)*		**cinqüenta euros**	

Many English words that start with **sp** or **st** have an **e** in front of them in **português.**

❒ **a economia** *(eh-koh-noh-mee-ah)*	economy		______________
❒ **o espaço** *(es-pah-soo)*	space	**e** 	______________
❒ **esplêndido** *(es-plehn-jee-doo)*	splendid		______________
❒ **o esporte** *(es-por-chee)*	sport		______________

Review **os números dez** *(dehsh)* through **mil** again. **Agora** *(now)*, **como** *(koh-moo)* *(how)* do you say "twenty-two" **ou** *(oh)* "fifty-three" **em português** *(por-too-gaysh)*? Put the numbers together in a logical sequence just as you do in English. See if you can say **e** *(eh)* write out **os números** on this **página** *(pah-zhee-nah)* *(page)*. The answers **estão** *(es-town)* *(are)* at the bottom of the **página** *(pah-zhee-nah)*.

1. ______________________ (25 = 20 and 5)

2. ______________________ (83 = 80 and 3)

3. ______________________ (47 = 40 and 7)

4. noventa e seis (96 = 90 and 6)

Now, **como** would you say the following **em português** *(por-too-gaysh)*?

5. ______________________ (I have 80 reais.)

6. ______________________ (We have 72 reais.)

To ask how much something costs **em português** *(por-too-gaysh)*, one asks — **Quanto** *(kwahn-too)* **custa** *(koos-tah)* **isso?** *(ees-soo)*

Now you try it. ______________________ (How much does that cost?)

Answer the following questions based on the numbers in parentheses.

7. **Quanto** *(kwahn-too)* **custa** *(koos-tah)* *(costs)* **isso?** *(ees-soo)* *(that)* **Custa** *(it) costs* ______________________ (10) **reais** *(heh-eyes)*.

8. **Quanto custa isso?** *(ees-soo)* **Custa** *(koos-tah)* ______________________ (20) **reais** *(heh-eyes)*.

9. **Quanto custa o livro?** *(lee-vroo)* *(book)* **O livro custa** ______________________ (17) **reais.**

10. **Quanto custa o cartão postal?** *(kar-town) (pohs-tahl)* *(postcard)* **O cartão postal custa** *(kar-town) (pohs-tahl)* ____________ (2) **reais.**

ANSWERS

1. vinte e cinco
2. oitenta e três
3. quarenta e sete
4. noventa e seis
5. Eu tenho oitenta reais.
6. Nós temos setenta e dois reais.
7. dez
8. vinte
9. dezessete
10. dois

8 Hoje, Amanhã e Ontem

(oh-zhee) (ah-mahn-yahn) (ohn-tame)
Hoje, Amanhã e Ontem
today tomorrow and yesterday

(kah-lehn-dah-ree-oo)
o calendário
calendar

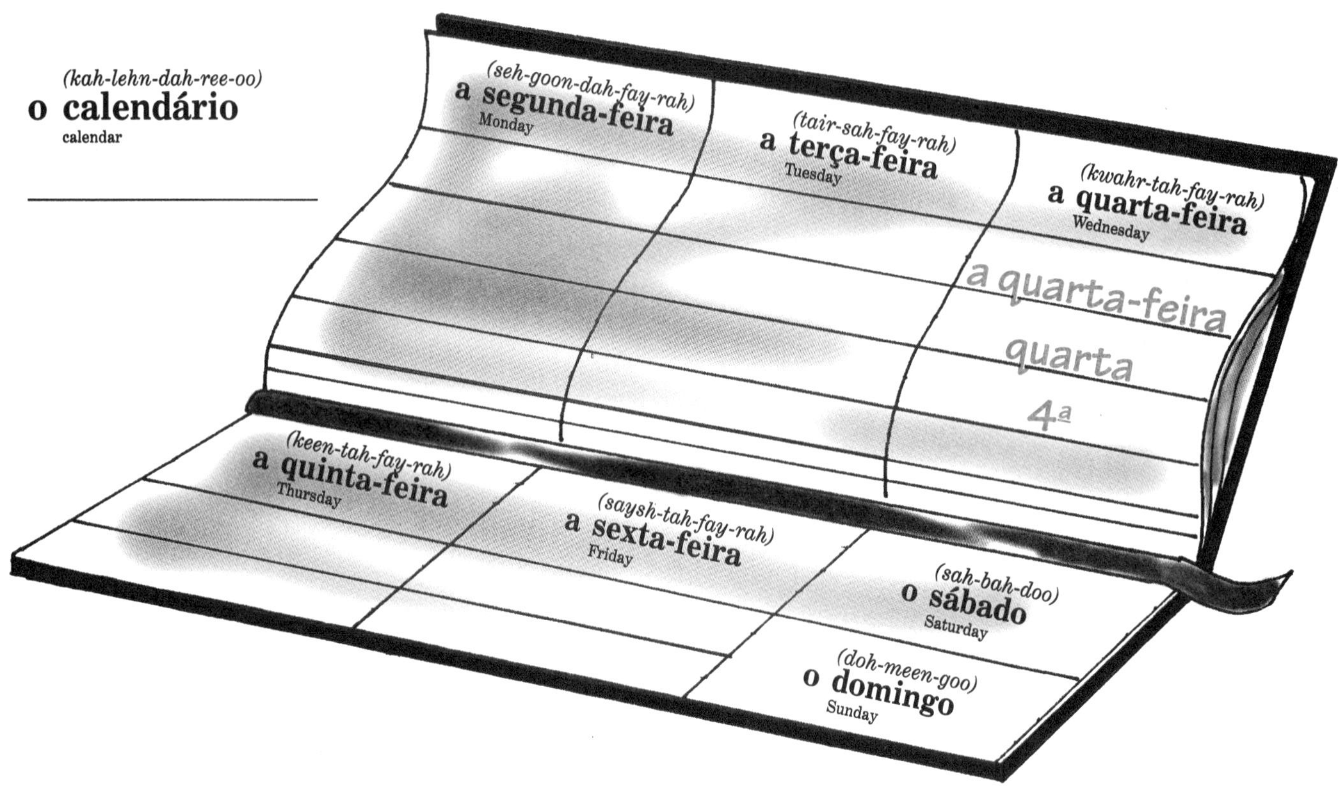

Learn the days of the week by writing them in **o calendário** *(kah-lehn-dah-ree-oo)* above **e** *(eh)* then move on to the **quatro** *(kwah-troo)* (four) parts to each **dia** *(jee-ah)* (day). Often "**feira**" *(fay-rah)* is dropped when referring to the days of the week. You will also see **os dias** *(ohs) (jee-ahs)* (days) abbreviated simply as **dom., 2ª, 3ª, 4ª, 5ª, 6ª** and **sab.**

(mahn-yahn) **a manhã** — morning

(tar-jee) **a tarde** — afternoon

(noy-chee) **a noite** — evening

(noy-chee) **a noite** — night

- ❒ **a estabilidade** *(es-tah-bee-lee-dah-jee)* ..... stability
- ❒ **a estação** *(es-tah-sown)* .... station
- ❒ **o estado** *(es-tah-doo)* .... state
- ❒ **a estátua** *(es-tah-too-ah)* .... statue
- ❒ **o/a estudante** *(es-too-dahn-chee)* .... student

e

It is **muito** (mwee-too) very **importante** (eem-por-tahn-chee) important to know the days of the week **e** (eh) the various parts of the day as well as these **três** (traysh) **palavras** (pah-lah-vrahs).

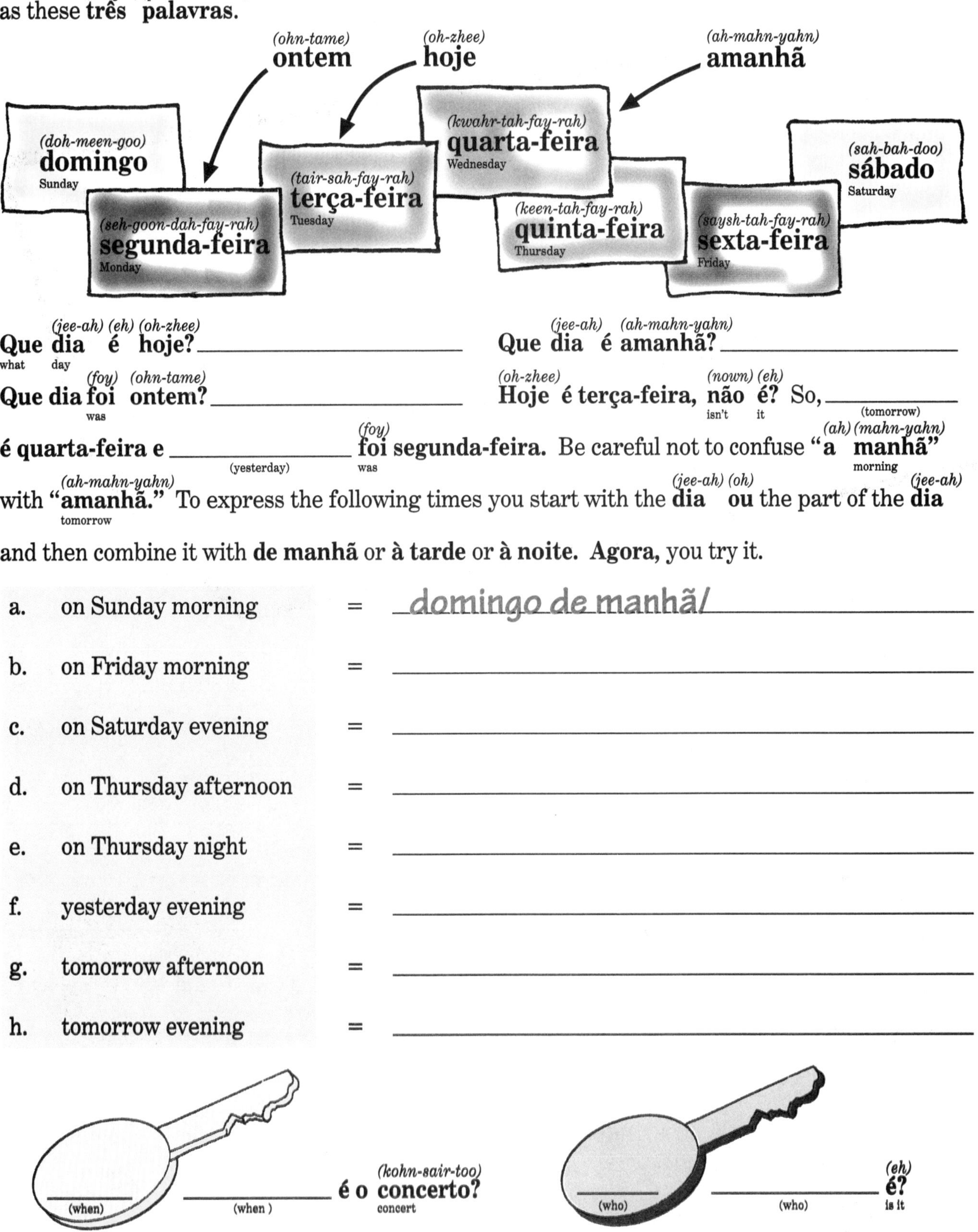

Que what **dia** (jee-ah) day **é** (eh) **hoje** (oh-zhee)**?** ______________________ **Que dia** (jee-ah) **é amanhã** (ah-mahn-yahn)**?** ______________________

Que dia foi (foy) was **ontem** (ohn-tame)**?** ______________________ **Hoje** (oh-zhee) **é terça-feira, não** (nown) isn't **é** (eh) it**?** So, ______________ (tomorrow)

é quarta-feira e ______________ (yesterday) **foi** (foy) was **segunda-feira.** Be careful not to confuse "**a** (ah) **manhã**" (mahn-yahn) morning with "**amanhã**" (ah-mahn-yahn) tomorrow. To express the following times you start with the **dia** (jee-ah) **ou** (oh) the part of the **dia** (jee-ah) and then combine it with **de manhã** or **à tarde** or **à noite. Agora,** you try it.

a. on Sunday morning = domingo de manhã/ ______________________

b. on Friday morning = ______________________

c. on Saturday evening = ______________________

d. on Thursday afternoon = ______________________

e. on Thursday night = ______________________

f. yesterday evening = ______________________

g. tomorrow afternoon = ______________________

h. tomorrow evening = ______________________

______________ (when) ______________ (when) **é o concerto** (kohn-sair-too) concert**?**

______________ (who) ______________ (who) **é** (eh) is it**?**

ANSWERS

a. **domingo de manhã**
b. **sexta-feira de manhã**
c. **sábado à noite**
d. **quinta-feira à tarde**
e. **quinta-feira à noite**
f. **ontem à noite**
g. **amanhã à tarde**
h. **amanhã à noite**

Knowing the parts of **o** *(jee-ah)* **dia** (day) will help you to learn the various *(por-too-gay-zeesh)* **portugueses** greetings below. Practice these every day until your trip.

(bohm) (jee-ah)
bom dia ______________________________
good morning/good day

(boh-ah)(tar-jee)
boa tarde ______________________________
good afternoon

(boh-ah)(noy-chee)
boa noite ______________________________
good evening/good night

Take the next *(traysh)* **três** labels **e** stick them on the appropriate things in your *(kah-zah)* **casa** (house). Make sure you attach them to the correct items, as they are only **em** *(por-too-gaysh)* **português.** How about the bathroom mirror for "*(bohm)* **bom dia**"? *(oh)* **ou** (or) your alarm clock for "**boa** *(noy-chee)* **noite**"? Let's not forget,

(oi) (oh-lah)
oi / **olá** ______________________________
hello/hi

(chow) (ah-deh-oos)
tchau / **adeus** ______________________________
good-bye

(vy)
Como vai? ______________________________
how are you

(too-doo) (bame)
Tudo bem? ______________________________
how's it going

Now for some "*(seem)* **sim**" (yes) or "*(nown)* **não**" (no) questions –

Is the sky *(ah-zool)* **azul?** ____________ Is your car *(mar-hohm)* **marrom?** ____________

Is your favorite color *(vair-mel-yoo)* **vermelho?** ____________ Is today *(sah-bah-doo)* **sábado?** ____________

Do you own a *(kah-shor-hoo)* **cachorro?** ____________ Do you own a *(gah-too)* **gato?** ____________

You are about one-fourth of your way through this **livro** (book) **e** it is a good time to quickly review **as palavras** you have learned before doing the crossword puzzle on the next *(pah-zhee-nah)* **página.** Have fun **e** *(boh-ah) (sor-chee)* **boa sorte!** (good luck)

ANSWERS TO THE CROSSWORD PUZZLE

ACROSS
1. custa
3. bicicleta
6. mesa
7. sim
8. quem
10. tenho
12. inglês
15. telefone
18. dez
21. estado
23. hoje
25. correspondência
28. abril
32. real
33. amanhã
35. salada
37. janela
38. um
40. chocolate
42. noite
43. dia
44. ontem
45. três
46. ativo

DOWN
1. calma
2. tapete
3. banco
4. cheque
5. cadeira
7. segunda-feira
9. treze
11. nós
13. selos
14. ingresso
16. doutor
17. trem
19. zero
20. cozinha
22. trinta
24. sala
26. eu
27. por que
29. rosa
30. marrom
31. cachorro
34. menina
36. sábado
39. seis
40. casa
41. como
43. de

PALAVRAS CRUZADAS
(kroo-zah-dah)

crossword puzzle

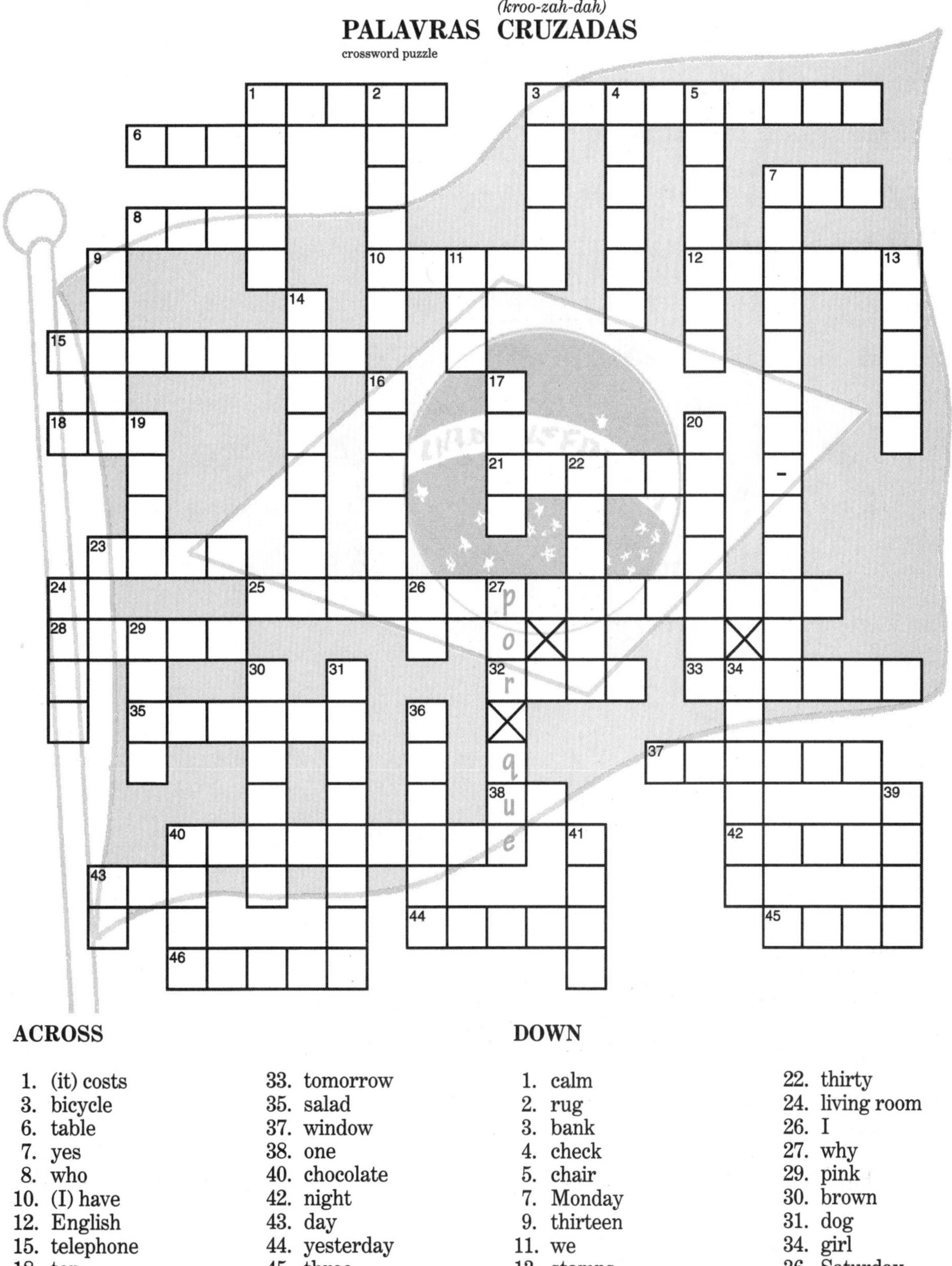

ACROSS

1. (it) costs
3. bicycle
6. table
7. yes
8. who
10. (I) have
12. English
15. telephone
18. ten
21. state
23. today
25. mail
28. April
32. Brazilian currency
33. tomorrow
35. salad
37. window
38. one
40. chocolate
42. night
43. day
44. yesterday
45. three
46. active

DOWN

1. calm
2. rug
3. bank
4. check
5. chair
7. Monday
9. thirteen
11. we
13. stamps
14. ticket
16. doctor (title)
17. train
19. zero
20. kitchen
22. thirty
24. living room
26. I
27. why
29. pink
30. brown
31. dog
34. girl
36. Saturday
39. six
40. house
41. how
43. of, from

❒	**elétrico** *(eh-leh-tree-koo)*	electric	____________
❒	**enorme** *(eh-nor-mee)*	enormous	____________
❒	**entrar** *(ehn-trar)*	to enter	**e** ____________
❒	**o erro** *(air-hoo)*	error	____________
❒	**o e-mail** *(ee-may-oo)*	e-mail	____________

9 Em, de, sobre . . .

(ehm) **Em,** (in) *(dee)* **de,** (from) *(soh-bree)* **sobre . . .** (on top of)

Portuguese prepositions (words like "in," "on," "through" and "next to") *(sown)* **são** (are) easy to learn, **e** they allow you to be *(preh-see-zoo)* **preciso** (precise) **com** a *(mee-nee-moo)* **mínimo** (minimum) of effort. Instead of having to point *(kwah-troo)* **quatro** times at a piece of yummy pastry you would like, you can explain precisely which one you want by saying **está** ((it) is) behind, in front of, next to *(oh)* **ou** under the piece of pastry that the salesperson is starting to pick up. Let's learn some of these little **palavras.**

(ehm) **em** (into/in) ____________________

(dee) **de*** (of/from) ____________________

(soh-bree) **sobre** (over/on/on top of) ____________________

(ehm-by-shoo) (dee) **embaixo de*** (under) / *(ah-by-shoo)* **abaixo** (below) ____________________

(ehn-tree) **entre** (between) entre, entre, entre

(ehm) (frehn-chee) (dee) **em frente de*** (in front of) ____________________

(ah-trahs) **atrás** (behind) ____________________

(doo) (lah-doo) (dee) **do lado de*** (next to) ____________________

(pah-rah) **para** (to) ____________________

(boh-loo) **o bolo,** (cake,) *(tor-tah)* **a torta,** (pie,) *(doh-see)* **o doce** (pastry!) ____________________

***** The pronunciation for **"de"** varies. You'll hear *(dee)*, *(jee)*, *(deh)* and *(jeh)*. The differences are very subtle. Note that **"de"** can combine with **"a"** (the) or **"o"** (the) to form *(de+a)* **"da"** (from the) and *(de+o)* **"do."** (from the) Also, *(ehm)* **"em"** combines with **"a"** or **"o"** to become *(em+a)* **"na"** (in the) or *(em+o)* **"no."** (in the)

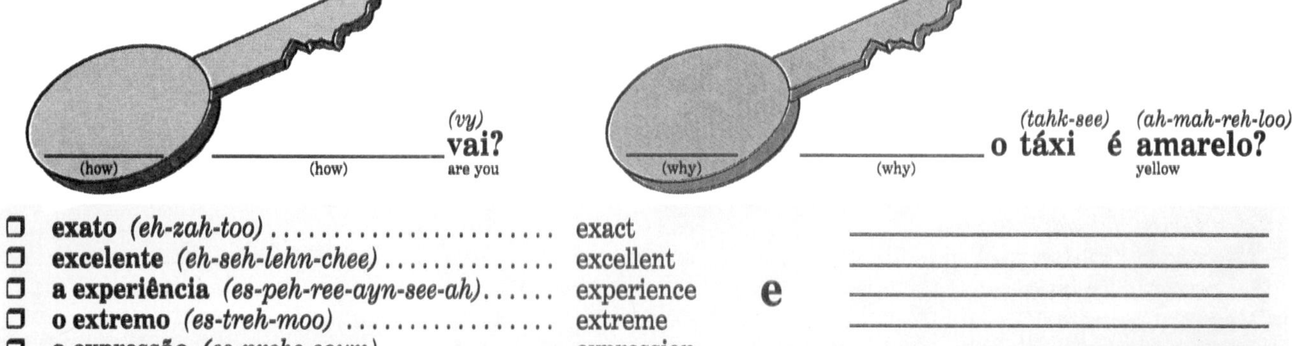

__________ (how) *(vy)* **vai?** (are you)

__________ (why) **o** *(tahk-see)* **táxi** **é** *(ah-mah-reh-loo)* **amarelo?** (yellow)

- ❒ **exato** *(eh-zah-too)* . . . . exact ____________
- ❒ **excelente** *(eh-seh-lehn-chee)* . . . . excellent ____________
- ❒ **a experiência** *(es-peh-ree-ayn-see-ah)* . . . . . experience ____________
- ❒ **o extremo** *(es-treh-moo)* . . . . extreme ____________
- ❒ **a expressão** *(es-prehs-sown)* . . . . expression ____________

e

O **doce** *(doh-see)* [pastry] está ______________ (on) **a mesa** *(meh-zah)* [table].

O **cachorro** *(kah-shor-hoo)* [dog] **preto** *(preh-too)* está ______________ (under the) **mesa.**

O **médico** *(meh-jee-koo)* [doctor] está ______________ (in the) **hotel** *(oh-tel)* **novo** *(noh-voo)* [new].

Onde *(ohn-jee)* **está o médico?** ______________

O **homem** *(oh-mehn)* [man] está ______________ (in front of the) **casa.**

Onde está o homem *(oh-mehn)***?** ______________

O **telefone** *(teh-leh-foh-nee)* [telephone] está ______________ (next to the) **porta** *(por-tah)* [door].

Onde está o telefone? ______________

Agora (now) fill in each blank on the picture below with the best possible one of these **pequenas** *(peh-kay-nahs)* (little) **palavras.** Will you be attending **um jogo de futebol** *(zhoh-goo) (deh) (foo-cheh-bohl)* (soccer game) while abroad? **Maracanã** *(mah-rah-kah-nahn)* **no Rio** is the largest stadium in the world **e** was built in 1950 for the World Cup Championship.

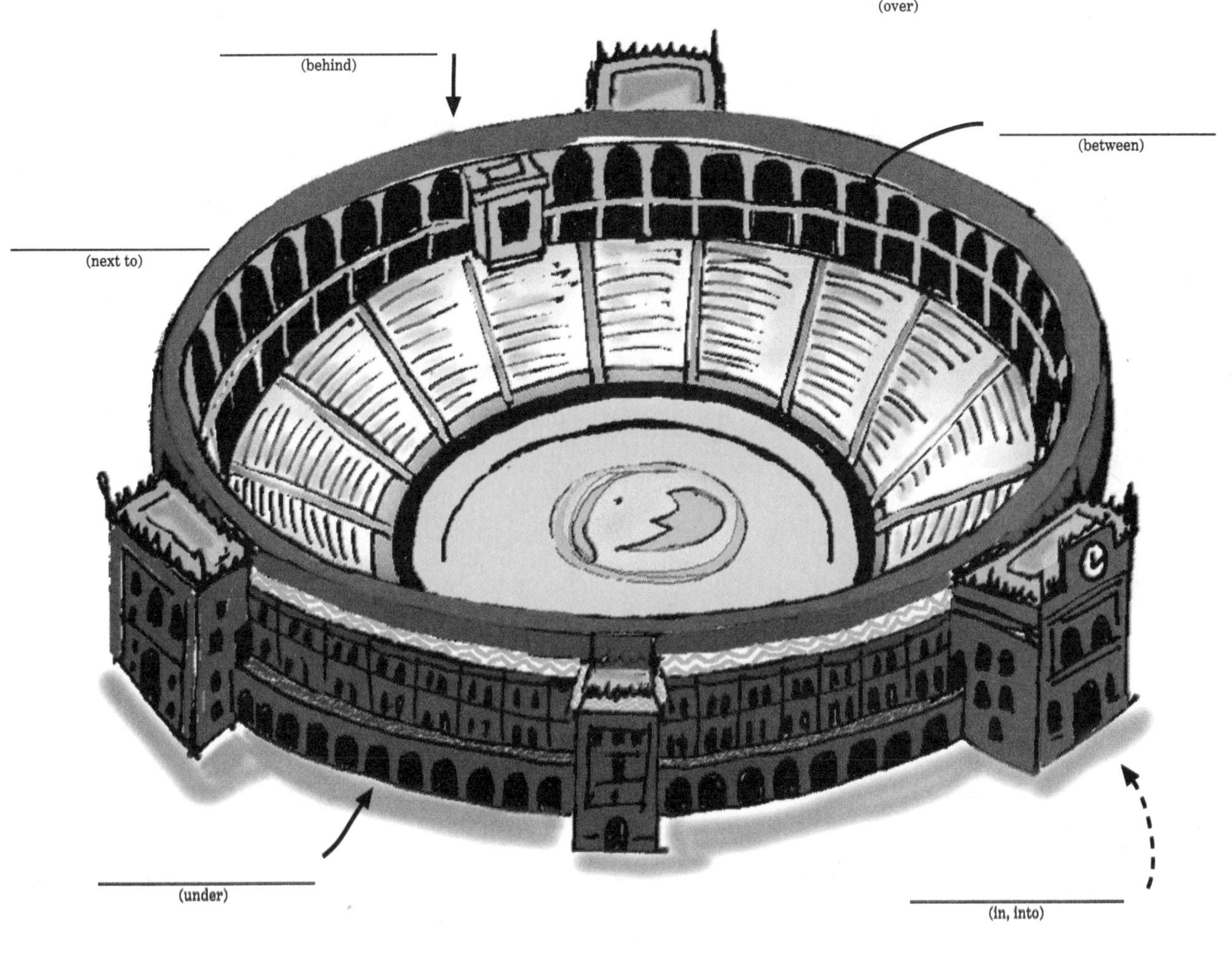

______________ (in front of)

❐	**a fama** *(fah-mah)*	fame	______________
❐	**a família** *(fah-mee-lee-ah)*	family	______________
❐	**famoso** *(fah-moh-zoo)*	famous **f**	______________
❐	**o favor** *(fah-vor)*	favor	______________
	– **(por favor)** = for a favor	please	______________

Janeiro, Fevereiro, Março

(zhah-nay-roo) (feh-veh-ray-roo) (mar-soo)
January, February, March

You have learned **os dias** *(jee-ahs)* (days) **da semana,** *(seh-mah-nah)* (of the week) so now **é hora** *(oh-rah)* (it is time) to learn **os mêses** *(may-zeesh)* (months) **do ano** *(doo)(ah-noo)* (of the year) **e** all the different kinds of **tempo.** *(tame-poo)* (weather)

(zhah-nay-roo) **janeiro**

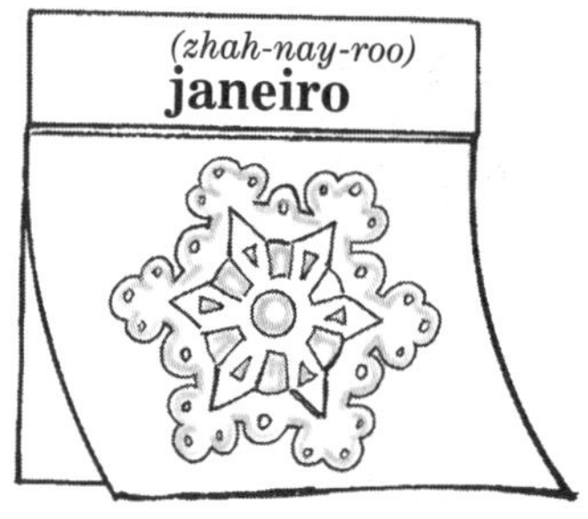

(feh-veh-ray-roo) **fevereiro**

(mar-soo) **março**

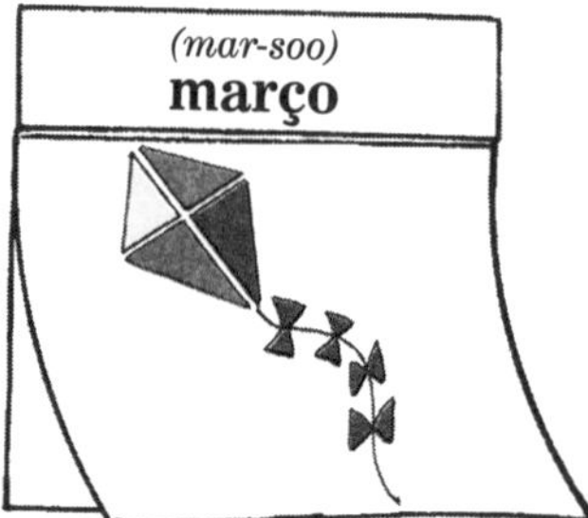

(ah-breel) **abril**

(my-oo) **maio**

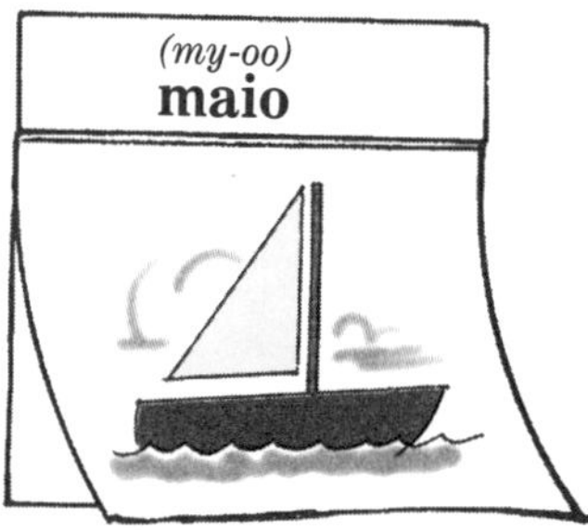

(zhoon-yoo) **junho**

(zhool-yoo) **julho**

(ah-gohs-too) **agosto**

(seh-tem-broo) **setembro**

(oh-too-broo) **outubro**

(noh-vem-broo) **novembro**

(deh-zem-broo) **dezembro**

When someone asks, "**Como está o tempo hoje?**" *(koh-moo) (es-tah) (tame-poo) (oh-zhee)* (how is the weather today) you have a variety of answers. Let's learn them but first, does this sound familiar?

(treen-tah) (jee-ahs) (tame) (seh-tem-broo) (ah-breel) (zhoon-yoo) (eh) (noh-vem-broo)
Trinta dias tem setembro, abril, junho e novembro . . .
(has)

- ❒ **o festival** *(fehs-chee-vahl)* .... festival
- ❒ **a figura** *(fee-goo-rah)* .... figure
- ❒ **o final** *(fee-nahl)* .... final
- ❒ **o folclore** *(fohl-kloh-ree)* .... folklore
- ❒ **a forma** *(for-mah)* .... form

f _______________

(tame-poo) (oh-zhee)
Como está o tempo hoje? ______
how is today

(neh-vah) (ehm) (zhah-nay-roo)
Neva em janeiro. ______
it snows in

(tahm-bame) (feh-veh-ray-roo)
Neva também em fevereiro. ______
also

(shoh-vee) (mar-soo)
Chove em março. ______
it rains

(tahm-bame)
Chove também em abril. ______

(vehn-tah) (my-oo)
Venta em maio. ______
it is windy

(tahm-bame) (zhoon-yoo)
Venta também em junho. ______

(fahs) (kah-lor) (zhool-yoo)
Faz calor em julho. ______
it makes heat (= it is hot)

(fahs) (ah-gohs-too)
Faz calor tambén em agosto. ______

(bohm) (tame-poo) (seh-tem-broo)
Faz bom tempo em setembro. ______
good

(ah) (neh-voh-ah) (oh-too-broo)
Há névoa em outubro. ______
there is fog

(fahs) (free-oh)
Faz frio em novembro. ______
cold

(mow) (tame-poo)
Faz mau tempo em dezembro. ______
bad

(oh-zhee)
Como está o tempo hoje? Chove hoje. Chove hoje. Chove hoje.

(hee-oo)
Como está o tempo no Rio? ______

Como está o tempo no Brasil? ______

Como está o tempo em Portugal? ______

- ❒ **a fortuna** *(for-too-nah)*.................. fortune ______
- ❒ **a fotografia** *(foh-toh-grah-fee-ah)* .... photograph ______
- ❒ **freqüente** *(freh-kwehn-chee)*.............. frequent ______
- ❒ **a fruta** *(froo-tah)*........................ fruit ______
- ❒ **o futuro** *(foo-too-roo)* .... future ______

f

Agora for the seasons **do** *(doo)* of the **ano** *(ah-noo)* year . . .

o inverno *(een-vair-noo)* winter

o verão *(veh-rown)* summer

o outono *(oh-toh-noo)* autumn

a primavera *(pree-mah-veh-rah)* spring

______________ ______________ ______________ ______________

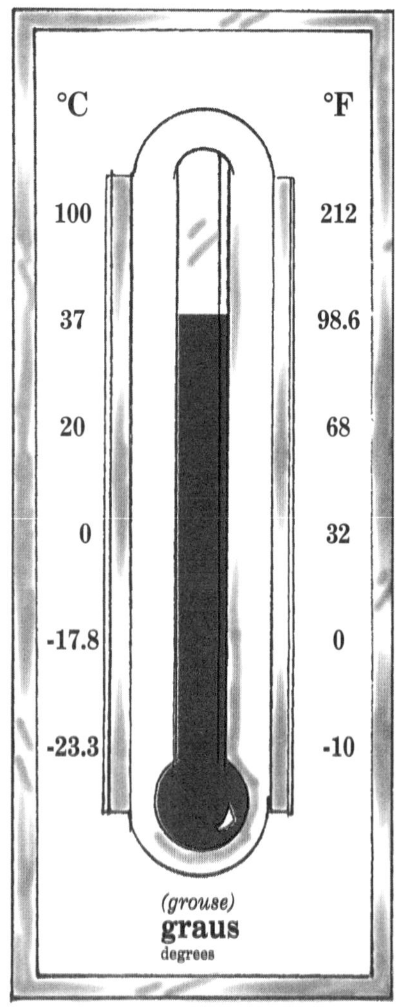

Remember that the seasons **no Brasil** are opposite those in North America as **Brasil** is in the southern hemisphere.

At this point, **é uma** *(oo-mah)* **boa** good **idéia** *(ee-day-ah)* idea to familiarize yourself **com as temperaturas** *(tame-peh-rah-too-rahs)* temperatures**.** Carefully study **o termômetro** *(tair-moh-meh-troo)* because **as temperaturas** *(tame-peh-rah-too-rahs)* **no Brasil** *(brah-zeel)* **e em Portugal** *(por-too-gahl)* are calculated on the basis of Centigrade (not Fahrenheit).

To convert °F to °C, subtract 32 and multiply by 0.55.

98.6 °F - 32 = 66.6 x 0.55 = 37 °C

To convert °C to °F, multiply by 1.8 and add 32.

37 °C x 1.8 = 66.6 + 32 = 98.6 °F

What is normal body temperature in **Centígrado?** *(sehn-chee-grah-doo)*

What is the freezing point in **Centígrado?**

g

- ❒ **a galáxia** *(gah-lahk-see-ah)*. . . . . galaxy ______________
- ❒ **a galeria** *(gah-leh-ree-ah)* . . . . gallery ______________
- ❒ **a glória** *(gloh-ree-ah)* . . . . glory ______________
- ❒ **grave** *(grah-vee)*. . . . . grave, serious ______________
- ❒ **o grupo** *(groo-poo)* . . . . group ______________

(kah-zah) (fah-mee-lee-ah) (heh-lee-zhee-own)
Casa, Família e Religião 11
home family religion

(noh) (brah-zeel)
No Brasil, not just the parents, but also the grandparents, aunts, uncles and cousins are all considered as close (fah-mee-lee-ah) **família** (family). Study the family tree below. Brazilians use (doh-nah) "**dona**" when addressing a woman as Miss, Mrs. (oh) **ou** as a general reflection of respect (**Dona Lucia Faria** or (sehn-yoh-rah) **Senhora** (Mrs.) **Faria**). For men, you would use (sehn-yor) "**senhor**" (Mr.) (**Senhor Faria**).

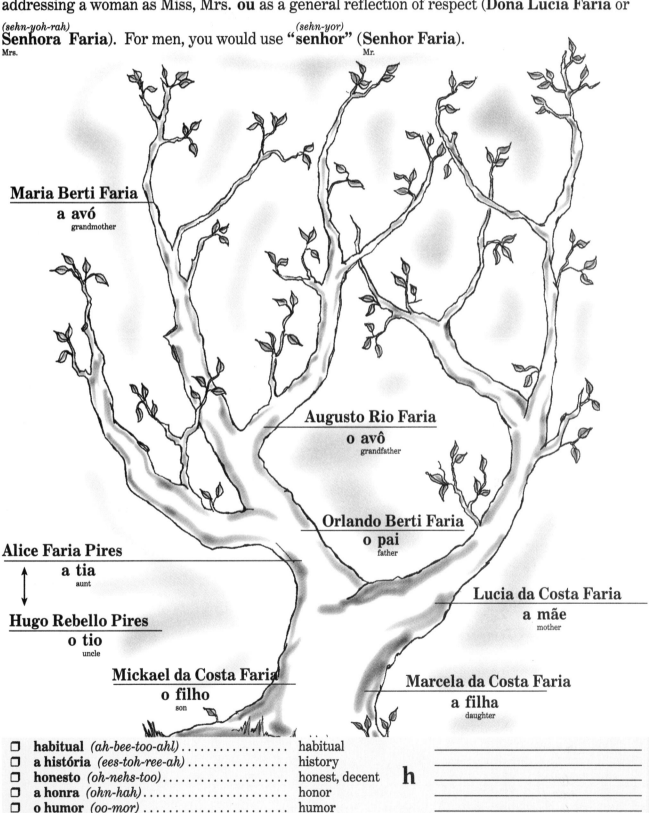

Maria Berti Faria
a avó
grandmother

Augusto Rio Faria
o avô
grandfather

Orlando Berti Faria
o pai
father

Alice Faria Pires
a tia
aunt

Hugo Rebello Pires
o tio
uncle

Lucia da Costa Faria
a mãe
mother

Mickael da Costa Faria
o filho
son

Marcela da Costa Faria
a filha
daughter

- ❒ **habitual** *(ah-bee-too-ahl)* .... habitual
- ❒ **a história** *(ees-toh-ree-ah)* .... history
- ❒ **honesto** *(oh-nehs-too)* .... honest, decent
- ❒ **a honra** *(ohn-hah)* .... honor
- ❒ **o humor** *(oo-mor)* .... humor

h

Let's learn how to identify a **família** *(fah-mee-lee-ah)* family by **nome** *(noh-mee)* name. Study the following **exemplos** *(eh-zame-ploosh)* examples carefully.

Qual é o seu nome? *(kwahl) (eh) (seh-oo) (noh-mee)* what is your name ______________

Meu nome é *(meh-oo) (noh-mee) (eh)* my name is ______________ (your name).

os pais *(piesh)* parents

o pai *(pie)* father ______________

Qual é o nome do pai? *(kwahl) (noh-mee) (doo) (pie)* what name of the father ______________

a mãe *(mah-een)* mother ______________

Qual é o nome da mãe? *(dah) (mah-een)* what of the mother ______________

os filhos *(feel-yoosh)* children

o filho e a filha = irmão e irmã *(feel-yoo) (feel-yah) (eer-mown) (eer-mahn)* brother sister

o filho *(feel-yoo)* son ______________

Qual é o nome do filho? *(kwahl) (noh-mee) (doo)* what name son ______________

a filha *(feel-yah)* daughter ______________

Qual é o nome da filha? daughter ______________

os parentes *(pah-rehn-cheesh)* relatives

o avô *(ah-voh)* grandfather ______________

Qual é o nome do avô? *(doo) (ah-voh)* grandfather ______________

a avó *(ah-voh)* grandmother ______________

Qual é o nome da avó? grandmother ______________

Now you ask —

______________ (What is your name?)

And answer —

______________ (My name is . . .)

i

- ❒ **a idéia** *(ee-day-ah)* .... idea ______________
- ❒ **a imaginação** *(ee-mah-zhee-nah-sown)*...... imagination ______________
- ❒ **a importância** *(eem-por-tahn-see-ah)* ...... importance ______________
- ❒ **impossível** *(eem-pohs-see-vel)*............. impossible ______________
- ❒ **incorreto** *(een-kor-heh-too)*............... incorrect ______________

(koh-zeen-yah)
A Cozinha
kitchen

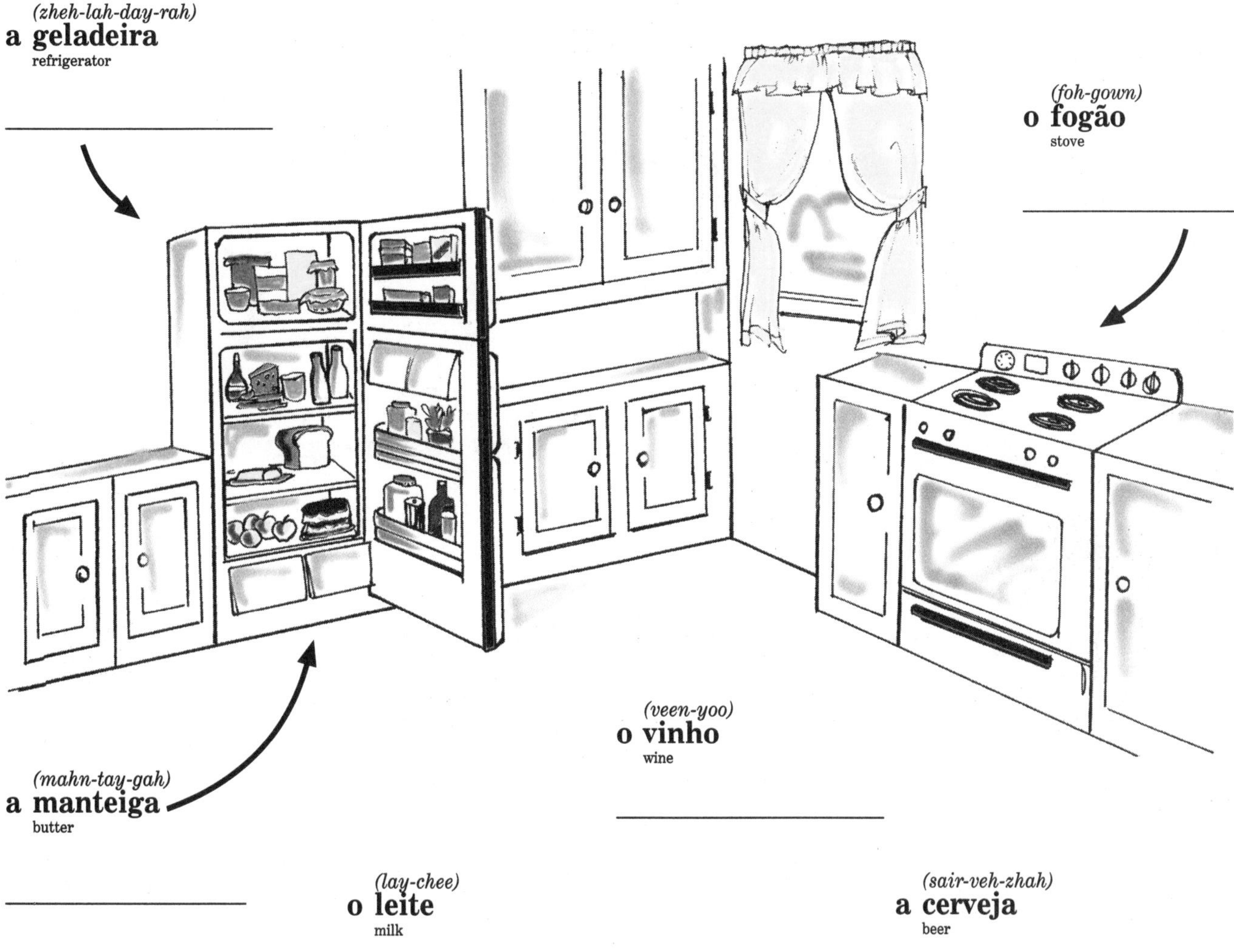

Answer these questions aloud.

Onde está a cerveja? *(ohn-jee)* *(sair-veh-zhah)* (beer) .... **A cerveja está na geladeira.** *(ah)* *(zheh-lah-day-rah)*

Onde está o leite? *(lay-chee)* (milk) **Onde está o vinho?** *(veen-yoo)* (wine) **Onde está a manteiga?** *(mahn-tay-gah)* (butter)

Agora abra *(ah-brah)* (open) your **livro** *(lee-vroo)* (book) to the **páginas** *(pah-zhee-nahs)* **com** the labels **e** remove the next group of labels **e** proceed to label all these **coisas** *(koy-zahs)* (things) in your **cozinha.** *(koh-zeen-yah)* (kitchen)

❒ **a influência** *(een-floo-ayn-see-ah)*	influence		______________
❒ **a informação** *(een-for-mah-sown)*	information		______________
❒ **inglês** *(een-glaysh)*	English	**i**	______________
❒ **a instrução** *(een-stroo-sown)*	instruction		______________
❒ **o instrumento** *(een-stroo-mehn-too)*	instrument		______________

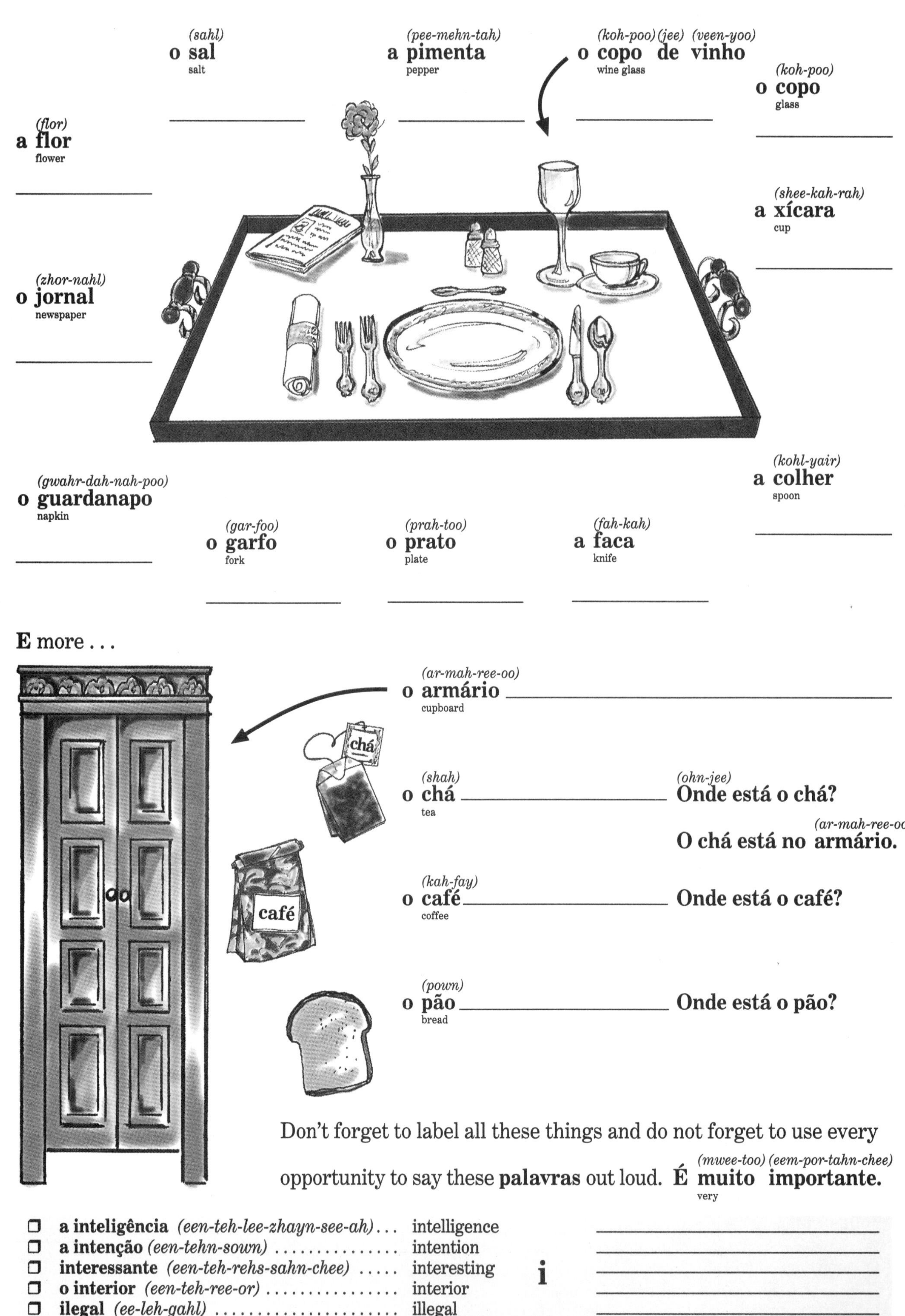

(sahl)
o sal
salt

(pee-mehn-tah)
a pimenta
pepper

(koh-poo) (jee) (veen-yoo)
o copo de vinho
wine glass

(koh-poo)
o copo
glass

(flor)
a flor
flower

(shee-kah-rah)
a xícara
cup

(zhor-nahl)
o jornal
newspaper

(kohl-yair)
a colher
spoon

(gwahr-dah-nah-poo)
o guardanapo
napkin

(gar-foo)
o garfo
fork

(prah-too)
o prato
plate

(fah-kah)
a faca
knife

E more . . .

(ar-mah-ree-oo)
o armário ______________
cupboard

(shah)
o chá ______________ *(ohn-jee)* **Onde está o chá?**
tea

O chá está no armário. *(ar-mah-ree-oo)*

(kah-fay)
o café ______________ **Onde está o café?**
coffee

(pown)
o pão ______________ **Onde está o pão?**
bread

Don't forget to label all these things and do not forget to use every opportunity to say these **palavras** out loud. **É** *(mwee-too)* **muito** (very) *(eem-por-tahn-chee)* **importante.**

i

- ❐ **a inteligência** *(een-teh-lee-zhayn-see-ah)*. . . intelligence ______________
- ❐ **a intenção** *(een-tehn-sown)* . . . . intention ______________
- ❐ **interessante** *(een-teh-rehs-sahn-chee)* . . . . . interesting ______________
- ❐ **o interior** *(een-teh-ree-or)* . . . . interior ______________
- ❐ **ilegal** *(ee-leh-gahl)* . . . . illegal ______________

(dehs-kool-pee) **desculpe**	*(seh-loo)* **o selo**	*(deh-zoh-doh-rahn-chee)* **o desodorante**	*(jeansh)* **o jeans**
(kah-mah) **a cama**	*(kar-town) (pohs-tahl)* **o cartão postal**	*(pehn-chee)* **o pente**	*(shorch)* **o short**
(trah-vehs-say-roo) **o travesseiro**	*(pahs-sah-por-chee)* **o passaporte**	*(kah-zah-koo)* **o casaco**	*(kah-mee-zeh-tah)* **a camiseta**
(koh-bair-tor) **o cobertor**	*(mah-lah)* **a mala**	*(gwahr-dah-shoo-vah)* **o guarda-chuva**	*(koo-eh-kah)* **a cueca**
(dehs-pair-tah-dor) **o despertador**	*(pahs-sah-zhame)* **a passagem**	*(kah-pah) (shoo-vah)* **a capa de chuva**	*(vehs-chee-doo)* **o vestido**
(es-pel-yoo) **o espelho**	*(bohl-sah)* **a bolsa**	*(loo-vahs)* **as luvas**	*(bloo-zah)* **a blusa**
(pee-ah) **a pia**	*(kar-tay-rah)* **a carteira**	*(vee-zay-rah)* **a viseira**	*(sy-ah)* **a saia**
(toh-ahl-yahs) **as toalhas**	*(jeen-yay-roo)* **o dinheiro**	*(shah-peh-oo) (pry-ah)* **o chapéu de praia**	*(soo-eh-tair)* **o suéter**
(vah-zoo) (sah-nee-tah-ree-oo) **o vaso sanitário**	*(kar-toynsh) (kreh-jee-too)* **os cartões de crédito**	*(boh-tahs)* **as botas**	*(kohm-bee-nah-sown)* **a combinação**
(shoo-vay-roo) **o chuveiro**	*(sheck-esh) (vee-ah-zhame)* **os cheques de viagem**	*(sah-pah-toosh)* **os sapatos**	*(soo-chee-own)* **o sutiã**
(lah-peesh) **o lápis**	*(mah-key-nah) (foh-toh-grah-fee-kah)* **a máquina fotográfica**	*(tay-nees)* **os tênis**	*(kahl-seen-yah)* **a calcinha**
(teh-leh-vee-zown) **a televisão**	*(feel-mee)* **o filme**	*(tair-noo)* **o terno**	*(may-ahs)* **as meias**
(kah-neh-tah) **a caneta**	*(soon-gah)* **a sunga**	*(grah-vah-tah)* **a gravata**	*(may-ah-kahl-sah)* **a meia-calça**
(heh-vees-tah) **a revista**	*(my-oh)* **o maiô**	*(kah-mee-zah)* **a camisa**	*(pee-zhah-mah)* **o pijama**
(lee-vroo) **o livro**	*(sahn-dah-lee-ahs)* **as sandálias**	*(lehn-soo)* **o lenço**	*(kah-mee-zoh-lah)* **a camisola**
(kohm-poo-tah-dor) **o computador**	*(oh-koo-loosh) (sohl)* **os óculos de sol**	*(zhah-kay-tah)* **a jaqueta**	*(hoh-pown) (bahn-yoo)* **o roupão de banho**
(oh-koo-loosh) **os óculos**	*(es-koh-vah) (dehn-chees)* **a escova de dentes**	*(kahl-sah)* **a calça**	*(shee-neh-loosh)* **os chinelos**
(pah-pel) **o papel**	*(pahs-tah) (dehn-chees)* **a pasta de dentes**	*(eh-oo) (soh)* **Eu sou de ______________.**	
(sehs-too) (pah-pel) **o cesto de papel**	*(sah-boh-neh-chee)* **o sabonete**	*(kair-oo) (ah-prehn-dair) (por-too-gaysh)* **Quero aprender português.**	
(kar-tah) **a carta**	*(ah-pah-rel-yoo) (bar-beh-ar)* **o aparelho de barbear**	*(meh-oo) (noh-mee) (eh)* **Meu nome é______________.**	

PLUS . . .

This book includes a number of other innovative features unique to the ***"10 minutes a day®"*** series. At the back of this book, you will find twelve pages of flash cards. Cut them out and flip through them at least once a day.

On pages 116, 117 and 118 you will find a beverage guide and a menu guide. Don't wait until your trip to use them. Clip out the menu guide and use it tonight at the dinner table. Take them both with you the next time you dine at your favorite Portuguese restaurant.

By using the special features in this book, you will be speaking Portuguese before you know it.

(boh-ah) (sor-chee)
Boa sorte!
good luck

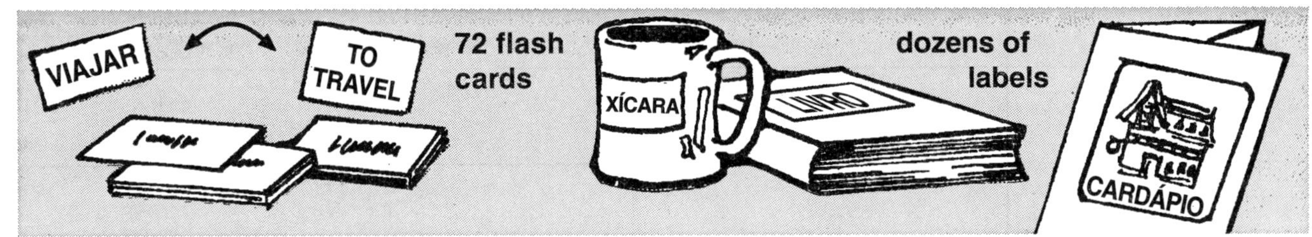

(heh-lee-zhee-own)
A Religião
religion

(brah-zeel) (vah-ree-eh-dah-jee) (heh-lee-zhee-oynsh)
No Brasil there is a wide **variedade** (variety) of accepted **religiões** (religions). However, a person is usually one of the following.

1. (kah-toh-lee-koo) **católico** (Catholic ♂) / (kah-toh-lee-kah) **católica** (Catholic ♀) ____________
2. (proh-tehs-tahn-chee) **protestante** (Protestant ♂/♀) ____________
3. (zhoo-deh-oo) **judeu** (Jewish ♂) / (zhoo-jee-ah) **judia** (Jewish ♀) ____________

É (is it) (oo-mah) **uma** (ee-greh-zhah) **igreja** (church) (brah-zee-lay-rah) **brasileira? Sim!**

É uma (ee-greh-zhah) **igreja católica?**

É uma (ee-greh-zhah) **igreja protestante?**

É uma (ee-greh-zhah) **igreja** (noh-vah) **nova?** (new)

É uma igreja (vel-yah) **velha?** (old)

There are different ways to say "I am" **em** (por-too-gaysh) **português:**

(eh-oo) **eu** (I) (soh) **sou** (am) ____________ (es-toh) **eu** (I) **estou** (am) ____________

Use "(eh-oo) **eu** (soh) **sou**" when you are telling your profession, religion, gender or a more permanent fact about yourself such as your nationality. Use "(eh-oo) **eu** (es-toh) **estou**" when you are telling something temporary such as your location or how you feel, for example, "(eh-oo) **Eu** (I) (es-toh) **estou** (am) (bame) **bem,**" (well) or simply, "**Estou** ((I) am) (bame) **bem.**" (well) Test yourself – write each sentence on the next page for more practice. Add your own personal variations as well.

_______ (how much) _______ (how much) **custa** (ees-soo) **isso?** (this)

❐ **a jaqueta** *(zhah-kay-tah)*	jacket	**j**	____________
❐ **o/a jornalista** *(zhor-nah-lees-tah)*	journalist		____________
❐ **julho** *(zhool-yoo)*	July		____________
❐ **junho** *(zhoon-yoo)*	June		____________
❐ **juvenil** *(zhoo-veh-neel)*	juvenile		____________

(soh) (kah-toh-lee-koo)
Eu sou católico. ________________
I am Catholic (♂)

(soh) (proh-tehs-tahn-chee)
Sou protestante. ________________
Protestant (♂) and (♀)

(kah-toh-lee-kah)
Sou católica. ________________
(I) am Catholic (♀)

(ah-meh-ree-kah-noo)
Sou americano. ________________
American (♂)

(soh) (zhoo-deh-oo)
Sou judeu. ________________
Jewish (♂)

(kah-nah-dehn-see)
Sou canadense. ________________
Canadian (♂) and (♀)

(zhoo-jee-ah)
Sou judia. ________________
Jewish (♀)

(es-toh) (hee-oo)
Estou no Rio. ________________
(I) am in

(es-toh) (eh-oo-roh-pah)
Eu estou na Europa. ________________
Europe

(sown) (pow-loo)
Estou em São Paulo. ________________
in

(ee-greh-zhah)
Estou na igreja. ________________
church

(por-too-gahl)
Estou em Portugal. ________________

(es-toh) (oh-tel)
Estou no hotel. ________________
in the

(hehs-tow-rahn-chee)
Estou no restaurante. ________________

(foh-mee)
Estou com fome. ________________
with hunger (= I am hungry)

(seh-jee)
Estou com sede. ________________
with thirst (= I am thirsty)

To negate any statement, simply add "**não**" *(nown)* (not/no) before the verb.

(nown) (proh-tehs-tahn-chee)
Não sou protestante. ________________
(I) am not

(nown) (es-toh) (seh-jee)
Não estou com sede. ________________
(I) am not

Go through and drill these sentences again but using "**não**" *(nown)*. **Agora**, take a piece of paper. Our **família** *(fah-mee-lee-ah)* from earlier had a reunion. Identify everyone below by writing **a palavra portuguesa** *(por-too-gay-zah)* **correta** *(kor-heh-tah)* (correct) for each person — **a mãe**, *(mah-een)* **o tio** and so on. Don't forget **o cachorro**! *(kah-shor-hoo)*

- ❒ **legal** *(leh-gahl)* .... legal
  - **legal** = used as slang .... cool
- ❒ **a lição** *(lee-sown)* .... lesson
- ❒ **o licor** *(lee-kor)* .... liquor
- ❒ **o limão** *(lee-mown)* .... lime

l

(ah-prehn-dair) Aprender! (to learn) 12

You have already used (doysh) **dois** very important verbs: **eu** (I) (kair-oo) **quero** (want) and **eu** (I) (tehn-yoo) **tenho** (have). Although you might be able to get by with only these verbs, let's assume you want to do better. First a quick review.

How do you say **"I"** em (por-too-gaysh) **português?** ________________

How do you say **"we"** em **português?** ________________

Compare these (doysh) **dois** (two) charts (mwee-too) **muito** (very) carefully **e** learn these **palavras** now.

I =	(eh-oo) **eu**	________________		we =	(noys) **nós**	________________
you =	(voh-say) **você**	________________		you (plural) =	(voh-saysh) **vocês**	________________
he =	(eh-lee) **ele**	________________		they =	(eh-leesh) **eles** (♂ or mixed)	________________
she =	(eh-lah) **ela**	________________		they =	(eh-lahs) **elas** (♀)	________________

Not too hard, is it? Draw lines between the matching **palavras** (een-glay-zahs) **inglesas** **e** (por-too-gay-zahs) **portuguesas** below to see if you can keep these **palavras** straight in your mind.

(noys) **nós**	I
(eh-leesh) **eles**	they (♀)
(eh-lee) **ele**	we
eu	he
(voh-say) **você**	you
ela	she
(eh-lahs) **elas**	they (♂)

- ❒ **a limonada** *(lee-moh-nah-dah)* .... lemonade ________________
- ❒ **a lista** *(lees-tah)* .... list ________________
- ❒ **o litro** *(lee-troo)* .... liter ________________
- ❒ **local** *(loh-kahl)* .... local ________________
- ❒ **longo** *(lohn-goo)* .... long ________________

l

Agora *(ah-goh-rah)* close **o livro** *(lee-vroo)* **e** write out both columns of this practice on a piece of **papel** *(pah-pel)* paper. How did **você** *(voh-say)* do? **Bem** *(bame)* good **ou** or **mal?** *(mahl)* bad **Agora** that **você** *(voh-say)* you know these **palavras, você** can say almost anything **em português** *(por-too-gaysh)* with one basic formula: the "plug-in" formula.

To demonstrate, let's take **seis** *(saysh)* six basic **e** practical verbs **e** see how the "plug-in" formula works. Write the verbs in the blanks after **você** *(voh-say)* have practiced saying them out loud many times.

(fah-lar) **falar** to speak	____________	*(kair-air)* **querer** to want	____________
(kohm-prar) **comprar** to buy	comprar, comprar	*(tair)* **ter** to have	____________
(ahn-dar) **andar** to walk	____________	*(veer)* **vir** to come	____________

Besides the familiar words already circled, can **você** find the above verbs in the puzzle below?

When **você** find them, write them in the blanks to the right.

A	R	O	H	A	F	I	J	X	T	N
F	A	L	A	R	I	T	A	R	E	O
D	N	D	U	O	Q	U	E	M	T	C
A	D	C	O	M	P	R	A	R	E	E
R	A	M	E	Q	U	E	R	E	R	U
O	R	D	V	X	U	T	S	E	I	S
V	E	N	I	R	L	E	B	I	E	L
X	O	A	R	S	E	D	O	N	D	E

1. ____________
2. ____________
3. ____________
4. ____________
5. ____________
6. ____________

m

- ❒ **mágico** *(mah-zhee-koo)* .... magic ____________
- ❒ **maio** *(my-oo)* .... May ____________
- ❒ **o mapa** *(mah-pah)* .... map ____________
- ❒ **a máquina** *(mah-kee-nah)* .... machine ____________
- ❒ **a marca** *(mar-kah)* .... mark ____________

Study the following patterns carefully.

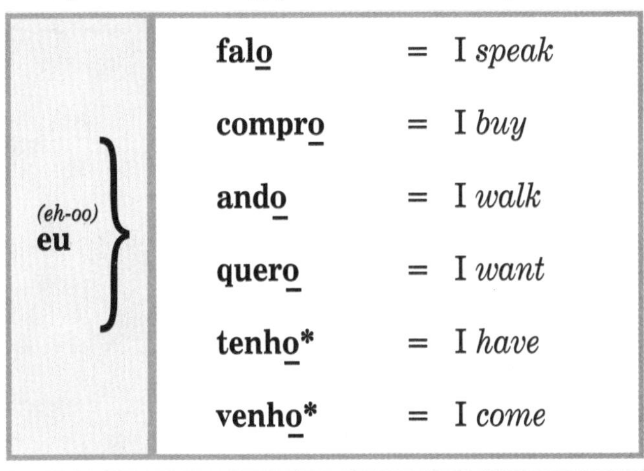

(eh-oo) **eu**		
	falo	= I *speak*
	compro	= I *buy*
	ando	= I *walk*
	quero	= I *want*
	tenho*	= I *have*
	venho*	= I *come*

(noys) **nós**		
	falamos	= we *speak*
	compramos	= we *buy*
	andamos	= we *walk*
	queremos	= we *want*
	temos	= we *have*
	vimos	= we *come*

Note:
- With all these verbs, the first thing you do is drop the final **"ar,"** **"er,"** or **"ir"** from the basic verb form or stem.
- With **"eu,"** add **"o"** to the basic verb form. * Some verbs are irregular. Think of **"o"** as the ending to go with **"eu."**
- With **"nós,"** add the vowel of the original ending plus "**mos**" (a+mos, e+mos, i+mos).

Some verbs just will not conform to the pattern! Do your best to learn them, but don't let them surprise you and don't worry. Speak slowly **e** clearly, **e** you will be perfectly understood whether you say **"eu veno"** or **"eu venho."** Portuguese speakers will be delighted that you have taken the time to learn their language.

Note:
- Portuguese has many different ways of saying "you" whereas in English we only use one word.
- **"Você"** *(voh-say)* will be used throughout this book and will be appropriate for most situations. **"Você"** (you) refers to one person.
- **"Vocês"** (you (plural)) refers to more than one person both in a formal and informal sense, as we might say, "you all."
- **"Tu"** (you (singular)) is a familiar form of address used primarily in Portugal as well as in some parts of Brasil and is generally reserved for family members and very close friends.

❒ **março** *(mar-soo)*	March	__________
❒ **masculino** *(mahs-koo-lee-noo)*	masculine	__________
❒ **a matemática** *(mah-teh-mah-chee-kah)*	mathematics	**m** __________
❒ **o matrimônio** *(mah-tree-moh-nee-oo)*	matrimony	__________
❒ **o mecânico** *(meh-kah-nee-koo)*	mechanic	__________

Here's your next group of patterns!

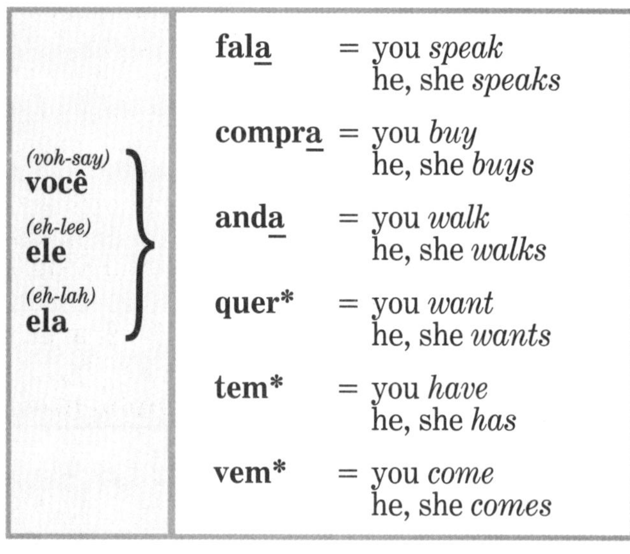

(voh-say) **você** *(eh-lee)* **ele** *(eh-lah)* **ela**	**fala**	= you *speak* he, she *speaks*
	compra	= you *buy* he, she *buys*
	anda	= you *walk* he, she *walks*
	quer*	= you *want* he, she *wants*
	tem*	= you *have* he, she *has*
	vem*	= you *come* he, she *comes*

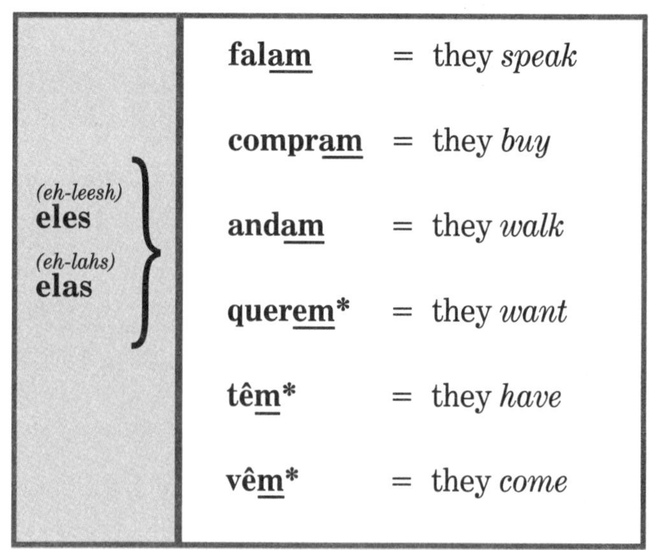

(eh-leesh) **eles** *(eh-lahs)* **elas**	**falam**	= they *speak*
	compram	= they *buy*
	andam	= they *walk*
	querem*	= they *want*
	têm*	= they *have*
	vêm*	= they *come*

Note:
- Again drop the final **"ar,"** **"er,"** or **"ir"** from the basic verb form or stem.
- With **"você,"** **"ele"** and **"ela,"** add **"a"** if the original ending was **"ar"** and **"e"** if the original ending was **"er"** or **"ir"** unless its one of those non-conformist verbs.
- With **"eles,"** and **"elas"** simply add **"m"** to the **"você,"** **"ele"** and **"ela"** form.

* Remember some verbs don't follow the patterns. Focus on the similarities.

(ah-key) (es-town) (saysh)
Aqui estão seis more verbs.
here are six

(ehn-trar) **entrar** _______________
to enter

(preh-see-zar) (dee) **precisar de** _______________
to need, to have need of

(ah-prehn-dair) **aprender** _______________
to learn

(vee-vair) **viver** _______________
to live

(vehn-dair) **vender** _______________
to sell

(heh-peh-cheer) **repetir** _______________
to repeat

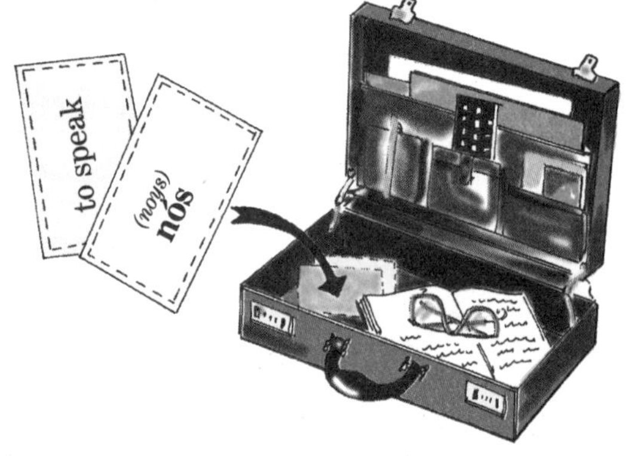

At the back of *(es-chee)* **este** (this) **livro, você** will find twelve **páginas** (pages) of flash cards to help you learn these **palavras novas** (new). Cut them out; carry them in your briefcase, purse, pocket **ou** (or) knapsack; **e** review them whenever **você** have a free moment.

❒ **a medicina** *(meh-jee-see-nah)* . . . . medicine _______________
❒ **o mediterrâneo** *(meh-jee-tair-hah-neh-oo)* . . . Mediterranean _______________
❒ **a melodia** *(meh-loh-jee-ah)* . . . . melody **m** _______________
❒ **o menu** *(meh-noo)* . . . . menu _______________
❒ **o mercado** *(mair-kah-doo)* . . . . market _______________

Agora, it is your turn to practice what **você** have learned. Fill in the following blanks with the correct form of the verb. Each time **você** write out the sentence, be sure to say it aloud.

(fah-lar)
falar
to speak

Bom dia!

Eu ____________________ *(por-too-gaysh)* **português.**

Você ____________________ *(een-glaysh)* **inglês.**

Ele / Ela fala/ ____________________ *(zhah-poh-naysh)* **japonês.** (Japanese)

Nós ____________________ *(frahn-saysh)* **françês.** (French)

Eles / Elas ____________________ *(es-pahn-yohl)* **espanhol.** (Spanish)

(kohm-prar)
comprar
to buy

Eu ____________________ **um livro.** (book)

Você compra/ ____________________ **um** *(heh-loh-zhee-oo)* **relógio.** (watch/clock)

Ele / Ela ____________________ **uma salada.**

Nós ____________________ **um** *(kar-hoo)* **carro.**

Eles / Elas ____________________ *(doysh) (een-grehs-soos)* **dois ingressos de** *(teh-ah-troo)* **teatro.** (theater)

(ahn-dar)
andar
to walk

Eu ando/ ____________________ *(pah-rah)* **para** (to) **a** *(kah-zah)* **casa.**

Você ____________________ **para a** *(pry-ah)* **praia.** (beach)

Ele / Ela ____________________ **para o hotel.**

Nós ____________________ **para o banco.**

Eles / Elas ____________________ **para os** *(bahn-yay-roosh)* **banheiros.** (restrooms)

(kair-air)
querer
to want

Eu ____________________ *(koh-poo)* **um copo** *(jee)* **de vinho** *(cheen-too)* **tinto.** (red)

Você quer/ ____________________ **um copo de vinho branco.** (white)

Ele / Ela quer/ ____________________ **um copo de vinho** *(hoh-zay)* **rosé.** (rosé)

Nós ____________________ *(traysh)* **três copos de** *(ah-gwah)* **água.** (water)

Eles / Elas querem/ ____________________ **cinco copos de** *(soo-koo)* **suco.** (juice)

(tair)
ter
to have

Eu tenho/ ____________________ *(keen-yehn-toosh)* **quinhentos** *(heh-eyes)* **reais.**

Você tem/ ____________________ *(doysh)* **dois mil reais.**

Ele / Ela ____________________ **dez** *(doh-lah-reesh)* **dólares americanos.**

Nós temos/ ____________________ *(heh-eyes)* **reais.**

Eles / Elas têm/ ____________________ *(doh-lah-reesh)* **dólares.**

(veer)
vir
to come

Eu venho/ ____________________ **do** (from) **Brasil.**

Você vem/ ____________________ **da** *(ee-tah-lee-ah)* **Itália.**

Ele / Ela ____________________ **do** *(kah-nah-dah)* **Canadá.**

Nós vimos/ ____________________ **da** *(een-glah-tair-hah)* **Inglaterra.** (England)

Eles / Elas vêm/ ____________________ **da** *(es-pahn-yah)* **Espanha.** (Spain)

❐ **o metrô** *(meh-troh)*	subway		____________
❐ **metropolitano** *(meh-troh-poh-lee-tah-noo)*	metropolitan		____________
❐ **o ministro** *(mee-nees-troo)*	minister (government)		____________
❐ **o minuto** *(mee-noo-too)*	minute	**m**	____________
❐ **moderno** *(moh-dair-noo)*	modern		____________

Now take a break, walk around the room, take a deep breath **e** do the next *(saysh)* **seis** verbs.

(ehn-trar)
entrar
to enter

Eu ____________ **no** *(oh-tel)* **hotel.** (into the)

Você ____________ **no banco.**

Ele / Ela entra/ ____________ **no** *(hehs-tow-rahn-chee)* **restaurante.**

Nós ____________ **na casa.**

Eles / Elas ____________ **no** *(kwahr-too)* **quarto.** (bedroom)

(vee-vair)
viver
to live

Eu ____________ **nos** *(es-tah-doosh)* **Estados** *(oo-nee-doosh)* **Unidos.** (in the / Unites States)

Você ____________ **na** *(eh-oo-roh-pah)* **Europa.** (in)

Ele / Ela ____________ **no Canadá.** (in)

Nós vivemos/ ____________ **no** *(meh-shee-koo)* **México.**

Eles / Elas ____________ **na Espanha.**

(preh-see-zar) (dee)
precisar de
to need, to have need of

Eu ____________ **um** *(koh-poo)* **copo de** *(ah-gwah)* **água.** (water)

Você precisa de/ ____________ **uma** *(sair-veh-zhah)* **cerveja.** (beer)

Ele / Ela ____________ **um copo de** *(veen-yoo)* **vinho.** (wine)

Nós ____________ *(doo-ahs)* **duas** *(shee-kah-rahs)* **xícaras de chá.** (two cups tea)

Eles / Elas ____________ **três xícaras de café.**

(vehn-dair)
vender
to sell

Eu ____________ *(lee-vroosh)* **livros.**

Você vende/ ____________ *(kar-hoosh)* **carros.** (cars)

Ele / Ela ____________ *(kar-toynsh)* **cartões** *(pohs-tiesh)* **postais.** (postcards)

Nós ____________ **ingressos.**

Eles / Elas ____________ *(seh-loosh)* **selos.** (stamps)

(ah-prehn-dair)
aprender
to learn

Eu ____________ *(por-too-gaysh)* **português.**

Você ____________ *(een-glaysh)* **inglês.**

Ele / Ela ____________ *(ah-leh-mown)* **alemão.** (German)

Nós ____________ *(frahn-saysh)* **francês.** (French)

Eles / Elas aprendem/ ____________ *(shee-naysh)* **chinês.** (Chinese)

(heh-peh-cheer)
repetir
to repeat

Alô? Alô? Alô?

Eu repito/ ____________ **a palavra.**

Você ____________ **o** *(ehn-deh-reh-soo)* **endereço.** (address)

Ele / Ela repete/ ____________ **o nome.**

Nós repetimos/ ____________ **as** *(jee-reh-soynsh)* **direções.** (directions)

Eles / Elas *(nown)* **não** repetem/ ____________ **nada.** (nothing)

- ❒ **o momento** *(moh-mehn-too)* .... moment ____________
- ❒ **o monastério** *(moh-nahs-teh-ree-oo)* .... monastery ____________
- ❒ **a montanha** *(mohn-tahn-yah)* .... mountain ____________
- ❒ **o museu** *(moo-zeh-oo)* .... museum ____________
- ❒ **a música** *(moo-zee-kah)* .... music ____________

m

(seem) **Sim,** (yes) it is hard to get used to all those **palavras novas** *(new)*. Just keep practicing **e** before **você** know it, **você** will be using them naturally. **Agora** is a perfect time to turn to the back of this **livro**, clip out your verb flash cards **e** start flashing. Don't skip over your free **palavras** either. Check them off in the box provided as **você** *(ah-prehn-jee)* **aprende** (learn) each one. See if **você** can fill in the blanks below. **As** *(hehs-pohs-tahs)* **respostas** (answers) are at the bottom of **a** *(pah-zhee-nah)* **página** (page).

1. ____
(I speak Portuguese.)

2. ____
(We learn Portuguese.)

3. ____
(She needs ten reais.)

4. ____
(He comes from Canada.)

5. ____
(They live in the United States.)

6. ____
(You buy a book.)

In the following Steps, *(voh-say)* **você** will be introduced to more verbs **e você** should drill them in exactly the same way as **você** did in this section. Look up **as palavras novas** in your *(jee-see-oh-nah-ree-oo)* **dicionário** (dictionary) **e** make up your own sentences. Try out your **palavras novas** for that's how you make them yours to use on your holiday. Remember, the more **você** practice **agora,** the more enjoyable your trip will be.

(boh-ah) (sor-chee)
Boa sorte!
good luck

AS RESPOSTAS

1. Eu falo português.
2. Nós aprendemos português.
3. Ela precisa de dez reais.
4. Ele vem do Canadá.
5. Eles (or Elas) vivem nos Estados Unidos.
6. Você compra um livro.

13 Que horas são?

(kay) (oh-rahs) (sown)
Que horas são?
what time is it

Você know how to tell **os dias** (jee-ahs) days **da semana** (seh-mah-nah) week **e os mêses** (may-zeesh) months **do ano,** (ah-noo) year so now let's learn to tell time. As a traveler, **você** need to be able to tell time in order to make **reservas** (heh-zair-vahs) reservations, **e** to catch **trens** (trains) trains **e ônibus** (ow-nee-boos) buses. **Aqui estão** (es-town) are the "basics." Keep in mind that the 24-hour clock system is frequently used.

What time is it?	=	**Que horas são?** (kay) (oh-rahs) (sown) ______
	=	**Você tem horas?** (voh-say) (tame) do you have the time ______
minutes	=	**minutos** (mee-noo-toosh) ______
half past	=	(the hour) + **e meia** (eh) (may-ah) ______
noon	=	**meio-dia** (may-oo-jee-ah) ______
midnight	=	**meia-noite** (may-ah-noy-chee) ______
a quarter	=	**quinze** (keen-zee) 15 (minutes) ______
a quarter before	=	**quinze para às** (ahs) + (the hour) ______
a quarter after	=	(the hour) + **e quinze** ______

Agora quiz yourself. Fill in the missing letters below.

minutes = m _ n _ t _ s

half past = _ X m _ _ _

a quarter = q _ _ _ _ e

noon = m _ _ o - _ _ a

midnight = m _ _ a - _ _ _ _ e

and finally

What time is it? = Q _ _ X _ o _ _ s X _ ã _ ?

- ❑ **a nação** *(nah-sown)* .... nation ______
- ❑ **natural** *(nah-too-rahl)* .... natural ______
- ❑ **naturalmente** *(nah-too-rahl-mehn-chee)* ... naturally **n** ______
- ❑ **não** *(nown)* .... no, not ______
- ❑ **náutico** *(now-chee-koo)* .... nautical ______

Agora, **como** (how) are these **palavras** used? Study **os** *(eh-zame-ploosh)* **exemplos** (examples) *(ah-by-shoo)* **abaixo.** (below) When **você** think it through, it really is not too difficult. Just notice that the pattern changes after the halfway mark. Notice that the phrase "o'clock" is not used.

(sown) **São** (it is) **cinco** *(oh-rahs)* **horas.**	5:00	São cinco horas. São cinco horas.
São cinco e *(dehsh)* **dez.**	5:10	
São cinco e *(keen-zee)* **quinze.**	5:15	
São cinco e *(veen-chee)* **vinte.**	5:20	
São cinco e *(may-ah)* **meia.** (half past five)	5:30	
São vinte para (before) **às** *(saysh)* **seis.**	5:40	
São quinze para às seis.	5:45	
São dez para às seis.	5:50	
São seis horas.	6:00	

See how *(eem-por-tahn-chee)* **importante é** (it is) to learn **os** *(noo-meh-roosh)* **números?** Answer the following *(pair-goon-tahs)* **perguntas** (questions) based on the *(heh-loh-zhee-oosh)* **relógios** (clocks) below.

1. 8:00 ____________________
2. 7:15 ____________________
3. 4:30 ____________________
4. 9:20 ____________________

AS RESPOSTAS

1. **São oito horas.**
2. **São sete e quinze.**
3. **São quatro e meia.**
4. **São nove e vinte.**

When **você** answer an "**A** *(ah)* (at) **que** *(kay)* (what) **horas?**" *(oh-rahs)* (time) question, say "**às**" *(ahs)* (at) before **você** give the time.

1. **A** *(ah)* (at) **que** *(kay)* (what) **horas** *(oh-rahs)* (time) **chega** *(sheh-gah)* (arrives) **o trem?** *(trame)* (train) ___às seis___ (at 6:00)

2. **A que horas chega o ônibus?** *(ow-nee-boos)* ______________ (at 7:30)

3. **A que horas começa** *(koh-meh-sah)* (begins/commences) **o concerto?** *(kohn-sair-too)* ______________ (at 20:00)

4. **A que horas começa o filme?** *(feel-mee)* (film) ______________ (at 21:00)

5. **A que horas abre** *(ah-bree)* (opens) **o restaurante?** *(hehs-tow-rahn-chee)* ______________ (at 11:30)

6. **A que horas abre o banco?** ______________ (at 8:30)

7. **A que horas fecha** *(feh-shah)* (closes) **o restaurante?** *(hehs-tow-rahn-chee)* ______________ (at 2:00)

8. **A que horas fecha** *(feh-shah)* **o banco?** ______________ (at 16:00)

Agora a quick quiz. Fill in the blanks **com** the correct **números.**

9. **Um minuto** *(mee-noo-too)* (minute) **tem** *(tame)* ______ (?) **segundos.** *(seh-goon-doosh)* (seconds)

10. **Uma hora** (hour) **tem** ______ (?) **minutos.** *(mee-noo-toosh)*

11. **Uma semana** *(seh-mah-nah)* (week) **tem** ______ (?) **dias.** *(jee-ahs)*

12. **Um ano** *(ah-noo)* (year) **tem** ______ (?) **mêses.** *(may-zeesh)* (months)

13. **Um ano tem** ______ (?) **semanas.**

14. **Um ano tem** ______ (?) **dias.** *(jee-ahs)*

AS RESPOSTAS

1. **às seis**
2. **às sete e meia**
3. **às vinte**
4. **às vinte e uma**
5. **às onze e meia**
6. **às oito e meia**
7. **às duas horas**
8. **às dezesseis horas**
9. **sessenta**
10. **sessenta**
11. **sete**
12. **doze**
13. **cinqüenta e duas**
14. **trezentos e sessenta e cinco**

Do **você** remember your greetings from earlier? It is a good time to review them as they will always be **muito** (mwee-too) *very* **importante.** (eem-por-tahn-chee)

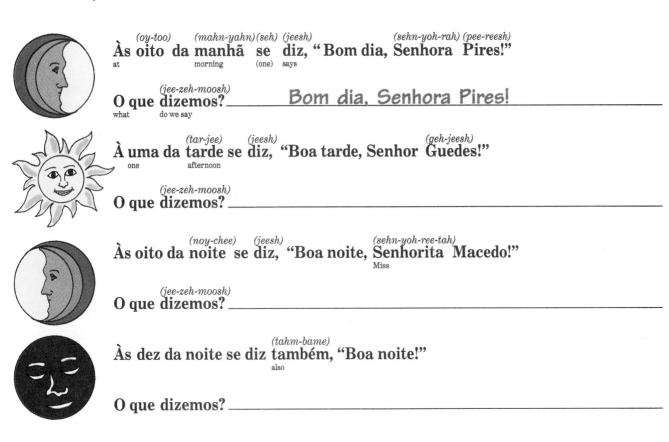

Às *at* **oito** (oy-too) **da manhã** (mahn-yahn) *morning* **se** (seh) *(one)* **diz,** (jeesh) *says* **"Bom dia, Senhora** (sehn-yoh-rah) **Pires!"** (pee-reesh)

O que *what* **dizemos?** (jee-zeh-moosh) *do we say* Bom dia, Senhora Pires!

À uma *one* **da tarde** (tar-jee) *afternoon* **se diz,** (jeesh) **"Boa tarde, Senhor Guedes!"** (geh-jeesh)

O que dizemos? (jee-zeh-moosh) ____________________

Às oito da noite (noy-chee) **se diz,** (jeesh) **"Boa noite, Senhorita** (sehn-yoh-ree-tah) *Miss* **Macedo!"**

O que dizemos? (jee-zeh-moosh) ____________________

Às dez da noite se diz também, (tahm-bame) *also* **"Boa noite!"**

O que dizemos? ____________________

Você have probably already noticed that plurals are *generally* formed by adding "s" after the final vowel.

(ah) (bee-see-kleh-tah) **a bicicleta** *bicycle*	(ahs) (bee-see-kleh-tahs) **as bicicletas**
(teh-leh-foh-nee) **o telefone**	(teh-leh-foh-neesh) **os telefones**
(heh-loh-zhee-oo) **o relógio** *clock/watch*	(heh-loh-zhee-oosh) **os relógios**

Em português adjectives agree with the gender and number of the nouns they modify **e** they generally come after the noun.

a bicicleta vermelha (vair-mel-yah) *red*	**as bicicletas vermelhas** (vair-mel-yahs)
o telefone preto (preh-too) *black*	**os telefones pretos** (preh-toosh)
o relógio (heh-loh-zhee-oo) **novo** (noh-voo) *new*	**os relógios novos** (noh-voosh)

❒ **necessário** *(neh-sehs-sah-ree-oo)*	necessary		____________
❒ **normal** *(nor-mahl)*	normal		____________
❒ **o norte** *(nor-chee)*	north	**O**	____________
❒ **november** *(noh-vem-bair)*	November		____________
❒ **o número** *(noo-meh-roo)*	number		____________

Aqui *(es-town)* **estão** (are) the new verbs for Step 13.

(koh-mair) **comer** (to eat) ______________________ *(beh-bair)* **beber** (to drink) ______________________

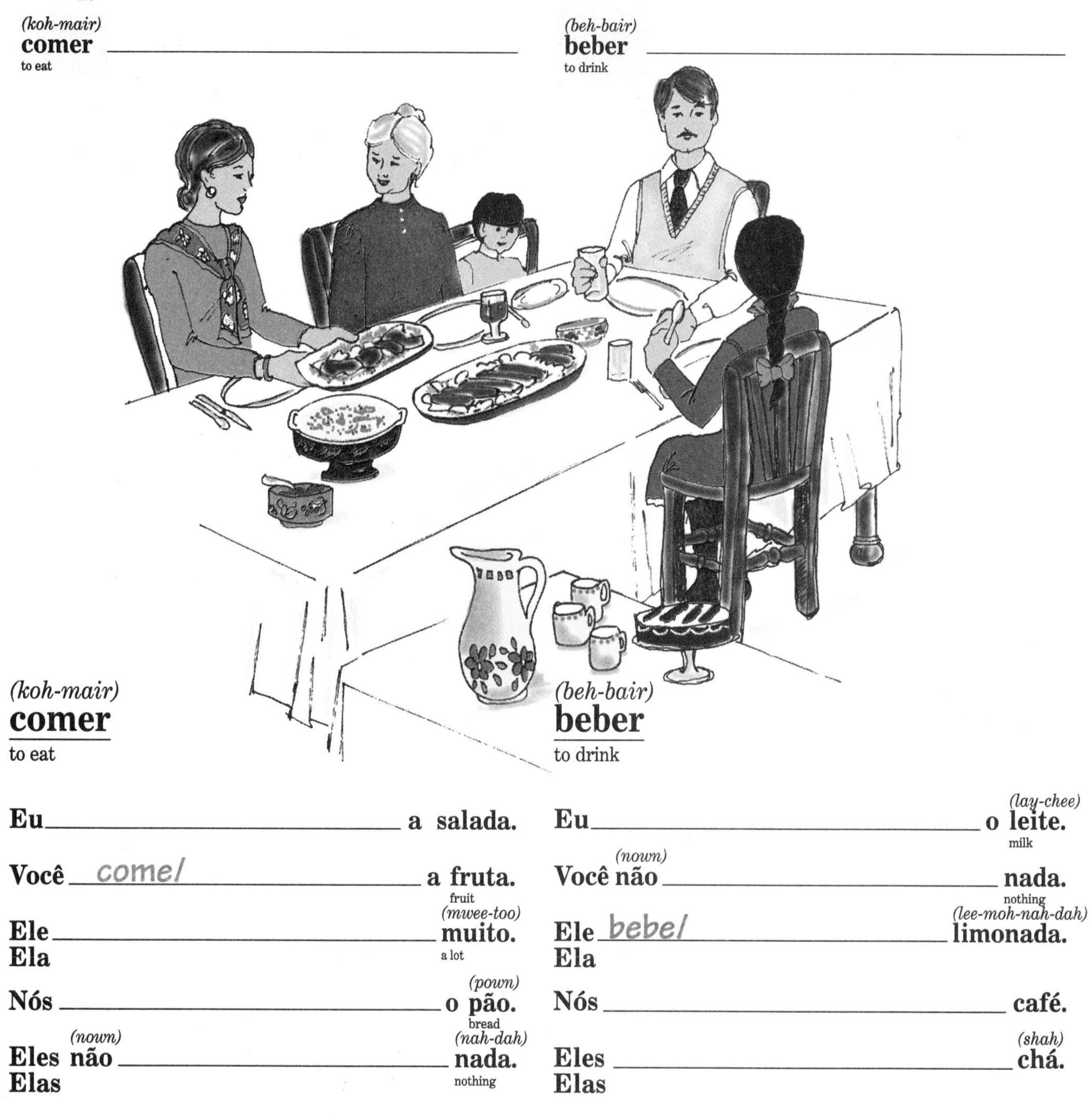

(koh-mair) **comer** to eat		*(beh-bair)* **beber** to drink	
Eu ______________	**a salada.**	**Eu** ______________	**o** *(lay-chee)* **leite.** (milk)
Você come/ ______________	**a fruta.** (fruit)	**Você** *(noun)* **não** ______________	**nada.** (nothing)
Ele / **Ela** ______________	*(mwee-too)* **muito.** (a lot)	**Ele** / **Ela** bebe/ ______________	*(lee-moh-nah-dah)* **limonada.**
Nós ______________	**o** *(pown)* **pão.** (bread)	**Nós** ______________	**café.**
Eles / **Elas** *(noun)* **não** ______________	*(nah-dah)* **nada.** (nothing)	**Eles** / **Elas** ______________	*(shah)* **chá.**

Você have learned that to negate a statement, simply add **não** before the verb. Notice in the examples above, that when you use the word "*(nah-dah)* **nada**," (nothing) you also add "**não**" before the verb.

(eh-oo) **Eu** *(noun)* **não** *(koh-moo)* **como** (eat) **nada.** (nothing)	OR	**Não como nada.**
(noys) **Nós** (we) **não compramos** (buy) **nada.** (nothing)		**Não compramos nada.**

- ❒ **o objeto** *(ohb-zheh-too)*.................... object
- ❒ **a ocasião** *(oh-kah-zee-own)*.............. occasion
- ❒ **o oceano** *(oh-seh-ah-noo)*................. ocean
- ❒ **o ocidente** *(oh-see-dehn-chee)*........... occident, west
- ❒ **ocupado** *(oh-koo-pah-doo)*................ occupied

O ______________

(voh-say)
Você have learned a lot of material in the last few steps **e** that means it is time to quiz yourself. Don't panic, this is just for you **e** no one else needs to know how **você** did. Remember, this is a chance to review, find out what **você** remember **e** what **você** need to spend more time on. After **você** have finished, check your **respostas** *(hehs-pohs-tahs)* in the glossary at the back of this book.

Circle the correct answers.

café -	tea	coffee
sim -	yes	no
tia -	aunt	uncle
ou -	and	or
aprender -	to drink	to learn
noite -	morning	night
terça-feira -	Friday	Tuesday
falar -	to live	to speak
verão -	summer	winter
dinheiro -	money	page
dez -	nine	ten
muito -	a lot	bread

família -	seven	family
filhos -	children	grandfather
leite -	butter	milk
sal -	pepper	salt
embaixo de -	under	over
homem -	man	doctor
junho -	June	July
cozinha -	kitchen	religion
tenho -	I want	I have
comprar -	to order	to buy
ontem -	yesterday	tomorrow
bom -	good	yellow

Como vai? *(vy)* What time is it? How are you? Well, how are you after this quiz?

- ❒ **a ópera** *(oh-peh-rah)* . . . . opera ______________
- ❒ **a operação** *(oh-peh-rah-sown)* . . . . operation ______________
- ❒ **a opção** *(ohp-sown)* . . . . option **O** ______________
- ❒ **a oportunidade** *(oh-por-too-nee-dah-jee)* . . . opportunity ______________
- ❒ **a oposição** *(oh-poh-zee-sown)* . . . . opposition ______________

14 Norte - Sul, Leste - Oeste

(nor-chee) **Norte** (north) - *(sool)* **Sul,** (south) *(lehs-chee)* **Leste** (east) - *(oh-ehs-chee)* **Oeste** (west)

If **você** are looking at **um** *(mah-pah)* **mapa** (map) **e você** see the following **palavras,** it should not be too difficult to figure out what they mean. Take an educated guess.

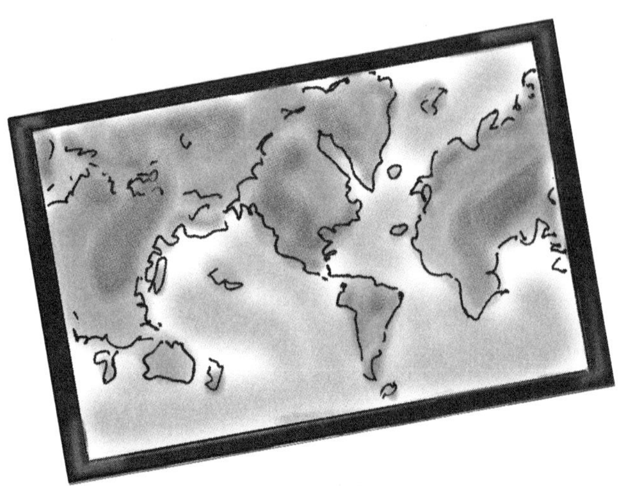

(ah-meh-ree-kah) (doo) (nor-chee) **América do Norte**	*(sool)* **América do Sul**
(poh-loo) **Pólo Norte**	**Pólo Sul**
(kohs-tah) (lehs-chee) **a costa do leste**	*(oh-ehs-chee)* **a costa do oeste**
(eer-lahn-dah) **Irlanda do Norte**	*(ah-free-kah)* **África do Sul**

As palavras *(por-too-gay-zahs)* **portuguesas** "north," "south," "east," **e** "west" are easy to recognize due to their similarity to **inglês**. These **palavras** *(sown)* **são** (are) *(mwee-too)* **muito** *(eem-por-tahn-chees)* **importantes**. Learn them *(oh-zhee)* **hoje**!

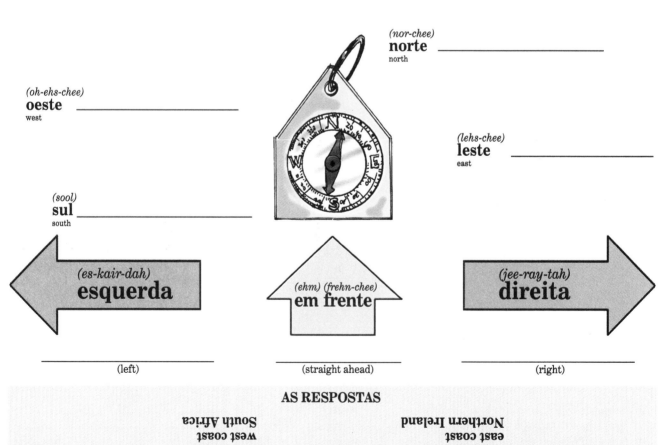

(nor-chee) **norte** (north) ____________________

(oh-ehs-chee) **oeste** (west) ____________________

(lehs-chee) **leste** (east) ____________________

(sool) **sul** (south) ____________________

(es-kair-dah) **esquerda** ____________________ (left)

(ehm) (frehn-chee) **em frente** ____________________ (straight ahead)

(jee-ray-tah) **direita** ____________________ (right)

AS RESPOSTAS

North America	South America
North Pole	South Pole
east coast	west coast
Northern Ireland	South Africa

These **palavras** can go a long way. Say them aloud each time you write them in the blanks below.

(por) (fah-vor)
por favor ______________________________
please/excuse me (to catch attention)

(kohm) (lee-sehn-sah)
com licença ______________________________
excuse me (when interupting)

(dehs-kool-pee)
desculpe ______________________________
excuse me (as in I am sorry)

(oh-bree-gah-doo) (oh-bree-gah-dah)
obrigado / obrigada ______________________________
thank you (♂) thank you (♀)

(jee) (nah-dah)
de nada ______________________________
you're welcome

Aqui estão *(doo-ahs)* **duas** (two) *(kohn-vair-sah-soynsh)* **conversações** (conversations) very *(chee-pee-kahs)* **típicas** (typical) **para** (for) someone who is trying to find something.

Write them out in the blanks below.

João: Por favor. Onde é o *(oh-tel)* Hotel *(koh-pah-kah-bah-nah)* Copacabana *(pah-lah-see)* Palace?

Por favor. Onde é o Hotel Copacabana Palace?

Carlos: *(vy)* Vai (go) em frente (straight ahead) e *(vee-ree)* vire (turn) na segunda (second) à esquerda (left).

____

O Hotel Copacabana *(pah-lah-see)* Palace é à *(jee-ray-tah)* direita.

____

Orlando: Por favor. Onde é o *(moo-zeh-oo)* Museu de *(ar-chees)* Artes?

____

Cristina: *(vee-ree)* Vire (turn) à *(jee-ray-tah)* direita e *(vy)* vai (go) em frente *(ah-proh-see-mah-dah-mehn-chee)* aproximadamente (approximately) *(same)* cem *(meh-troosh)* metros (meters).

____

O Museu de Artes é à esquerda.

____

O

- ❒ **ordinário** *(or-jee-nah-ree-oo)* .... ordinary ______________
- ❒ **oriental** *(oh-ree-ehn-tahl)* .... oriental ______________
- ❒ **original** *(oh-ree-zhee-nahl)* .... original ______________
- ❒ **a ostra** *(ohs-trah)* .... oyster ______________
- ❒ **oval** *(oh-vahl)* .... oval ______________

Are **você** lost? There is no need to be lost if **você** have learned the basic direction **palavras.** Do not try to memorize these *(kohn-vair-sah-soynsh)* **conversações** because **você** will never be looking for precisely these places. One day, **você** might need to ask *(jee-reh-soynsh)* **direções** (directions) to "**O Hotel** *(hee-oo)* **Rio** *(pah-lah-see)* **Palace**" or "*(hehs-tow-rahn-chee)* **Restaurante** *(kah-roh-lee-nee)* **Caroline.**" Learn the key direction **palavras e** be sure **você** can find your destination. **Você** may want to buy a guidebook to start planning which places **você** would like to visit. Practice asking *(jee-reh-soynsh)* **direções** to these special places. What if the person responding to your *(pair-goon-tah)* **pergunta** (question) answers too quickly for **você** to understand the entire reply? Practice saying,

(dehs-kool-pee) **Desculpe.** *(nown) (ehn-tehn-doo)* **Não entendo.** (I do not understand) *(poh-jee)* **Pode** (can you) *(heh-peh-cheer)* **repetir,** (repeat) **por favor?**

Agora, say it again **e** then write it out below.

____
(Excuse me. I do not understand. Can you repeat, please?)

(seem) **Sim,** (yes) **é** (it is) *(jee-fee-seel)* **difícil** (difficult) at first but don't give up! **Quando** (when) the directions are repeated, **você** will be able to understand if **você** have learned the key **palavras.** Let's review by writing them in the blanks below.

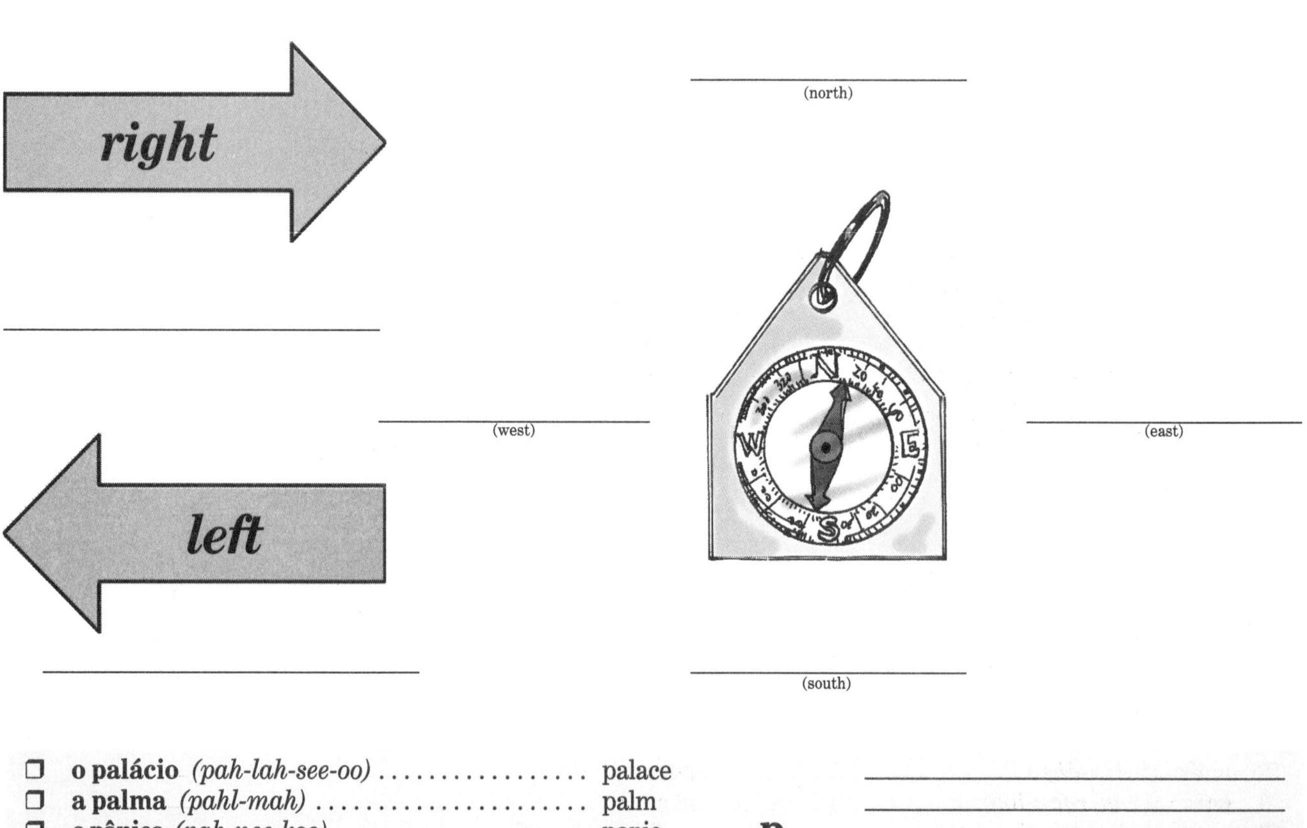

- ❐ **o palácio** *(pah-lah-see-oo)* .... palace
- ❐ **a palma** *(pahl-mah)* .... palm
- ❐ **o pânico** *(pah-nee-koo)* .... panic
- ❐ **o passaporte** *(pahs-sah-por-chee)* .... passport
- ❐ **a pausa** *(pow-zah)* .... pause

p

Aqui *(es-town)* **estão** (are) **quatro** verbs *(noh-voosh)* **novos.** (new)

(ehn-kohn-trar) **encontrar** to find, to meet ______________________

(ehn-tehn-dair) **entender** to understand ______________________

(mahn-dar) **mandar** to send ______________________

(es-kreh-vair) **escrever** to write ______________________

As always, say each sentence out loud. Say each **e** every **palavra** carefully, pronouncing each sound **em** *(por-too-gaysh)* **português** as well as **você** can.

(ehn-kohn-trar)
encontrar
to find, to meet

Eu ______________________ o hotel.

Você encontra/ ______________________ o *(hehs-tow-rahn-chee)* restaurante.

Ele / Ela ______________________ o banco.

Nós ______________________ o *(moo-zeh-oo)* museu.

Eles / Elas ______________________ o *(jeen-yay-roo)* dinheiro.

(ehn-tehn-dair)
entender
to understand

Eu entendo/ ______________________ *(por-too-gaysh)* português.

Você entende/ ______________________ *(een-glaysh)* inglês.

Ele / Ela ______________________ *(ah-leh-mown)* alemão. (German)

Nós ______________________ *(hoos-soo)* russo. (Russian)

Eles / Elas ______________________ *(frahn-saysh)* francês.

(mahn-dar)
mandar
to send

Eu ______________________ a *(kar-tah)* carta. (letter)

Você ______________________ o *(kar-town)* cartão *(pohs-tahl)* postal.

Ele / Ela manda/ ______________________ o *(lee-vroo)* livro.

Nós ______________________ *(doysh)* dois *(kar-toynsh)* cartões *(pohs-tiesh)* postais.

Eles / Elas ______________________ cinco cartas.

(es-kreh-vair)
escrever
to write

Eu ______________________ o *(ehn-deh-reh-soo)* endereço. (address)

Você escreve/ ______________________ *(mwee-too)* muito. (a lot)

Ele não / Ela ______________________ nada. (nothing)

Nós ______________________ *(doo-ahs)* duas cartas.

Eles / Elas ______________________ suas (their) *(ahs-see-nah-too-rahs)* assinaturas. (signatures)

p

- ❒ **a pêra** *(pair-ah)* .... pear ______________
- ❒ **perfeito** *(pair-fay-too)* .... perfect ______________
- ❒ **o perfume** *(pair-foo-mee)* .... perfume ______________
- ❒ **o/a pianista** *(pee-ah-nees-tah)* .... pianist ______________
- ❒ **o piano** *(pee-ah-noo)* .... piano ______________

15

(ehm) Em *(see-mah)* cima – *(ehm-by-shoo)* Embaixo
upstairs — downstairs

Aqui *(noys)* **nós** (we) *(ah-prehn-deh-moosh)* **aprendemos** (learn) *(mysh)* **mais palavras** (more). Imagine that this **é uma casa em** *(sown)* **São** *(pow-loo)* **Paulo.** Go to your *(kwahr-too)* **quarto** (bedroom) **e** look around **o quarto.** Let's learn the names of the things **no** (in) *(seh-oo)* **seu** (your) **quarto,** just like *(noys)* **nós** learned the various parts of **a casa.**

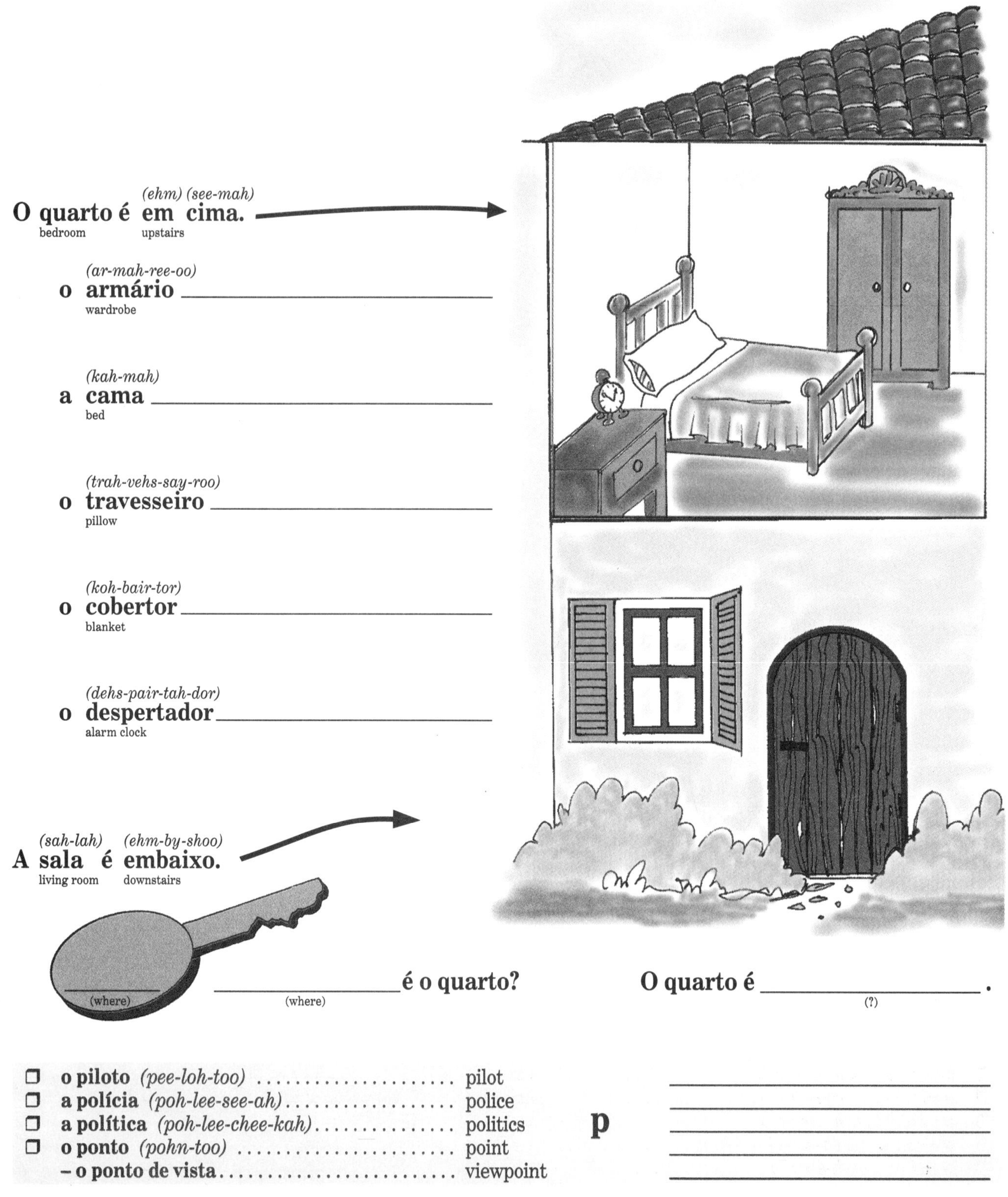

O quarto é *(ehm) (see-mah)* **em cima.**
bedroom — upstairs

o *(ar-mah-ree-oo)* **armário** (wardrobe) ______________________

a *(kah-mah)* **cama** (bed) ______________________

o *(trah-vehs-say-roo)* **travesseiro** (pillow) ______________________

o *(koh-bair-tor)* **cobertor** (blanket) ______________________

o *(dehs-pair-tah-dor)* **despertador** (alarm clock) ______________________

A *(sah-lah)* **sala** (living room) **é** *(ehm-by-shoo)* **embaixo** (downstairs).

(where)

______________ **é o quarto?** (where) **O quarto é** ______________ (?) **.**

❒	**o piloto** *(pee-loh-too)*	pilot
❒	**a polícia** *(poh-lee-see-ah)*	police
❒	**a política** *(poh-lee-chee-kah)*	politics
❒	**o ponto** *(pohn-too)*	point
	– o ponto de vista	viewpoint

p ______________________

Agora, remove the next **cinco** stickers **e** label these things **no** **seu** *(seh-oo)* (your) **quarto.** Let's move **para** (to) **o** (the) **banheiro** *(bahn-yay-roo)* **e** do the same thing. Restrooms may be marked with pictures **ou** simply with the letters **D** **ou** **C.** **Você** may also see the women's restroom labeled "**Damas**" *(dah-mahs)* **ou** "**Mulheres.**" *(mool-yair-eesh)* Either "**Cavalheiros**" *(kah-vahl-yay-roosh)* **ou** "**Homens**" *(oh-mehns)* is used to identify the men's restroom.

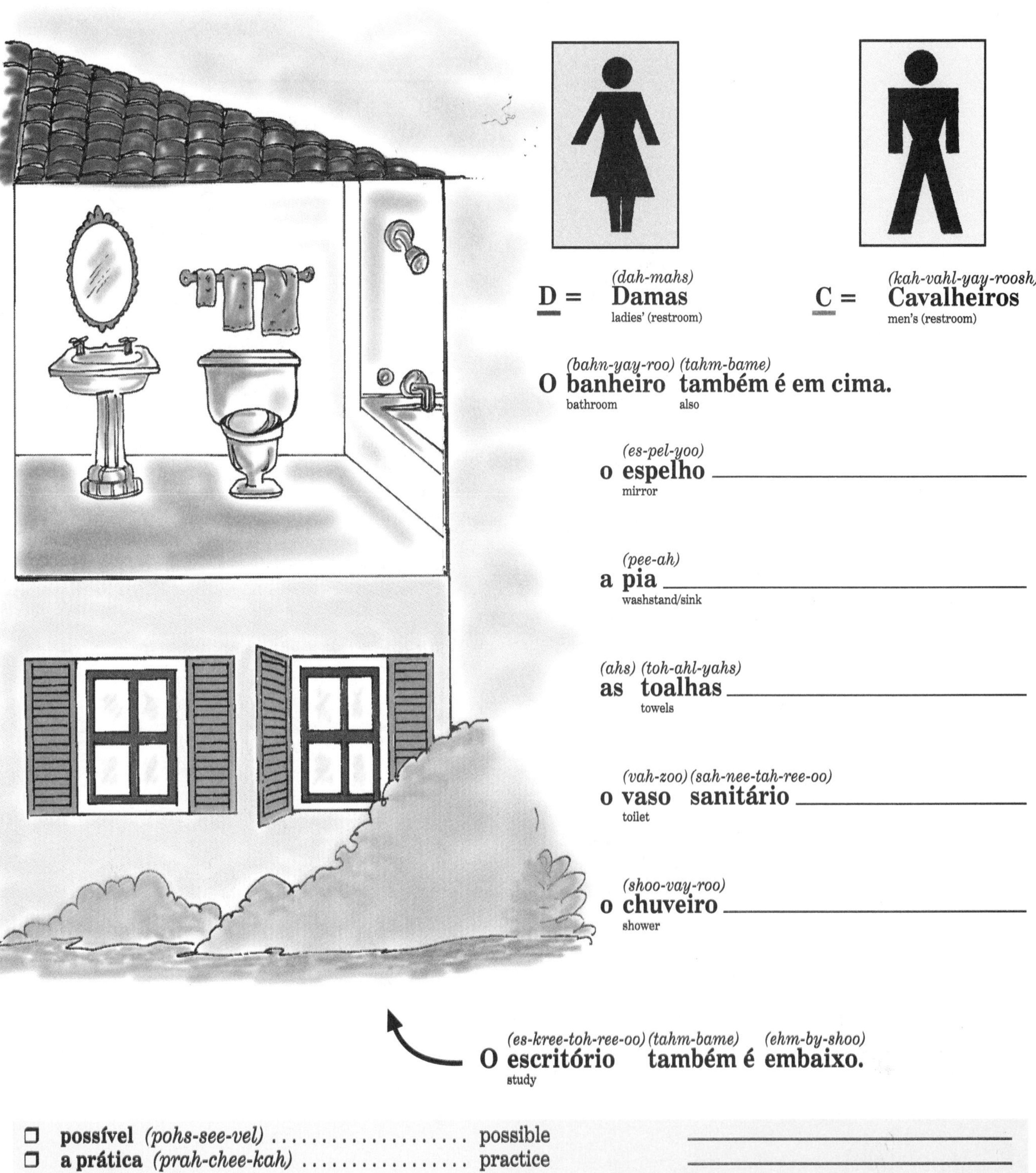

D = **Damas** *(dah-mahs)* — ladies' (restroom)

C = **Cavalheiros** *(kah-vahl-yay-roosh)* — men's (restroom)

O banheiro *(bahn-yay-roo)* (bathroom) **também** *(tahm-bame)* (also) **é em cima.**

o espelho *(es-pel-yoo)* (mirror) ____________________

a pia *(pee-ah)* (washstand/sink) ____________________

as toalhas *(ahs) (toh-ahl-yahs)* (towels) ____________________

o vaso sanitário *(vah-zoo) (sah-nee-tah-ree-oo)* (toilet) ____________________

o chuveiro *(shoo-vay-roo)* (shower) ____________________

O escritório *(es-kree-toh-ree-oo)* (study) **também** *(tahm-bame)* **é embaixo.** *(ehm-by-shoo)*

❒ **possível** *(pohs-see-vel)*	possible	____________________
❒ **a prática** *(prah-chee-kah)*	practice	____________________
❒ **preciso** *(preh-see-zoo)*	precise	**p** ____________________
❒ **precioso** *(preh-see-oh-zoo)*	precious	____________________
❒ **o preço** *(preh-soo)*	price	____________________

(noun)
Não forget to remove the next group of stickers **e** label these things in your **banheiro.** Okay, it is time to review. Here's a quick quiz to see what you remember.

men's (restroom)	*(ehm-by-shoo)* **embaixo**
I understand	*(kah-vahl-yay-roosh)* **cavalheiros**
downstairs	**por favor**
please	**eu** *(ehn-tehn-doo)* **entendo**
towels	*(heh-peh-cheer)* **repetir**
upstairs	**em** *(frehn-chee)* **frente**
bathroom/restroom	**damas**
to repeat	**as** *(toh-ahl-yahs)* **toalhas**
straight ahead	**em cima**
women's (restroom)	**o** *(bahn-yay-roo)* **banheiro**

p

- ❒ **o presente** *(preh-zehn-chee)* .... present, gift ____________________
- ❒ **principal** *(preen-see-pahl)*................. principal, main ____________________
- ❒ **o problema** *(proh-bleh-mah)*............... problem ____________________
- ❒ **o produto** *(proh-doo-too)* .... product ____________________
- ❒ **o professor** *(proh-fehs-sor)* .... professor ____________________

Next stop — **o** *(es-kree-toh-ree-oo)* **escritório,** (office) specifically **a** *(meh-zah)* **mesa** (table/desk) **do** *(es-kree-toh-ree-oo)* **escritório.** **O** *(kay)* **que está** *(soh-bree)* **sobre** (on) **a mesa?**

Let's identify **as** *(koy-zahs)* **coisas** (things) which one normally finds **sobre a mesa** or strewn about **o escritório.**

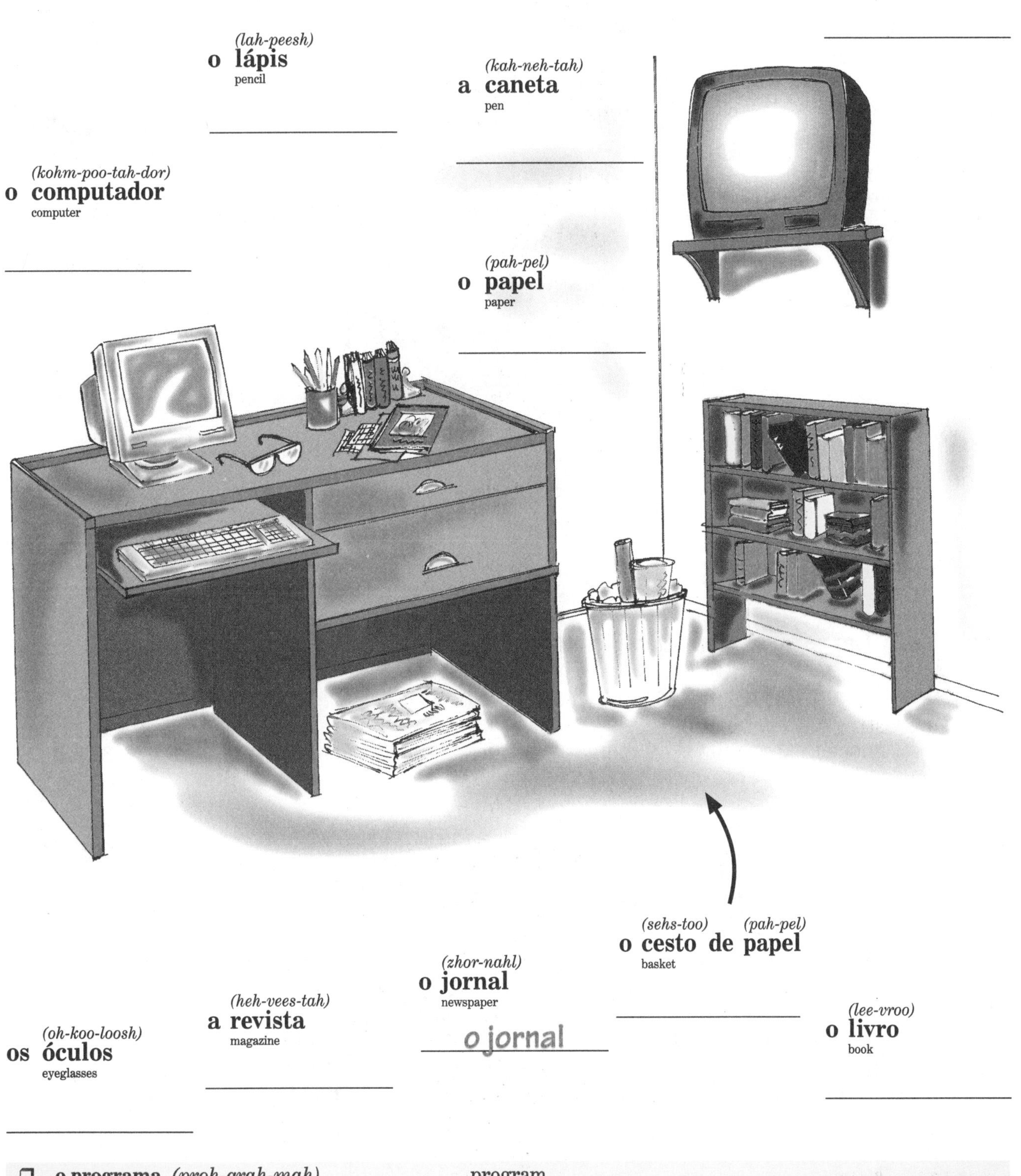

❒ **o programa** *(proh-grah-mah)*	program	_______________
❒ **proibido** *(proh-ee-bee-doo)*	prohibited, forbidden	_______________
❒ **a promessa** *(proh-mehs-sah)*	promise **p**	_______________
❒ **a pronúncia** *(proh-noon-see-ah)*	pronunciation	_______________
❒ **o público** *(poo-blee-koo)*	public	_______________

Don't forget these essentials!

(kar-tah)
a carta
letter

(seh-loo)
o selo
stamp

(kar-town) (pohs-tahl)
o cartão postal
postcard

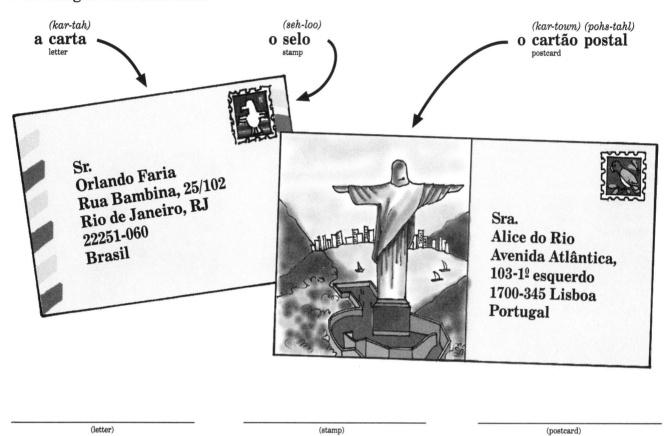

Sr.
Orlando Faria
Rua Bambina, 25/102
Rio de Janeiro, RJ
22251-060
Brasil

Sra.
Alice do Rio
Avenida Atlântica,
103-1º esquerdo
1700-345 Lisboa
Portugal

________________ (letter) ________________ (stamp) ________________ (postcard)

(kar-nah-vahl)
Carnaval no Brasil é a party celebrated by the entire country. The dates vary from **ano** to **ano,** but officially **Carnaval** starts **no sábado** before **e** finishes on Ash Wednesday. The parade of the *(es-koh-lahs)* *(sahm-bah)* **Escolas** (schools) **de Samba é** "the event" with thousands of people wearing glamorous costumes **e** dancing enthusiastically while competing for Brazil's "World Cup of **Carnaval.**"

Remember if you add **<u>não</u>** (not) before a verb **você** negate the sentence.

(kair-oo) *(koh-poo)* **Eu quero um copo de água.** want, glass, water	**Eu não quero um copo de água.** do not want

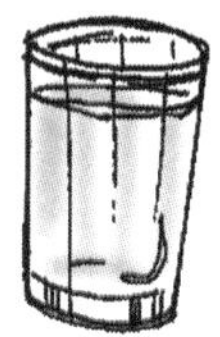

Em português, you may drop the subject of the sentence as long as the meaning remains clear.

Eu entendo português. (understand)	OR	**Entendo português.**
Nós vimos dos Estados Unidos. (come)		**Vimos dos Estados Unidos.**

r

- ❒ **o rádio** *(hah-joo)* .... radio ____________
- ❒ **a raça** *(hah-sah)* .... race ____________
- ❒ **o raio** *(hi-oo)* .... ray ____________
- ❒ **rápido** *(hah-pee-doo)* .... rapid ____________
- ❒ **a reação** *(heh-ah-sown)* .... reaction ____________

Simple, isn't it? **Agora**, after you fill in the blanks below, go back a second time and negate all these sentences by adding "**não**" *(nown)* before each verb. Then go back a third time **e** drop the subject. **Você** will see some verbs which do not conform to the patterns. Don't get discouraged! Just look at how much **você** have already learned **e** think ahead to beautiful **praias** *(pry-ahs)* beaches, **Pão de Açúcar** *(pown) (jeh) (ah-soo-kar)* Sugar Loaf, **e** new adventures **no Rio.**

(teh-leh-foh-nar) **telefonar** to phone, to call ____________

(dor-meer) **dormir** to sleep ____________

(pah-gar) **pagar** to pay, to pay for ____________

(mee) (dah) (por) (fah-vor) **me dá . . . por favor** give me please ____________

(teh-leh-foh-nar)
telefonar
to phone, to call

Eu ____________ **para o Canadá.** (to)

Você ____________ **para os Estados Unidos.**

Ele / Ela telefona/ ____________ **para a Itália.**

Nós ____________ **para a Inglaterra.**

Eles / Elas ____________ **à cobrar.** *(koh-brar)* collect

(pah-gar)
pagar
to pay, to pay for

Eu pago/ ____________ **a conta.** *(kohn-tah)* bill

Você ____________ **os ingressos do teatro.** *(een-grehs-soos)* tickets *(teh-ah-troo)* theater

Ele / Ela ____________ **os ingressos do balé.** *(bah-lay)* ballet

Nós ____________ **os ingressos do museu.** *(moo-zeh-oo)*

Eles / Elas ____________ **os ingressos do concerto.** *(kohn-sair-too)* concert

(dor-meer)
dormir
to sleep

Eu durmo/ ____________ **no quarto.** *(kwahr-too)* bedroom

Você dorme/ ____________ **no hotel.**

Ele / Ela ____________ **na casa.**

Nós dormimos/ ____________ **embaixo do cobertor.** *(ehm-by-shoo)* under *(koh-bair-tor)* blanket

Eles / Elas dormem/ ____________ **sem os travesseiros.** *(same)* without *(trah-vehs-say-roosh)* pillows

(mee) (dah) (fah-vor)
me dá . . . por favor
give me please

Me dá/ ____________ **a conta,** *(kohn-tah)* bill por favor/ ____________.

____________ **o menu,** *(meh-noo)* ____________.

____________ **o ingresso,** *(een-grehs-soo)* ____________.

____________ **o endereço,** *(ehn-deh-reh-soo)* address ____________.

____________ **o nome,** ____________.

❒ **a rebelião** *(heh-beh-lee-own)*	rebellion		____________
❒ **receber** *(heh-seh-bair)*	to receive		____________
❒ **regular** *(heh-goo-lar)*	regular	**r**	____________
❒ **a relação** *(heh-lah-sown)*	relation		____________
❒ **a religião** *(heh-lee-zhee-own)*	religion		____________

Before **você** proceed with the next step, **por favor** identify all the items **abaixo.** *(ah-by-shoo)* below

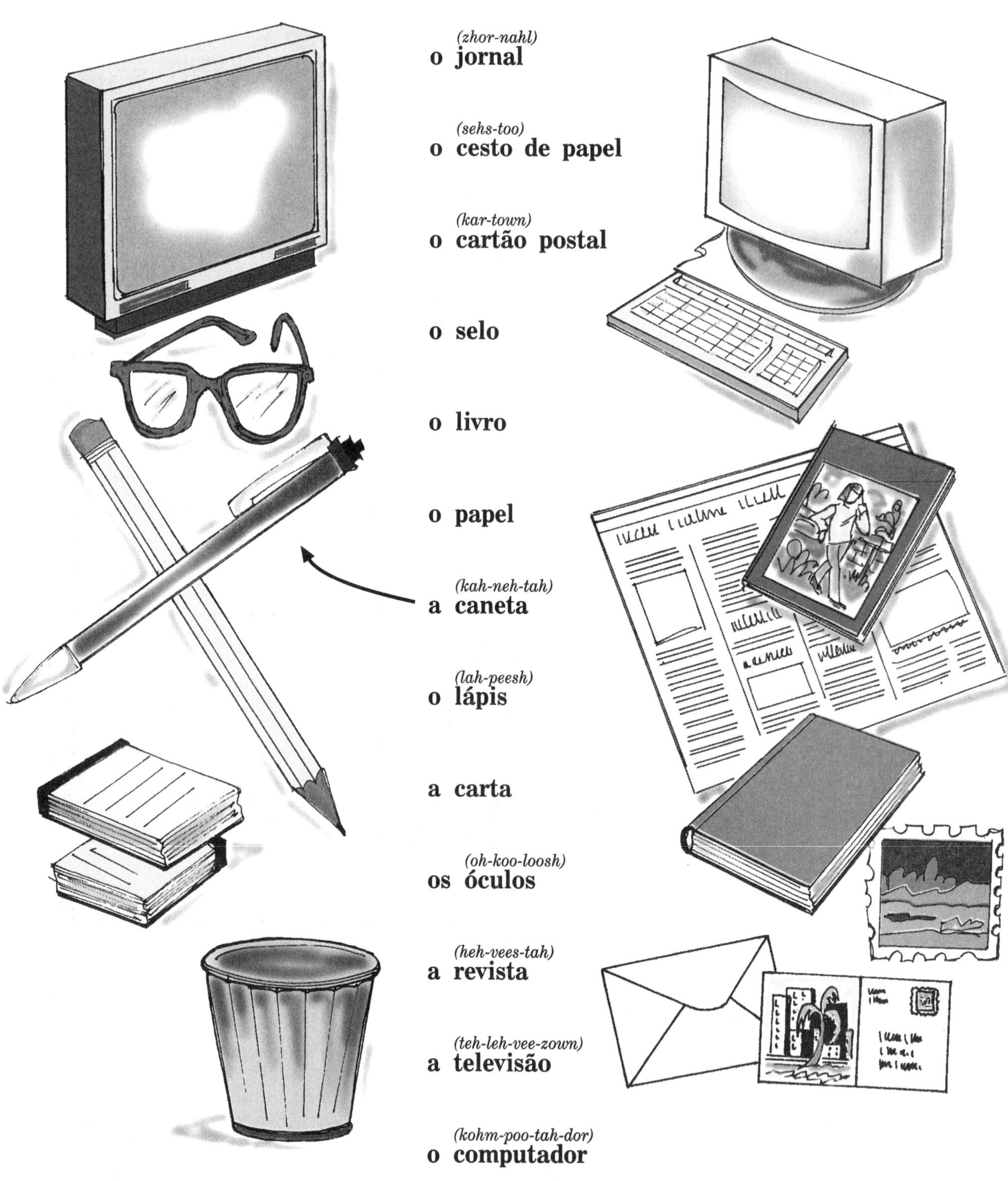

(zhor-nahl)
o jornal

(sehs-too)
o cesto de papel

(kar-town)
o cartão postal

o selo

o livro

o papel

(kah-neh-tah)
a caneta

(lah-peesh)
o lápis

a carta

(oh-koo-loosh)
os óculos

(heh-vees-tah)
a revista

(teh-leh-vee-zown)
a televisão

(kohm-poo-tah-dor)
o computador

- ❒ **relaxado** *(heh-lah-shah-doo)*................ relaxed
- ❒ **repetir** *(heh-peh-cheer)* .... to repeat
  - **– Repita por favor!** .... Please repeat!
- ❒ **a república** *(heh-poo-blee-kah)*........... republic
- ❒ **a reserva** *(heh-zair-vah)* .... reservation

r

(kor-hay-oo) O Correio (mail/post office) — 16

Agora você know how to count, how to ask **perguntas** *(pair-goon-tahs)* (questions), how to use verbs **com** the "plug-in" formula **e** how to describe something, be it the location of **um hotel ou a cor** (color) **de uma casa**. Let's take the basics that **você** have learned **e** expand them in special areas that will be most helpful in your travels. What does everyone do on a vacation? Send **cartões** *(kar-toynsh)* **postais,** *(pohs-tiesh)* of course! Let's learn exactly how **a** (the) **agência** *(ah-zhayn-see-ah)* **do correio,** *(kor-hay-oo)* (post office) or simply **"correio"** *(kor-hay-oo)* works.

O correio *(kor-hay-oo)* (post office) is where **você** buy **selos,** *(seh-loosh)* send **pacotes,** *(pah-koh-chees)* (packages) **cartas e cartões postais.** *(kar-toynsh)(pohs-tiesh)* In large cities, **você** can send **um fax** *(fahks)* **ou e-mail** *(ee-may-oo)* **do correio. No correio você** can also buy **um cartão de telefone** *(kar-town) (teh-leh-foh-nee)* (phone card) **e** make **cópias.** *(koh-pee-ahs)* (copies)

❒ **o restaurante** *(hehs-tow-rahn-chee)*	restautant		______________
❒ **a revolução** *(heh-voh-loo-sown)*	revolution		______________
❒ **romano** *(hoh-mah-noo)*	Roman	**r**	______________
❒ **romântico** *(hoh-mahn-chee-koo)*	romantic		______________
❒ **o rubi** *(hoo-bee)*	ruby		______________

Aqui estão the necessary **palavras para o correio.** Practice them aloud **e** write them in the blanks.

(kar-tah)
a carta
letter

(kar-town) (pohs-tahl)
o cartão postal
postcard

(pah-koh-chee)
o pacote
package

(ee-may-oo)
o e-mail
e-mail

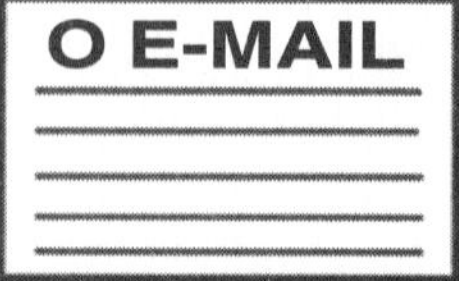

(vee-ah) (ah-air-ee-ah)
via aérea
by airmail

(fahks)
o fax
fax

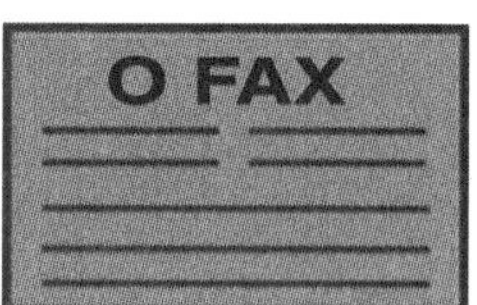

(seh-loo)
o selo
stamp

(kah-bee-nee) (teh-leh-foh-nee-kah)
a cabine telefônica /
telephone booth

(oh-rel-yown)
o orelhão

(ky-shah) (kor-hay-oo)
a caixa do correio
mailbox

(teh-leh-foh-nee)
o telefone
telephone

S

- ❐ **o sal** *(sahl)* .... salt
- ❐ **o salário** *(sah-lah-ree-oo)* .... salary
- ❐ **o salmão** *(sahl-moun)* .... salmon
- ❐ **o santo** *(sahn-too)* .... saint
- ❐ **a sardinha** *(sar-jeen-yah)* .... sardine

Next step — **você** ask *(pair-goon-tahs)* **perguntas** like those *(ah-by-shoo)* **abaixo,** depending on what **você** *(kair)* **quer.** Repeat these sentences aloud many times.

(ohn-jee) (kohm-proo) (seh-loosh)
Onde compro selos? ______________________
(compro = do I buy)

(kar-town)
Onde compro um cartão postal? ______________________

(ah) (teh-leh-foh-nee)
Onde há um telefone? ______________________
(há = is there)

(ah) (ky-shah) (kor-hay-oo)
Onde há uma caixa do correio? ______________________
(há = is there; caixa do correio = mailbox)

Onde há uma cabine telefônica? ______________________
(cabine telefônica = telephone booth)

(pohs-soo) (mahn-dar) (pah-koh-chee)
Onde posso mandar um pacote? ______________________
(posso = can I; mandar = send)

(fah-zair) (shah-mah-dah) (loh-kahl)
Onde posso fazer uma chamada local? ______________________
(posso = can I; fazer = make; chamada = call)

Quanto custa isso? Quanto custa isso? Quanto custa isso?

Agora, quiz yourself. See if **você** can translate the following thoughts into **português.**

1. Where is there a telephone booth? ______________________
2. Where can I phone to the U.S.A.? ______________________
3. Where can I make a local telephone call? ______________________
4. Where is the post office? ______________________
5. Where can I buy stamps? ______________________
6. Airmail stamps? ______________________
7. Where can I send a package? ______________________
8. Where can I send a fax? ______________________

AS RESPOSTAS

1. **Onde há uma cabine telefônica?**
2. **Onde posso telefonar para os Estados Unidos?**
3. **Onde posso fazer uma chamada local?**
4. **Onde é o correio?**
5. **Onde posso comprar selos?**
6. **Selos por via aérea?**
7. **Onde posso mandar un pacote?**
8. **Onde posso mandar un fax?**

Aqui estão *(mysh)* **mais** (more) *(vair-boosh)* **verbos.** (verbs)

(fah-zair) **fazer** (to make, to do) ______________________

(jee-zair) **dizer** (to say) ______________________

(vair) **ver** (to see) ______________________

(eer) **ir** (to go) ______________________

Practice these verbs by not only filling in the blanks, but by saying them aloud many, many times until you are comfortable with the sounds **e** the words.

(fah-zair)
fazer
to make, to do

Eu faço/ ______________ *(too-doo)* **tudo.** (everything)

Você não faz/ ______________ **nada.** (nothing)

Ele não / **Ela** ______________ *(mwee-too)* **muito.**

Nós não fazemos/ ______________ **a cama.**

Eles / **Elas** fazem/ ______________ **o café.**

(jee-zair)
dizer
to say

Oi!

Eu digo/ ______________ *(oy)* **"oi."** (hi)

Você diz/ ______________ **"sim."**

Ele / **Ela** ______________ **"não."**

Nós dizemos/ ______________ *(chow)* **"tchau" ou** *(ah-deh-oos)* **"adeus."**

Eles não / **Elas** dizem/ ______________ **nada.**

(vair)
ver
to see

Eu vejo/ ______________ **o** *(mair-kah-doo)* **mercado.** (market)

Você vê/ ______________ **o Museu de** *(ar-chees)* **Artes.**

Ele / **Ela** ______________ **o Teatro** *(moo-nee-see-pahl)* **Municipal.** (Municipal Theater)

Nós vemos/ ______________ **o** *(oh-seh-ah-noo)* **Oceano** (Ocean) *(aht-lahn-chee-koo)* **Atlântico.** (Atlantic)

Eles / **Elas** vêem/ ______________ **as** *(mohn-tahn-yahs)* **montanhas.** (mountains)

(eer)
ir
to go

Eu vou/ ______________ **à** *(pry-ah)* **praia.** (beach)

Você vai/ ______________ *(ah-oh)* **ao concerto.**

Ele / **Ela** vai/ ______________ **ao hotel.**

Nós vamos/ ______________ **à** *(see-dah-jee)* **cidade.** (city)

Eles / **Elas** vão/ ______________ **à** *(ee-greh-zhah)* **igreja.** (church)

- ❒ **a secretária** *(seh-kreh-tah-ree-ah)*........... secretary (♀) ______________
- ❒ **o secretário** *(seh-kreh-tah-ree-oo)*........... secretary (♂) ______________
- ❒ **a seleção** *(seh-leh-sown)*.................. selection **S** ______________
- ❒ **a sensação** *(sehn-sah-sown)*............... sensation ______________
- ❒ **o serviço** *(sair-vee-soo)*.................. service ______________

Basic Traffic Signs and Conversions 17

Some of these signs you probably recognize, but take a couple of minutes to review them anyway.

(see-gah) *(frehn-chee)*
siga em frente
go straight ahead

(ahl-fane-deh-gah)
alfândega
customs

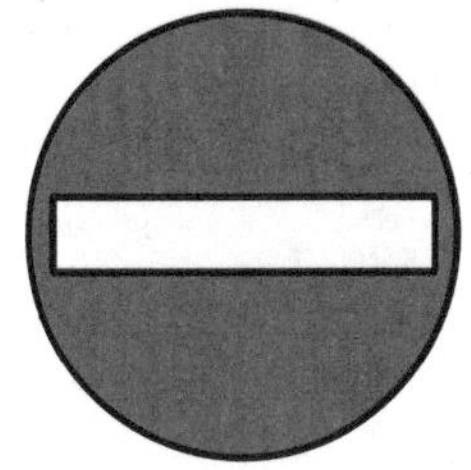

(ehn-trah-dah) *(proh-ee-bee-dah)*
entrada proibida
no entrance

(ah-air-oh-por-too)
aeroporto
airport

(proh-ee-bee-doo) *(vee-rar)* *(es-kair-dah)*
proibido virar à esquerda
no left turn

(veh-loh-see-dah-jee) *(mah-see-mah)*
velocidade máxima
speed limit

(proh-ee-bee-doo)(es-tah-see-oh-nar)
proibido estacionar
no parking

(proh-ee-bee-doo) *(ool-trah-pahs-sar)*
proibido ultrapassar
no passing

(pah-ree)
pare
stop

(dehs-vee-oo)
DESVIO
detour

What follows are approximate conversions, so when you order something by liters, kilograms or grams you will have an idea of what to expect and not find yourself being handed one piece of candy when you thought you ordered an entire bag.

To Convert		Do the Math		
liters (l) to gallons,	multiply by 0.26	4 liters x 0.26	=	1.04 gallons
gallons to liters,	multiply by 3.79	10 gal. x 3.79	=	37.9 liters
kilograms (kg) to pounds,	multiply by 2.2	2 kilograms x 2.2	=	4.4 pounds
pounds to kilos,	multiply by 0.46	10 pounds x 0.46	=	4.6 kg
grams (g) to ounces,	multiply by 0.035	100 grams x 0.035	=	3.5 oz.
ounces to grams,	multiply by 28.35	10 oz. x 28.35	=	283.5 g.
meters (m) to feet,	multiply by 3.28	2 meters x 3.28	=	6.56 feet
feet to meters,	multiply by 0.3	6 feet x 0.3	=	1.8 meters

For fun, take your weight in pounds and convert it into kilograms. It sounds better that way, doesn't it? How many kilometers is it from your home to school, to work, to the post office?

The Simple Versions		
one liter	=	approximately one US quart
four liters	=	approximately one US gallon
one kilo	=	approximately 2.2 pounds
100 grams	=	approximately 3.5 ounces
500 grams	=	slightly more than one pound
one meter	=	slightly more than three feet

The distance between **Nova York e Rio de Janeiro é** approximately 4,799 miles. How many kilometers would that be? It is 5,745 miles between **Rio de Janeiro e Londres.** How many kilometers is that?

kilometers (km.) to miles,	multiply by 0.62	1000 km. x 0.62	=	620 miles
miles to kilometers,	multiply by 1.6	1000 miles x 1.6	=	1,600 km.

Inches 1	2	3	4	5	6	7

To convert centimeters into inches, multiply by 0.39 Example: 9 cm. x 0.39 = 3.51 in.

To convert inches into centimeters, multiply by 2.54 Example: 4 in. x 2.54 = 10.16 cm.

cm 1	2	3	4	5	6	7	8	9	10	11	12	13	14	15	16	17	18

A Conta
(kohn-tah) — bill

(seem) (tahm-bame) (ah)
Sim, também há (there are) bills to pay **no Brasil e em Portugal. Você** have just finished your delicious dinner **e você quer** (kair) (want) **pagar a conta. O que você faz?** (do) **Voce chama** (shah-mah) **o garçom** (gar-sohm) (waiter) **ou a garçonete** (gar-soh-neh-chee) (waitress)**. O garçom** (gar-sohm) (waiter) will normally reel off what **você** have eaten while writing rapidly. **Ele** (eh-lee) will then place a piece **de papel** on **a mesa e dizer** (jee-zair)**, "São** (sown) **trinta reais** (heh-eyes) **no total** (toh-tahl)**." Você** will pay **o garçom ou** perhaps **você** will pay **o caixa** (ky-shah) (cashier)**.**

Garçom! Por favor, a conta.
Sim, pois não. (poysh) of course

Being a seasoned traveler, **você** know that tipping as **nós** (noys) know it **nos Estados Unidos** can vary from country to country. **No Brasil** a 10% service charge is usually included on **a conta,** but you can always add a little more for your **garçom sobre a mesa** if you wish. When **você** dine out on **sua** (your) **viagem** (vee-ah-zhame) (trip)**,** it is always a good idea to make a reservation. It can be difficult to get into a popular **restaurante** (hehs-tow-rahn-chee)**.** Nevertheless, the experience is well worth the trouble **você** might encounter to obtain a reservation. **E** remember, **você sabe** (sah-bee) (know) enough **português** to make a reservation. Just speak slowly and clearly.

			S
❒ **setembro** *(seh-tem-broo)*	September		______
❒ **severo** *(seh-veh-roo)*	severe		______
❒ **o silêncio** *(see-lane-see-oo)*	silence		______
❒ **simples** *(seem-pleesh)*	simple		______
❒ **simultâneo** *(see-mool-tah-neh-oo)*	simultaneous		______

Remember these key **palavras** when dining out, be it **no Brasil ou em Portugal.**

(gar-sohm) **o garçom** ______ waiter	*(gar-soh-neh-chee)* **a garçonete** ______ waitress
(kohn-tah) **a conta** a conta, a conta ______ bill	*(gor-zheh-tah)* **a gorjeta** ______ tip
(kar-dah-pee-oo) *(meh-noo)* **o cardápio / o menu** ______ menu	*(troh-koo)* **o troco** ______ change
(dehs-kool-pee) **desculpe** ______ excuse me	*(oh-bree-gah-doo)(oh-bree-gah-dah)* **obrigado / obrigada** ______ thank you (♂) thank you (♀)
(fah-vor) **por favor** ______ please	*(mee)(dah)* *(dah-mee)* **me dá / da-me** ______ give me (Brazil) give me (Portugal)

Aqui está a sample *(kohn-vair-sah-sown)* **conversação** involving paying **a conta** in a hotel.

Carlos: **Por favor, quero pagar a conta.** (pagar = to pay)

Por favor, quero pagar a conta.

(zheh-rehn-chee) Gerente (manager): *(noo-meh-roo)* *(ah-par-tah-mehn-too)* **O número do apartamento, por favor?** (apartamento = hotel room)

______

Carlos: *(treh-zehn-toosh)* **Apartamento trezentos e dez.**

______

Gerente: **Obrigado. Um momento senhor.**

______

Gerente: **Aqui está a conta.**

______

If **você** have any problems **com números,** just ask someone to write out **os números,** so that **você** can be sure you understand everything correctly, **"Por favor,** *(es-kreh-vah)* **escreva os números!"** (escreva = write out)

Practice: ______
(Please write out the numbers! Thank you.)

- ❒ **a sinfonia** *(seen-foh-nee-ah)* .... symphony ______
- ❒ **o sistema** *(sees-teh-mah)* .... system ______
- ❒ **social** *(soh-see-ahl)* .... social **S** ______
- ❒ **o sofá** *(soh-fah)* .... sofa ______
- ❒ **sólido** *(soh-lee-doo)* .... solid ______

Agora, let's take a break from **as contas e o** *(jeen-yay-roo)* **dinheiro** (money) **e** learn some **novas** fun **palavras. Você** can always practice these **palavras** by using your flash cards at the back of this **livro.** Carry these flash cards in your purse, pocket, briefcase **ou** knapsack **e** *use them!*

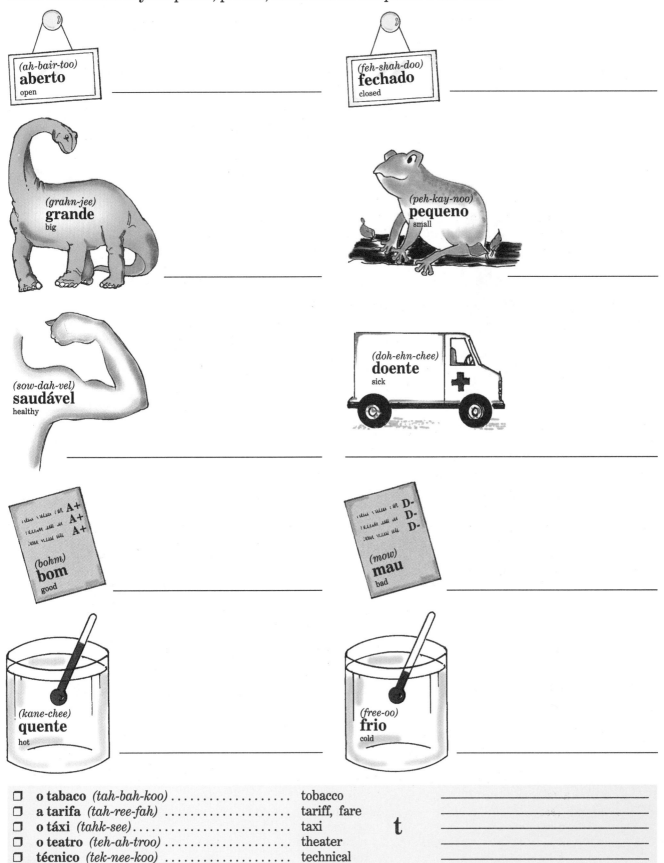

(ah-bair-too) **aberto** open ______________

(feh-shah-doo) **fechado** closed ______________

(grahn-jee) **grande** big ______________

(peh-kay-noo) **pequeno** small ______________

(sow-dah-vel) **saudável** healthy ______________

(doh-ehn-chee) **doente** sick ______________

(bohm) **bom** good ______________

(mow) **mau** bad ______________

(kane-chee) **quente** hot ______________

(free-oo) **frio** cold ______________

❒ **o tabaco** *(tah-bah-koo)*	tobacco		______________
❒ **a tarifa** *(tah-ree-fah)*	tariff, fare		______________
❒ **o táxi** *(tahk-see)*	taxi	**t**	______________
❒ **o teatro** *(teh-ah-troo)*	theater		______________
❒ **técnico** *(tek-nee-koo)*	technical		______________

(koor-too)
curto ______________________
short

(lohn-goo)
longo ______________________
long

(deh-vah-gar)
devagar ______________________
slow

(hah-pee-doo)
rápido ______________________
fast

(ahl-too)
alto ______________________
tall, high

(by-shoo)
baixo ______________________
short, low

(vel-yoo)
velho ______________________
old

(zhoh-vame)
jovem ______________________
young

(kah-roo)
caro ______________________
expensive

(bah-rah-too)
barato ______________________
inexpensive

(hee-koo)
rico ______________________
rich

(poh-bree)
pobre ______________________
poor

(mwee-too)
muito ______________________
a lot

(poh-koo)
pouco ______________________
a little

❒ **o telefone** *(teh-leh-foh-nee)* .... telephone ______________
❒ **o telegrama** *(teh-leh-grah-mah)* .... telegram ______________
❒ **a televisão** *(teh-leh-vee-zown)* .... television **t** ______________
❒ **a temperatura** *(tame-peh-rah-too-rah)* ..... temperature ______________
❒ **o terminal** *(tair-mee-nahl)* .... terminal ______________

Aqui estão *(mysh)* mais verbos novos.

(sah-bair) **saber** to know (fact) / (how to) ______

(poh-dair) **poder** to be able to, can ______

(lair) **ler** to read ______

(tair) (kay) **ter que** to have to, must ______

Study the patterns **abaixo** closely, as **você** will use these verbs a lot.

Avenida Atlântica

(sah-bair)
saber
to know (fact), to know (how to)

Eu sei/ ______ *(too-doo)* **tudo.** (everything)

Você ______ o *(ehn-deh-reh-soo)* **endereço.** (address)

Ele / Ela sabe/ ______ **falar português.** (to speak)

Nós ______ o nome do hotel.

Eles / Elas ______ falar francês.

Meu nome é Elena.

(poh-dair)
poder
to be able to, can

Eu posso/ ______ falar *(es-pahn-yohl)* **espanhol.**

Você pode/ ______ *(ehn-tehn-dair)* **entender** (understand) **português.**

Ele / Ela ______ *(lair)* **ler** (read) **português.**

Nós podemos/ ______ falar inglês.

Eles / Elas podem/ ______ entender *(ah-leh-mown)* **alemão.**

(lair)
ler
to read

Eu leio/ ______ o livro.

Você lê/ ______ a *(heh-vees-tah)* **revista.** (magazine)

Ele / Ela ______ o *(kar-dah-pee-oo)* **cardápio.** (menu)

Nós lemos/ ______ muito.

Eles / Elas lêem/ ______ o *(zhor-nahl)* **jornal.** (newspaper)

(tair) (kay)
ter que
to have to, must

Eu tenho que/ ______ *(ah-prehn-dair)* **aprender português.**

Você ______ ler o livro.

Ele / Ela tem que/ ______ comer agora.

Nós ______ visitar a Bahia.

Eles / Elas têm que/ ______ pagar a conta.

- ❒ **o termômetro** *(tair-moh-meh-troo)* .... thermometer
- ❒ **típico** *(chee-pee-koo)* .... typical
- ❒ **o tomate** *(toh-mah-chee)* .... tomato
- ❒ **o total** *(toh-tahl)* .... total
- ❒ **o tráfego** *(trah-feh-goo)* .... traffic

t ______

Notice that "**poder**," "**ter que**," **e** "**querer**" can be combined with another verb.

(kair-oo)
Eu quero pagar.
want

(koh-mair)
Eu quero comer.
to eat

(noys) (poh-deh-moosh) (lair)
Nós podemos ler português.
can

Nós podemos pagar a conta.

(tame) (eer)
Ele tem que ir.
must/has to — go

Ele tem que pagar a conta.

(kair-oo) (ah-prehn-dair) (por-too-gaysh)
Quero aprender português.
(I) want

Posso aprender português.
(I) can

Tenho que aprender português.
(I) must

(poh-jee) *(ah-by-shoo)*
Você pode translate the sentences **para o português ? As respostas estão abaixo.**
can — into

1. I can speak Portuguese. ______________________
2. They can pay the bill. ______________________
3. He has to pay the bill. ______________________
4. We know the answer. Nós sabemos a resposta.
5. She knows a lot. ______________________
6. We can read Portuguese. ______________________
7. I cannot eat a lot. ______________________
8. We are not able to (cannot) understand French. ______________________
9. I want to visit Lisbon. ______________________
10. She reads the newspaper. ______________________

AS RESPOSTAS

1. **Posso falar português.**
2. **Eles podem pagar a conta.**
3. **Ele tem que pagar a conta.**
4. **Nós sabemos a resposta.**
5. **Ela sabe muito.**
6. **Nós podemos ler português.**
7. **Eu não posso comer muito.**
8. **Nós não podemos entender francês.**
9. **Eu quero visitar Lisboa.**
10. **Ela lê o jornal.**

(leen-yahs) *(ehn-tree)* *(ah-by-shoo)*
Agora, draw **linhas** (lines) **entre** (between) the opposites **abaixo.** (below) **Não** forget to say them out loud. Use these **palavras** every day to describe **coisas** *(koy-zahs)* **em sua** (your) **casa, em sua escola** *(es-koh-lah)* (school) **e em seu** *(seh-oo)* (your) **escritório.** (office)

(grahn-jee) **grande**	*(ehm) (see-mah)* **em cima**
(es-kair-dah) **esquerda**	*(ah-bair-too)* **aberto**
(zhoh-vame) **jovem**	*(koor-too)* **curto**
(poh-bree) **pobre**	*(bah-rah-too)* **barato**
(sow-dah-vel) **saudável**	*(poh-koo)* **pouco**
(lohn-goo) **longo**	*(doh-ehn-chee)* **doente**
(mwee-too) **muito**	*(hah-pee-doo)* **rápido**
(bohm) **bom**	*(vel-yoo)* **velho**
(kane-chee) **quente**	*(peh-kay-noo)* **pequeno**
(ehm-by-shoo) **embaixo**	*(jee-ray-tah)* **direita**
(deh-vah-gar) **devagar**	*(free-oo)* **frio**
(kah-roo) **caro**	*(hee-koo)* **rico**
(feh-shah-doo) **fechado**	*(mow)* **mau**

Futebol *(foo-cheh-bohl)* (soccer) **é** the most popular sport **no Brasil. Nos domingos você** will see thousands of fans streaming to their local club **ou para a Maracanã no Rio.** Even if **futebol** *(foo-cheh-bohl)* is not your favorite **esporte,** *(es-por-chee)* (sport) don't miss **a oportunidade** *(oh-por-too-nee-dah-jee)* (opportunity) to join in.

- ❒ **trágico** *(trah-zhee-koo)* . . . . tragic
- ❒ **tranqüilo** *(trahn-kwee-loo)* . . . . tranquil, quiet
- ❒ **transparente** *(trahns-pah-rehn-chee)* . . . . transparent
- ❒ **transportar** *(trahns-por-tar)* . . . . . . to transport
- ❒ **o trem** *(trame)* . . . . train

t

19

(vee-ah-zhar) Viajar, Viajar, Viajar
to travel

(ohn-tame) **Ontem** em *(brah-zee-lee-ah)* **Brasília!** — yesterday

(oh-zhee) **Hoje** no *(hee-oo)* **Rio!** — today

(ah-mahn-yahn) **Amanhã** em *(sown)* **São** *(pow-loo)* **Paulo!** — tomorrow

If you know a few key **palavras,** traveling can be easy in both **Brasil e Portugal. O português** is spoken by millions of people around the world with each country adding its own character **e** flavor to the language. Keep in mind that **Brasil** alone has a population of over 150 million people!

Como você *(vee-ah-zhah)* **viaja?**

Pedro *(vee-ah-zhah)* **viaja** (travels) *(jee)* **de** *(kar-hoo)* **carro.**

(klow-jee-ah) **Cláudia viaja** *(jee)* **de** *(trame)* **trem.**

Ana viaja de *(ah-vee-own)* **avião.** (airplane)

(zhoh-zeh) **José viaja de** *(bar-koo)* **barco.** (boat)

(zhoh-own) **João viaja de** *(moh-toh-see-kleh-tah)* **motocicleta.**

Maria viaja de *(ow-nee-boos)* **ônibus.**

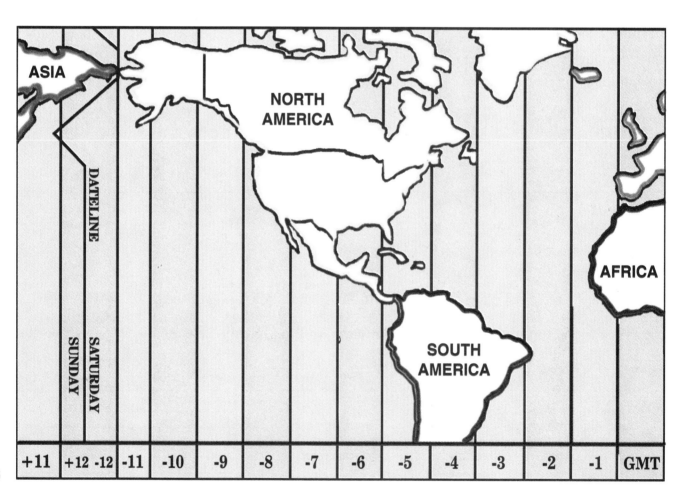

Quando você are traveling, **você** will want to tell others your nationality **e você** will meet people from all corners of the world. Can you guess where someone is from if they say one of the following? **As respostas** are in your glossary beginning on page 108.

Eu sou da Inglaterra. ______________________
(sou = am, da = from)

Sou da Itália. ______________________

Sou do Peru. *(peh-roo)* ______________________

Sou da Espanha. ______________________

Sou da Bélgica. *(bel-zhee-kah)* ______________________

Sou da Suíça. *(swee-sah)* ______________________

Sou de Honduras. *(ohn-doo-rahs)* ______________________

Sou da Bolívia. ______________________

Sou da Argentina. *(ar-zhehn-chee-nah)* ______________________

Nós somos da França. *(noys) (frahn-sah)* ______________________

Somos da Alemanha. *(ah-leh-mahn-yah)* ______________________

Somos do México. *(meh-shee-koo)* ______________________

Somos da Costa Rica. *(hee-kah)* ______________________

Ela é do Chile. *(shee-lee)* ______________________

Ele é de Cuba. *(koo-bah)* ______________________

Ela é de Portugal. ______________________

Ele é da Austrália. *(ows-trah-lee-ah)* ______________________

Eu sou do Canadá. ______________________

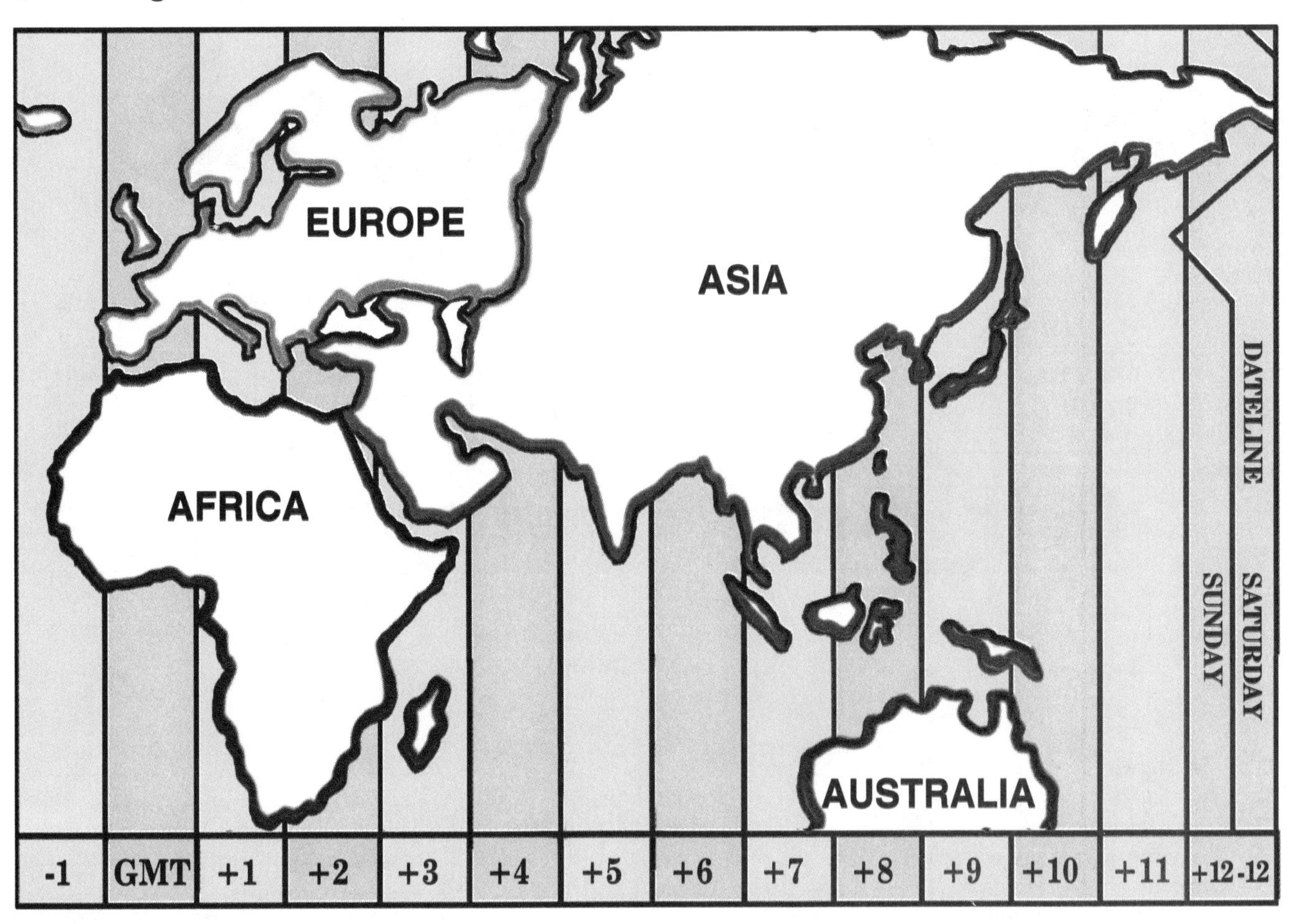

A **palavra** for "trip" is taken from **a palavra "viajar,"** *(vee-ah-zhar)* (to travel) which makes it easy: **a viagem.** *(vee-ah-zhame)* (the trip) **Muitas palavras** revolve around the concept of travel, which is exactly what **você quer** *(kair)* to do. Practice the following **palavras** many times. **Você** will see them often.

(vee-ah-zhar)
viajar ____________________
to travel

(vee-ah-zhahn-chee)
o viajante ____________________
traveler

(ah-zhayn-see-ah) (jeh) (vee-ah-zhehns)
a agência de viagens ____________________
travel agency

(boh-ah) (vee-ah-zhame)
Boa viagem! ____________________
have a good trip

If **você** choose **viajar de carro,** *(kar-hoo)* **aqui estão** a few key **palavras.**

(es-trah-dah)
a estrada ____________________
road

(ow-too-es-trah-dah)
a auto-estrada ____________________
freeway

(hoo-ah)
a rua ____________________
street

(kar-hoo) (ah-loo-gah-doo)
o carro alugado ____________________
rental car

(ah-loo-gehl) (kar-hoosh)
o aluguél de carros ____________________
car-rental agency

(pohs-too) (gah-zoh-lee-nah)
o posto de gasolina ____________________
service station

Abaixo há *(ah)* (there are) some basic signs which **você** should **também** learn to recognize quickly.

(ehn-trar)
entrar ____________________
to enter

(sah-eer)
sair ____________________
to exit

ENTRADA

SAÍDA

(ehn-trah-dah)
a entrada ____________________
entrance

(sah-ee-dah)
a saída ____________________
exit

(preen-see-pahl)
a entrada principal ____________________
main

(eh-mair-zhayn-see-ah)
a saída de emergência ____________________
emergency

EMPURRE

PUXE

(ehm-poor-hee)
empurre ____________________
push (doors)

(poo-shee)
puxe ____________________
pull (doors)

t

- ❒ **o triângulo** *(tree-ahn-goo-loo)* .... triangle ____________________
- ❒ **triunfante** *(tree-oon-fahn-chee)* .... triumphant ____________________
- ❒ **trivial** *(tree-vee-ahl)* .... trivial ____________________
- ❒ **a trompeta** *(trohm-peh-tah)* .... trumpet ____________________
- ❒ **tropical** *(troh-pee-kahl)* .... tropical ____________________

Let's learn the basic travel verbs. Take out a piece of paper **e** make up your own sentences with these **palavras novas.** Follow the same pattern **você** have in previous Steps. The patterns for the verb **"ir"** and **"fazer"** are on page 66.

(ah)
há* ______________________
there is, there are

(sheh-gar)
chegar ______________________
to arrive

(par-cheer)
partir ______________________
to depart

(peh-jeer)
pedir ______________________
to order, to request

(eer) (jee) (kar-hoo)
ir de carro ______________________
to drive, to go by car

(eer) (jee) (ah-vee-own)
ir de avião ______________________
to fly, to go by plane

(fah-zair) (mah-lah)
fazer a mala ______________________
to pack suitcase

(troh-kar)
trocar ______________________
to transfer (vehicles), to change (money)

* This verb doesn't need to be conjugated. It stays the same.

Aqui há *(ah)* some **palavras novas para a viagem** *(vee-ah-zhame)*.
trip

(ah-air-oh-por-too)
o aeroporto
airport

____

(plah-tah-for-mah)
a plataforma
platform

____

(oh-rah-ree-oo)
o horário
timetable

DO RIO À SÃO PAULO		
Partida	Nº do trem	Chegada
00:41	50	09:41
07:40	19	16:40
12:15	22	21:15
14:32	10	23:32
21:40	04	06:40

____

(es-tah-sown) (jee) (trame)
a estação de trem
train station

____

- ❒ **o tumulto** *(too-mool-too)* . . . . tumult ______________________
- ❒ **o túnel** *(too-nel)* . . . . tunnel ______________________
- ❒ **o/a turista** *(too-rees-tah)* . . . . tourist **t** ______________________
- ❒ **o turismo** *(too-rees-moo)* . . . . tourism ______________________
- ❒ **o tutor** *(too-tor)* . . . . tutor ______________________

Com *(es-tahs)* **estas** [these] **palavras, você está** ready for any **viagem**, anywhere. **Você** should have no problem **com** these verbs **novos**, just remember the basic "plug-in" formula **você** have already learned. Use that knowledge to translate the following thoughts **para o português** [into]**. As respostas estão abaixo.**

1. I fly to Rio. ______________________________
2. I transfer (planes) in São Paulo. ______________________________
3. He drives to Fortaleza. Ele vai de carro para Fortaleza.
4. We leave tomorrow. ______________________________
5. We buy tickets to Manaus. ______________________________
6. They drive to Minas Gerais. ______________________________
7. Where is the plane to Vitória? ______________________________
8. How can I go to Portugal? With Air TAP or with Varig? ______________________________

Aqui há some **palavras** *(eem-por-tahn-chees)* **importantes para o** *(vee-ah-zhahn-chee)* **viajante** [traveler].

RIO - MANAUS		
Partida	**Nº do trem**	**Chegada**
00:41	50	09:41
07:40	19	16:40
12:15	22	21:15
14:32	10	23:32
21:40	04	06:40

(oh-koo-pah-doo) **ocupado** [occupied] ______________________________

(lee-vree) **livre** [free] ______________________________

(vah-gown) **o vagão** [compartment, wagon] ______________________________

(ahs-sehn-too) **o assento** [seat] ______________________________

(par-chee-dah) **a partida** [departure] ______________________________

(sheh-gah-dah) **a chegada** [arrival] ______________________________

(een-tair-nah-see-oh-nahl) **internacional** [foreign, international] ______________________________

(doh-mehs-chee-koo) **doméstico** [domestic, internal (of the country)] ______________________________

AS RESPOSTAS

1. **Eu vou de avião para o Rio.**
2. **Eu troco de avião em São Paulo.**
3. **Ele vai de carro para Fortaleza.**
4. **Nós partimos amanhã.**
5. **Nós compramos passagens para Manaus.**
6. **Eles vão de carro para Minas Gerais.**
7. **Onde está o avião para Vitória?**
8. **Como posso ir para Portugal? Com a Air TAP ou com a Varig?**

Increase your travel **palavras** by writing out **as palavras abaixo e** practicing the sample sentences out loud. Practice asking *(pair-goon-tahs)* **perguntas com "onde."** It will help you later.

(pah-rah)
para ____________________
to
Onde está o avião para Iguaçu?

(ah-vee-own)
o avião ____________________
plane
Onde está o avião para Brasília?

(por-town)
o portão ____________________
gate
Onde é o portão número oito?

(bahl-kown)
o balcão ____________________
counter
Onde é o balcão número nove?

(seh-sown) (pair-jee-doosh) (ah-shah-doosh)
a seção de perdidos e achados ____________________
lost-and-found office
Onde é a seção de perdidos e achados?

(kar-heh-gah-dor)
o carregador Onde está o carregador?
porter
Onde está o carregador?

(heh-seh-bee-mehn-too) (jee) (bah-gah-zhame)
o recebimento de bagagem ____________________
baggage claim
Onde é o recebimento de bagagem?

(ah-zhayn-see-ah) (jeh) (kahm-bee-oo)
a agência de câmbio ____________________
money-exchange office
Onde há uma agência de câmbio?

(sah-lah) (es-peh-rah)
a sala de espera ____________________
waiting room
Onde é a sala de espera?

(kor-heh-dor)
o corredor ____________________
aisle
Eu quero um assento no corredor.

(zhah-neh-lah)
a janela ____________________
window
Eu quero um assento na janela.

(seh-sown) (jee) (nown) (foo-mahn-chees)
a seção de não fumantes ____________________
non-smoking section
Há uma seção de não fumantes?

________ (when) ________ (when) *(sheh-gah)* **chega o trem?**

________ (how) ________ (how) *(vy)* **vai?**

- ❒ **último** *(ool-chee-moo)* .... ultimate, last ____________________
- ❒ **a união** *(oo-nee-own)* .... union ____________________
- ❒ **o uniforme** *(oo-nee-for-mee)* .... uniform **u** ____________________
- ❒ **a universidade** *(oo-nee-vair-see-dah-jee)* ... university ____________________
- ❒ **urgente** *(oor-zhehn-chee)* .... urgent ____________________

Você pode (poh-jee) ler as seguintes (seh-geen-chees) frases (frah-zeesh)?
can read following phrases

Agora você está sentado *(sehn-tah-doo)* (seated) **no avião** *(ah-vee-own)* **e você vai** (go/fly) **de avião para o Brasil. Você tem o dinheiro, as passagens, o passaporte** *(pahs-sah-por-chee)* **e as malas** (suitcases)**. Você tem um assento no corredor. Ele tem um assento na janela. Agora você é turista. Você chega** *(sheh-gah)* **amanhã às 8:00. Boa viagem! Boa sorte!**

Não há muitos trens no Brasil. Because of its size, **você** will probably use **aviões** *(ah-vee-oynsh)* (planes) to get from one end of the country to the other. However, **há trens entre** some cities. **No Rio há** *(ah)* (there is) **também** a cogwheel **trem** that goes up to **Corcovado** *(kor-koh-vah-doo)*. It is most likely that **você** will do most of your traveling either **de ônibus ou de avião.**

- ❒ **usado** *(oo-zah-doo)* .... used ____________________
- ❒ **usar** *(oo-zar)* .... to use ____________________
- ❒ **usual** *(oo-zoo-ahl)* .... usual **u** ____________________
- ❒ **o utensílio** *(oo-tehn-see-lee-oo)* .... utensil ____________________
- ❒ **a utilidade** *(oo-chee-lee-dah-jee)* .... utility ____________________

Knowing these travel **palavras** will make your holiday twice as enjoyable **e** at least three times as easy. Drill yourself on this Step by selecting other destinations **e** ask your own **perguntas** about **trens, ônibus, ou aviões** *(ah-vee-oynsh)* that go there. Select **as palavras novas de** your **dicionário** *(jee-see-oh-nah-ree-oo)* **e** ask your own questions beginning with **quando**, **onde**, **e** **quanto custa.** **As respostas** to the crossword puzzle are at the bottom of the next page.

ACROSS

1. (I) read
6. ladies (restroom)
7. platform
9. well
10. to know
11. tip
14. (I) need
17. to enter
18. time
19. what
23. monetary unit of **Brasil**
25. restaurant
27. to travel
28. to buy
31. to write
33. cold
34. she
35. nothing
36. (I) want

DOWN

1. pencil
2. one hundred
3. station
4. to do, to make
5. bad
6. sick
8. to repeat
12. hotel room
13. excuse me
15. computer
16. to drink
20. suitcase
21. to leave, to depart
22. bill
24. to say
26. number
29. give me
30. open
32. twenty
33. to speak

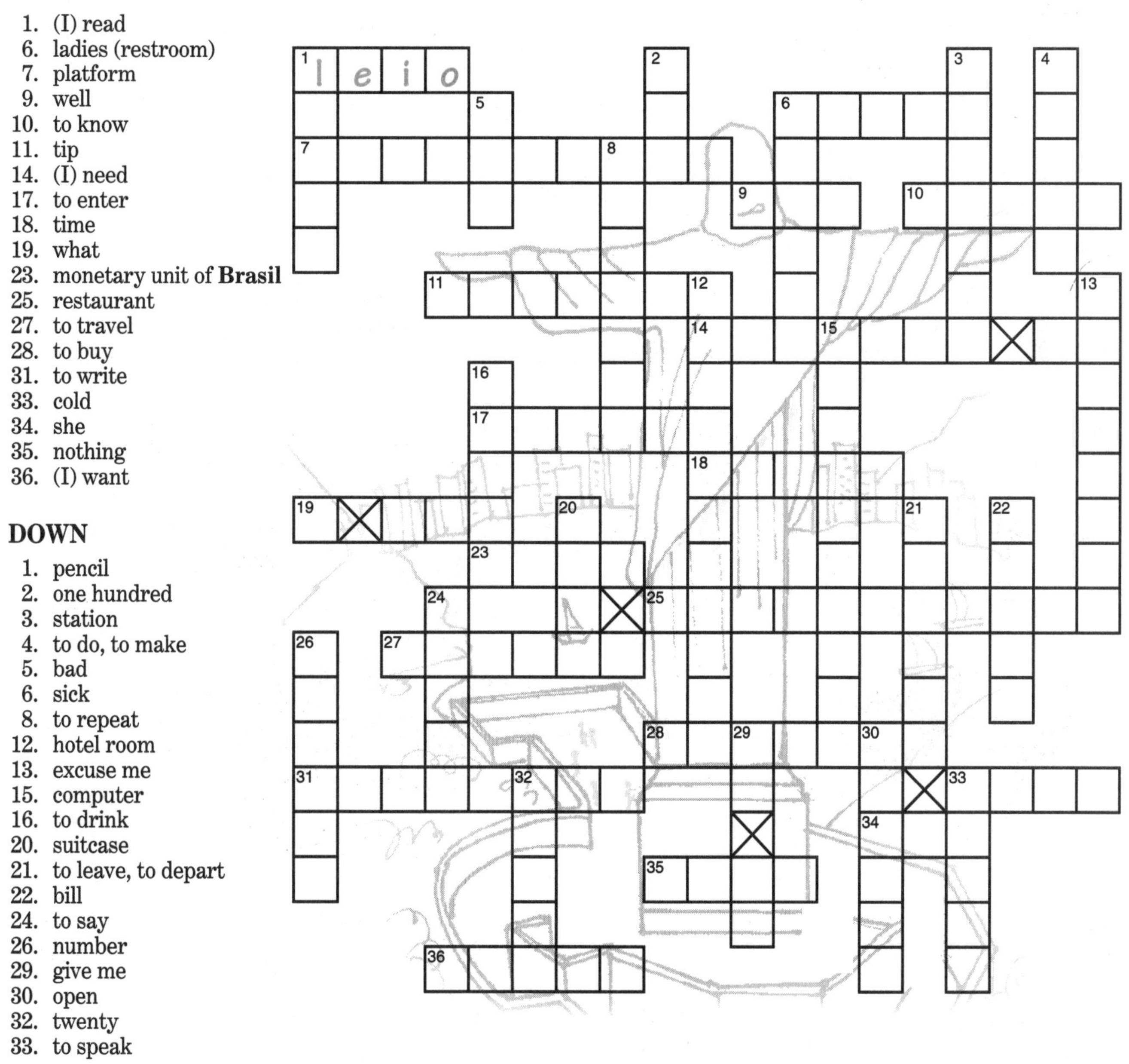

Corcovado is **uma montanha no Rio.** At its summit is the familiar statue of **Cristo Redentor.** It is this image which has become symbolic of the **cidade** of **Rio de Janeiro.**

V

- ❒ **a vacina** *(vah-see-nah)* .... vaccine ____________
- ❒ **a vaga** *(vah-gah)* .... vacancy ____________
- ❒ **válido** *(vah-lee-doo)* .... valid ____________
- ❒ **o vegetariano** *(veh-zheh-tah-ree-ah-noo)* ... vegetarian ____________
- ❒ **a vista** *(vees-tah)* .... view ____________

What about inquiring about the price of *(pahs-sah-zhehns)* **passagens?** (tickets) **Você** *(poh-jee)* **pode** (can) ask these **perguntas.**

Quanto custa uma passagem para a *(bah-ee-ah)* **Bahia?** ____________________

Quanto custa uma passagem para o Paraná? ____________________

Quanto custa uma passagem para a *(lees-boh-ah)* **Lisboa?** ____________________

a *(pahs-sah-zhame)* **passagem** *(jee)* **de** *(ee-dah)* **ida** (one-way ticket) ____________________

a passagem de ida e *(vohl-tah)* **volta** (round-trip ticket) ____________________

What about times of *(par-chee-dah)* **partida** (departure) **e** *(sheh-gah-dah)* **chegada?** (arrival) **Você pode perguntar** (ask) **isso também!**

A (a) **que** (what) **horas** (time) *(par-chee)* **parte** (departs) **o** *(ah-vee-own)* **avião para** *(mah-nows)* **Manaus?** ____________________

A que horas parte o avião para *(lohn-dreesh)* **Londres?** ____________________

A que horas *(sheh-gah)* **chega** (arrives) **o avião de Santiago?** ____________________

A que horas chega o avião de Angola? ____________________

A que horas *(par-chee)* **parte o avião para São Paulo?** ____________________

Você have just arrived **no Brasil. Você está no** *(ah-air-oh-por-too)* **aeroporto. Onde você** *(kair)* **quer** *(eer)* **ir? Para São Paulo? Para Minas?** Tell that to the person at **o** *(bahl-kown)* **balcão** (counter) selling **passagens**!

(kair-oo) **Quero** *(eer)* **ir** (go) **para Fortaleza.** ____________________

A que horas parte o avião para Fortaleza? ____________________

Quanto custa uma passagem para Fortaleza? ____________________

AS RESPOSTAS

ACROSS

1. leio
6. damas
7. plataforma
9. bem
10. saber
11. gorjeta
14. preciso de
17. entrar
18. tempo
19. o que
23. real
25. restaurante
27. viajar
28. comprar
31. escrever
33. frio
34. ela
35. nada
36. quero

DOWN

1. lápis
2. cem
3. estação
4. fazer
5. mau
6. doente
8. repetir
12. apartamento
13. desculpe
15. computador
16. beber
20. mala
21. partir
22. conta
24. dizer
26. número
29. me dá
30. aberto
32. vinte
33. falar

Agora that **você** know the words essential for traveling – be it throughout **Brasil ou Portugal,** what are some speciality items **você** might go in search of?

(ar-chee-goosh) *(koh-roo)*
os artigos de couro
leather goods

(bee-zhoo-teh-ree-ah) *(zhoy-ahs)*
a bijuteria / as jóias
jewelry / gems

(een-stroo-mehn-toosh) *(moo-zee-ky-eesh)*
os instrumentos musicais
musical instruments

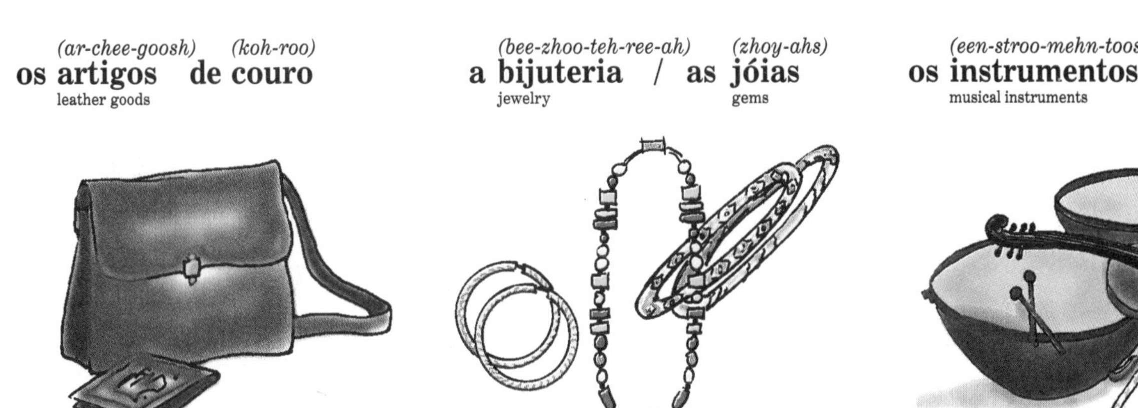

______________________ ______________________ ______________________

(ar-teh-zah-nah-too)
o artesanato
crafts

(seh-rah-mee-kah)
a cerâmica
ceramics

(ah-zoo-leh-zhoosh) *(peen-tah-doosh)* *(mown)*
os azulejos pintados à mão
hand-painted tiles

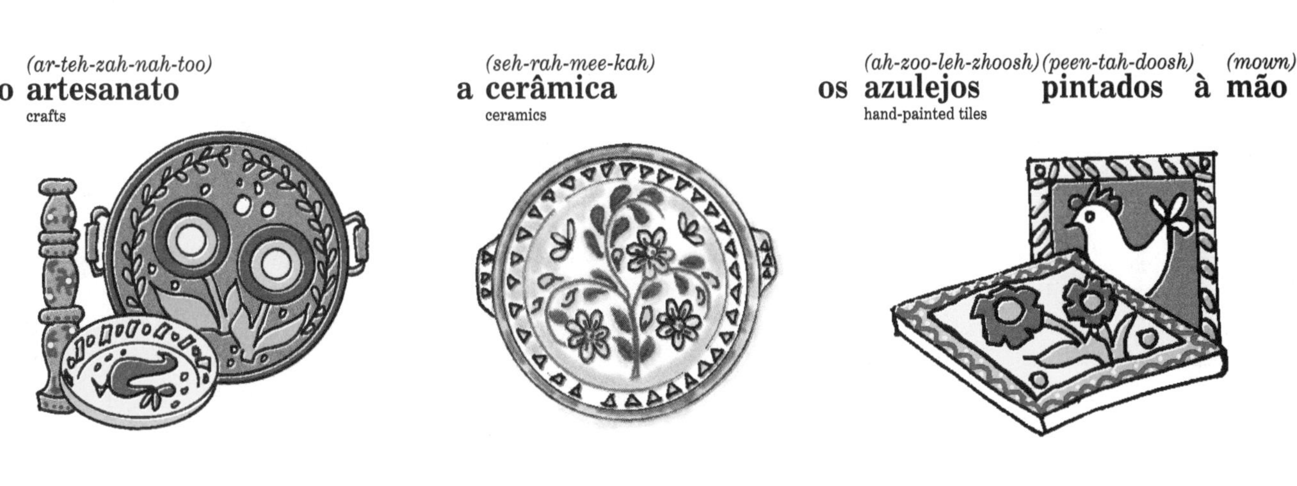

______________________ ______________________ ______________________

Consider using PORTUGUESE *a language map*® as well. PORTUGUESE *a language map*® is the perfect companion for your travels when **você** may not wish to take along this **livro**. Each section focuses on essentials for your *(vee-ah-zhame)* **viagem.** Your *Language Map*® is not meant to replace learning **português**, but will help you in the event **você** forget something and need a little bit of help. For more information about the *Language Map*® Series, please turn to page 132.

❒ **o vale** *(vah-lee)*	valley		______________
❒ **a vaidade** *(vy-dah-jee)*	vanity		______________
❒ **vários** *(vah-ree-oosh)*	various	**V**	______________
❒ **o vaso** *(vah-zoo)*	vase		______________
❒ **o Vaticano** *(vah-chee-kah-noo)*	the Vatican		______________

O Cardápio ou o Menu

(kar-dah-pee-oo) (meh-noo)
menu

Você está agora no Brasil ou em Portugal e você tem um **apartamento** (ah-par-tah-mehn-too) [hotel room]. Você está com **fome** (foh-mee) [hunger]. Onde **há** (ah) [is there] um bom restaurante? First of all, **há** (ah) [there are] different types of places to eat. Let's learn them.

o restaurante *(hehs-tow-rahn-chee)* ______________________

exactly what it says with a variety of meals

o café *(kah-fay)* ______________________

a coffee house **com** snacks **e** beverages

a lanchonete *(lahn-shoh-neh-chee)* ______________________

a type of **restaurante** where you find assorted sandwiches, snacks, ice cream **e** beverages.

o barzinho *(bar-zeen-yoo)* ______________________

a local street bar that generally stays open all day. People step in to have a **cafezinho ou chope** [draft beer] as well as other beverages. Snacks **e** phone cards can also be purchased here.

"Cafezinho" *(kah-fay-zeen-yoo)* is that little espresso-type drink which Brazilians drink over the counter **no barzinho ou** after any meal. **É** generally served black **com** some **açúcar** *(ah-soo-kar)* [sugar].

Before beginning your meal, be sure to wish those sharing your table – "**Bom apetite!**" *(bohm) (ah-peh-chee-chee)* [enjoy your meal] Your turn to practice now.

____
(enjoy your meal)

And at least one more time for practice!

____
(enjoy your meal)

V

- ❒ **o veículo** *(veh-ee-koo-loo)* .... vehicle ______________________
- ❒ **o vinagre** *(vee-nah-gree)* .... vinegar ______________________
- ❒ **o vinho** *(veen-yoo)* .... wine ______________________
- ❒ **o violino** *(vee-oh-lee-noo)* .... violin ______________________
- ❒ **a visa** *(vee-zah)* .... visa ______________________

Start imagining now all the new taste treats you will experience abroad. Try all of the different types of eating establishments mentioned on the previous page. Experiment. If **você** *(ehn-kohn-trar)* **encontrar um restaurante** that **você** would like to try, consider calling ahead to make **uma** *(heh-zair-vah)* **reserva:** (reservation)

(kair-oo) (heh-zair-var) (meh-zah)
"Quero reservar uma mesa, por favor."
(reservar = to reserve)

____
(I want to reserve a table, please.)

If **você precisa de um cardápio**, catch the attention of **o garçom**, saying,

"Garçom. O cardápio, por favor!"

____
(Waiter. The menu please!)

If your **garçom** asks if **você** enjoyed your meal, a smile **e** a **"Sim, muito obrigado,"** will tell him that you did.

Most *(hehs-tow-rahn-chees)* **restaurantes** *(brah-zee-lay-roosh)* **brasileiros** post **o cardápio** outside **ou** inside. Do not hesitate to ask to see **o cardápio** before being seated so **você sabe** what type of *(heh-fay-soynsh)* **refeições** (meals) **e** *(preh-soos)* **preços** (prices) **você** will encounter. Most **restaurantes** offer **um** *(es-peh-see-ahl)* **"especial** *(jee-ah)* **do dia."** (special meal of the day) Some **restaurantes** also offer **um** *(prah-too)* **"prato** *(fay-too)* **feito"** at lunchtime. This is a complete *(heh-fay-sown)* **refeição,** (meal) chosen by the chef for that day, usually at a very reasonable *(preh-soo)* **preço.** (price)

- ❒ **a visita** *(vee-zee-tah)* .... visit — **V** ______________________
- ❒ **visitar** *(vee-zee-tar)* .... to visit ______________________
- ❒ **o zodíaco** *(zoh-jee-ah-koo)* .... zodiac ______________________
- ❒ **a zona** *(zoh-nah)* .... zone — **Z** ______________________
- ❒ **a zoologia** *(zoh-oh-loh-zhee-ah)* .... zoology ______________________

No Brasil e em Portugal há (there are) **três** main meals to enjoy every day, plus perhaps **doces** *(doh-seesh)* (pastry) **para** (for) the tired traveler in **à tarde.** (afternoon)

o café da manhã *(kah-fay) (mahn-yahn)* (breakfast (Brazil)) / **o pequeno almoço** *(peh-kay-noo) (ahl-moh-soo)* (breakfast (Portugal)) ____________________

Em hotéis *(oh-tay-ees)* (hotels) **e pousadas** *(poh-zah-dahs)* (inns) this meal usually consists of coffee, tea, fresh orange juice, **pão,** butter, cheese **e** fruit. Check serving times before **você** retire for the night or you might miss out!

o almoço *(ahl-moh-soo)* (lunch) ____________________

generally served from 12:00 to 15:00

o jantar *(zhahn-tar)* (dinner) ____________________

generally served from 20:00 to midnight

Agora for a preview of delights to come . . . At the back of this **livro, você** will find a sample **cardápio** *(kar-dah-pee-oo)* **brasileiro.** *(brah-zee-lay-roo)* **Leia** *(lay-ah)* (read) **o cardápio hoje** *(oh-zhee)* (today) **e aprenda** *(ah-prehn-dah)* (learn) **as palavras novas!** When **você** are ready to leave on your **viagem,** *(vee-ah-zhame)* cut out **o cardápio**, fold it, **e** carry it in your pocket, wallet **ou** purse. Before you go, how do **você** say these **três** phrases which are **muito importantes para** the hungry **viajante?** *(vee-ah-zhahn-chee)* (traveler)

Excuse me. I want to reserve a table, please. ____________________

Waiter! A menu, please! ____________________

Enjoy your meal! ____________________

(who)

________ (who) **come** (eats) **a salada?**

________ (who) **bebe o suco?** *(soo-koo)* (juice)

________ (who) **viaja** *(vee-ah-zhah)* **para Angola?**

Learning the following should help you to identify what kind of meat **você** have ordered **e como** it will be prepared.

- ❒ **vaca** *(vah-kah)* .... beef ____________
- ❒ **vitela** *(vee-teh-lah)* .... veal ____________
- ❒ **porco** *(por-koo)* .... pork ____________
- ❒ **carneiro** *(kar-nay-roo)*.................. mutton ____________

O cardápio below has the main categories **você** will find in most restaurants. Learn them **hoje** *(oh-zhee)* so that **você** will easily recognize them when you dine **em Portugal ou no Brasil.** Be sure to write the words in the blanks below.

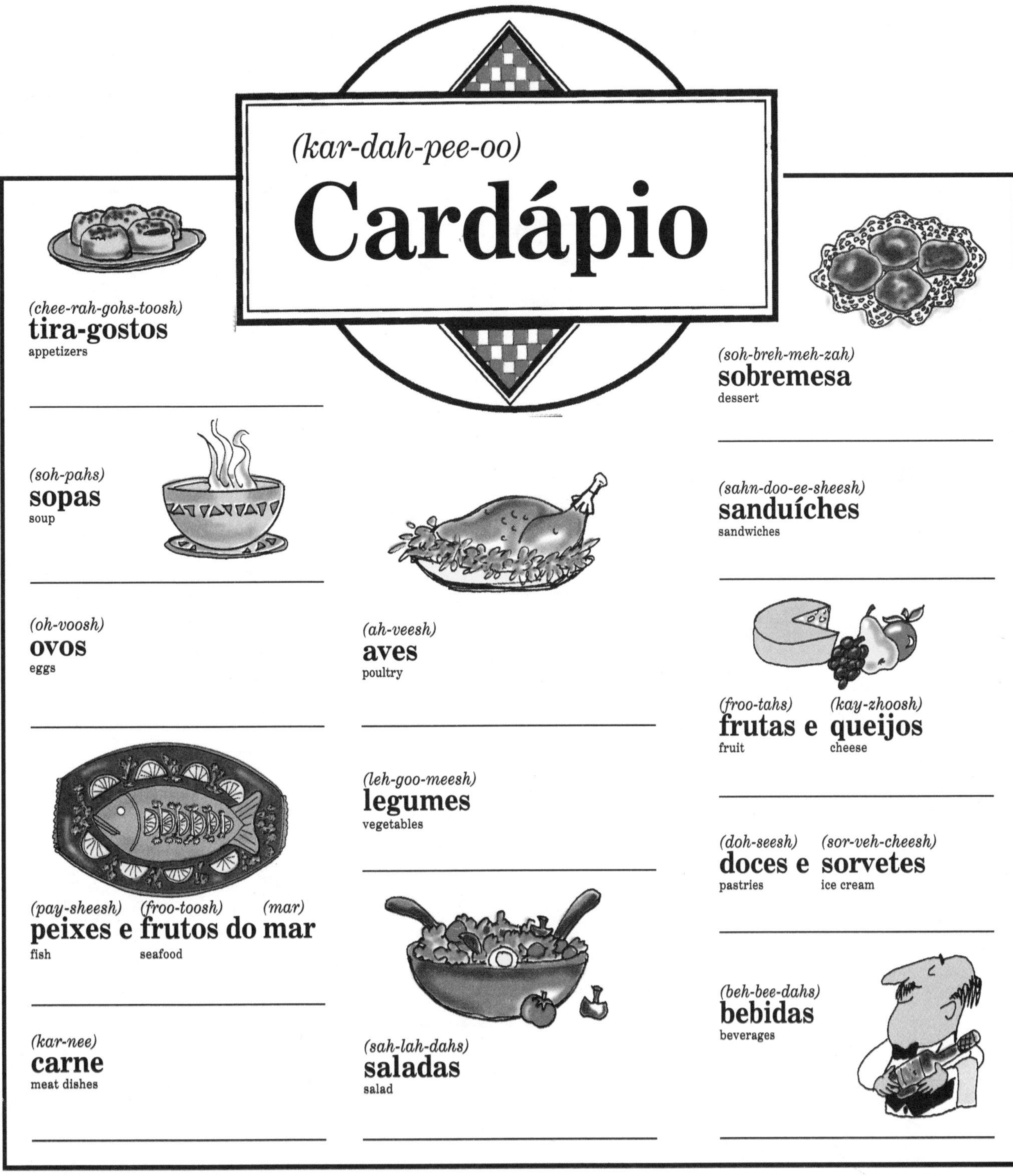

(kar-dah-pee-oo)
Cardápio
(chee-rah-gohs-toosh)
tira-gostos
appetizers
(soh-pahs)
sopas
soup
(oh-voosh)
ovos
eggs
(pay-sheesh) (froo-toosh) (mar)
peixes e frutos do mar
fish seafood
(kar-nee)
carne
meat dishes
(ah-veesh)
aves
poultry
(leh-goo-meesh)
legumes
vegetables
(sah-lah-dahs)
saladas
salad
(soh-breh-meh-zah)
sobremesa
dessert
(sahn-doo-ee-sheesh)
sanduíches
sandwiches
(froo-tahs) (kay-zhoosh)
frutas e queijos
fruit cheese
(doh-seesh) (sor-veh-cheesh)
doces e sorvetes
pastries ice cream
(beh-bee-dahs)
bebidas
beverages

- ❒ **frango** *(frahn-goo)* .... chicken ________________
- ❒ **cordeiro** *(kor-day-roo)* .... lamb ________________
- ❒ **churrasco** *(shoor-hahs-koo)* .... barbeque ________________
- ❒ **frito** *(free-too)* .... fried ________________
- ❒ **assado** *(ahs-sah-doo)* .... roasted ________________

Você (tahm-bame) **também** will get (leh-goo-meesh) **legumes** (vegetables) **com** your (heh-fay-sown) **refeição**, (meal) **e** perhaps **uma salada** (mees-tah) **mista** (mixed). **Um dia** at an open-air (fay-rah) **feira** (market) will teach you **os nomes** for all the different kinds of **legumes e frutas,** plus it will be a delightful experience for you. **Você** (poh-jee) **pode** always consult your menu guide at the back of this **livro** if **você** forget **os nomes** (kor-heh-toosh) **corretos**. **Agora você** are seated **e o garçom** (waiter) arrives.

O cardápio, por favor!
E para beber?
Um copo de vinho branco, por favor.

O café da (mahn-yahn) **manhã** (breakfast) **é um** (poh-koo) **pouco** (little) (jee-feh-rehn-chee) **diferente** because **é** fairly standardized **e você** will frequently take it at your (poh-zah-dah) **pousada** (guest house), as **está** ((it) is) (een-kloo-ee-doo) **incluído** (included) **no** (preh-soo) **preço** (price) **do quarto** (room). **Abaixo** is a sample of what **você pode** expect to greet you **de manhã**.

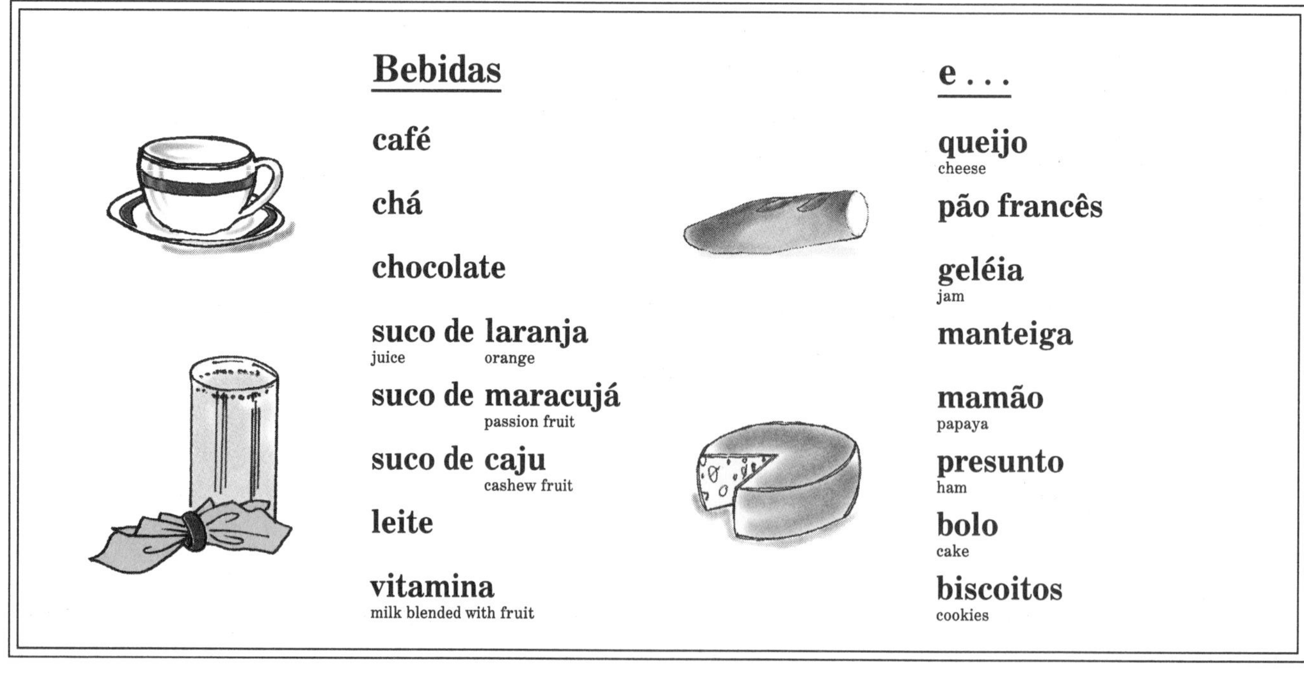

Bebidas
café
chá
chocolate
suco de laranja
juice orange
suco de maracujá
passion fruit
suco de caju
cashew fruit
leite
vitamina
milk blended with fruit
e . . .
queijo
cheese
pão francês
geléia
jam
manteiga
mamão
papaya
presunto
ham
bolo
cake
biscoitos
cookies

- ❐ **cozido** (koh-zee-doo) . . . . cooked ______
- ❐ **cozido no vapor** (koh-zee-doo)(noh)(vah-por) . . . . steamed ______
- ❐ **ao forno** (ah-oh)(for-noo) . . . . baked ______
- ❐ **grelhado** (grel-yah-doo) . . . . grilled ______
- ❐ **à milanesa** (ah)(mee-lah-neh-zah) . . . . in batter ______

Aqui está an example of what **você** might select for your evening meal. Using your menu guide on pages 117 and 118, as well as what **você** have learned in this Step, fill in the blanks *in English* with what **você** believe your **garçom** will bring you. **As respostas estão** below.
answers

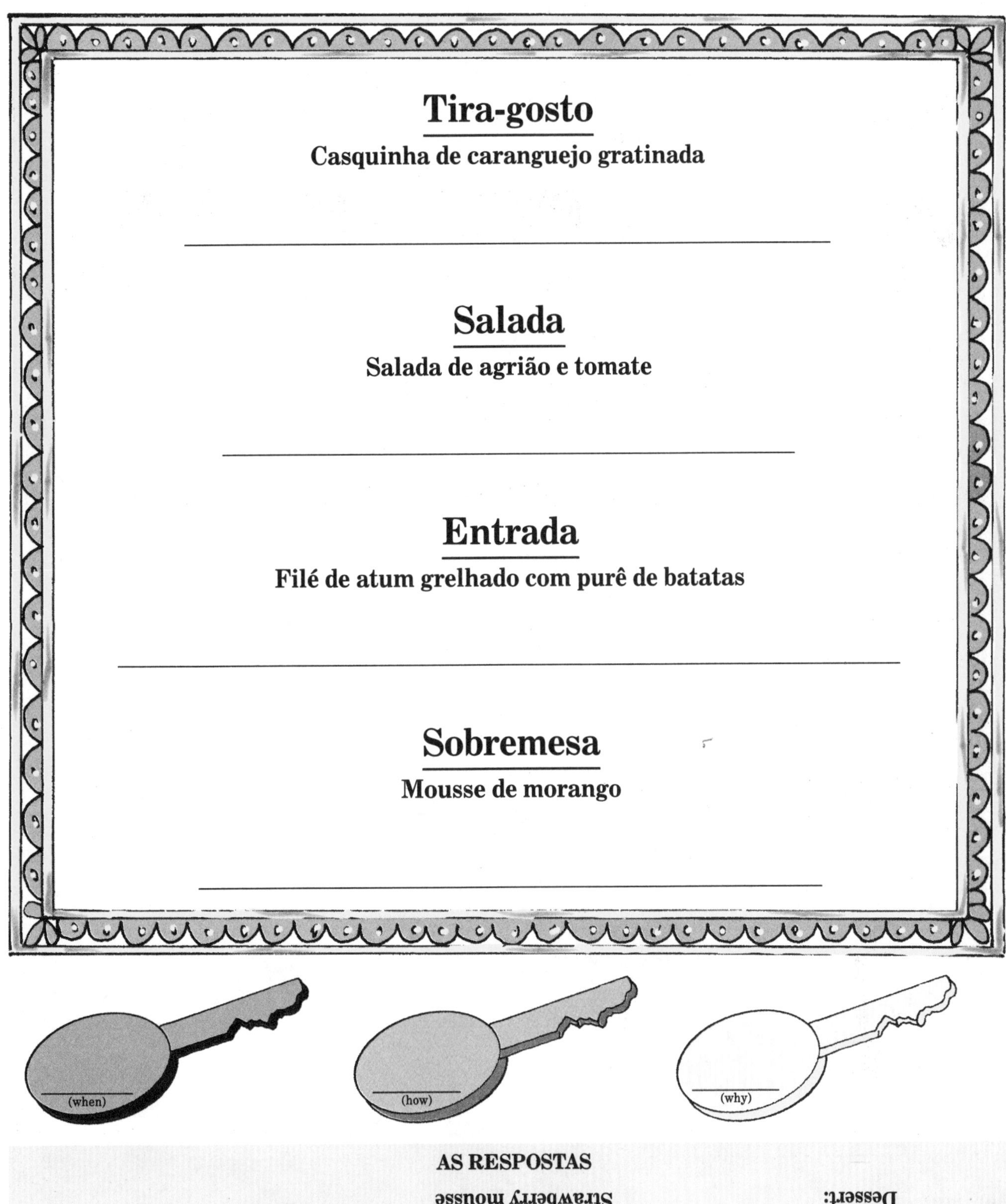

Tira-gosto
Casquinha de caranguejo gratinada
Salada
Salada de agrião e tomate
Entrada
Filé de atum grelhado com purê de batatas
Sobremesa
Mousse de morango
(when)
(how)
(why)

AS RESPOSTAS

Appetizer:	Grated deviled crab
Salad:	Watercress and tomato salad
Entree:	Grilled filet of tuna with mashed potatoes
Dessert:	Strawberry mousse

Agora é a good time for a quick review. Draw lines between **as palavras portuguesas e** their English equivalents.

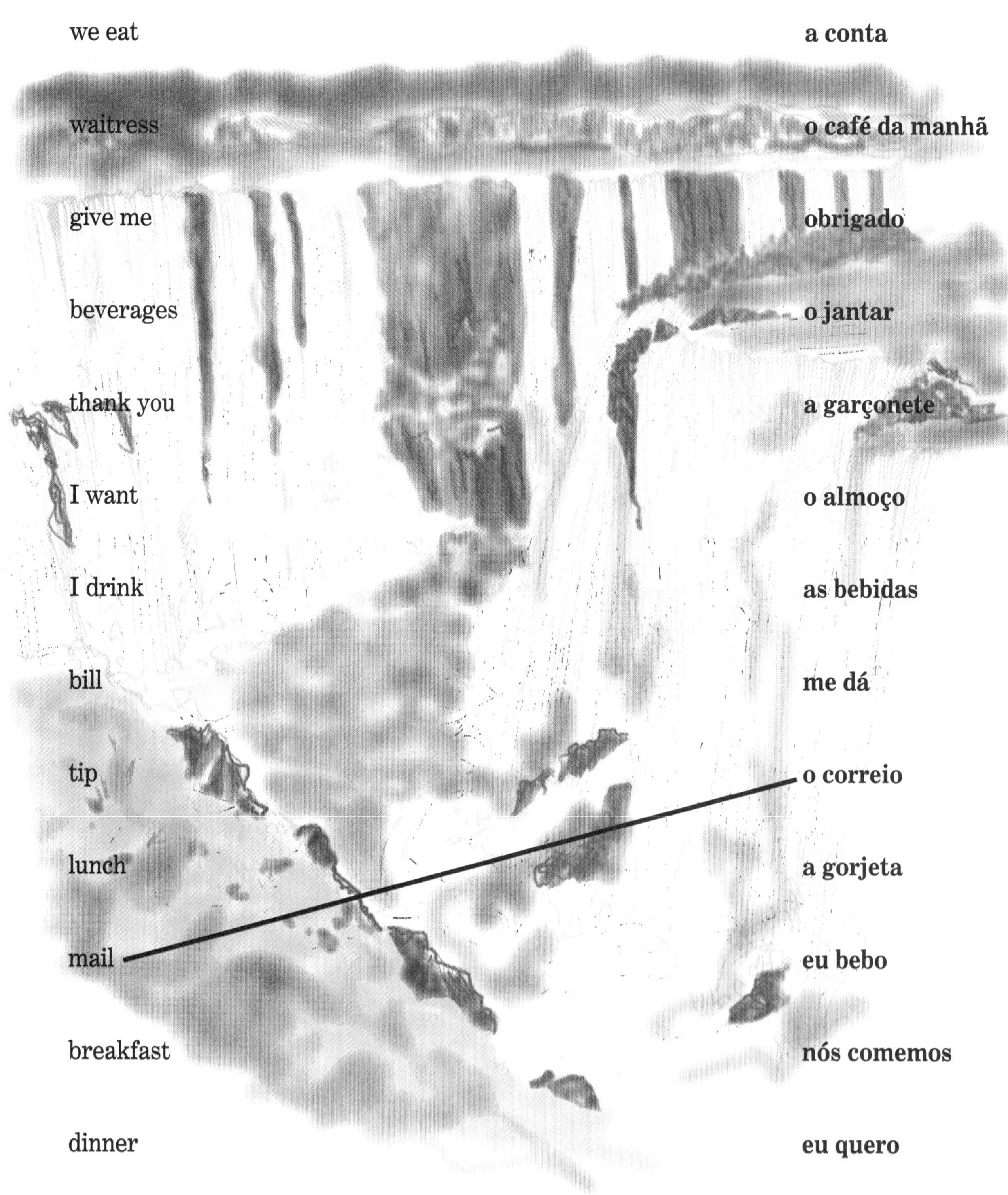

we eat	**a conta**
waitress	**o café da manhã**
give me	**obrigado**
beverages	**o jantar**
thank you	**a garçonete**
I want	**o almoço**
I drink	**as bebidas**
bill	**me dá**
tip	**o correio**
lunch	**a gorjeta**
mail	**eu bebo**
breakfast	**nós comemos**
dinner	**eu quero**

Aqui are free telephone calls.

- ❒ **informação** *(een-for-mah-sown)* .... information 102
- ❒ **polícia** *(poh-lee-see-ah)* .... police 190
- ❒ **ambulância** *(ahm-boo-lahn-see-ah)* .... ambulance 192
- ❒ **incêndio** *(een-same-jee-oo)* .... fire 193

O Telefone (teh-leh-foh-nee) telephone

What is different about **o telefone no Brasil ou em Portugal?** Well, **você** never notice such things until **você quer** (kair) to use them. **Os telefones** (teh-leh-foh-neesh) allow you to call **amigos** (ah-mee-goosh) friends, reserve **ingressos** tickets **de teatro, de balé** (bah-lay) ballet, **ou de concerto**, make calls **de urgência** (oor-zhayn-see-ah) urgency, check on the hours of **um museu** (moo-zeh-oo), rent **um carro, e** all those other things which **nós fazemos** (fah-zeh-moosh) do on a daily basis. It **também** gives you a certain amount of freedom when **você pode fazer** make your own calls.

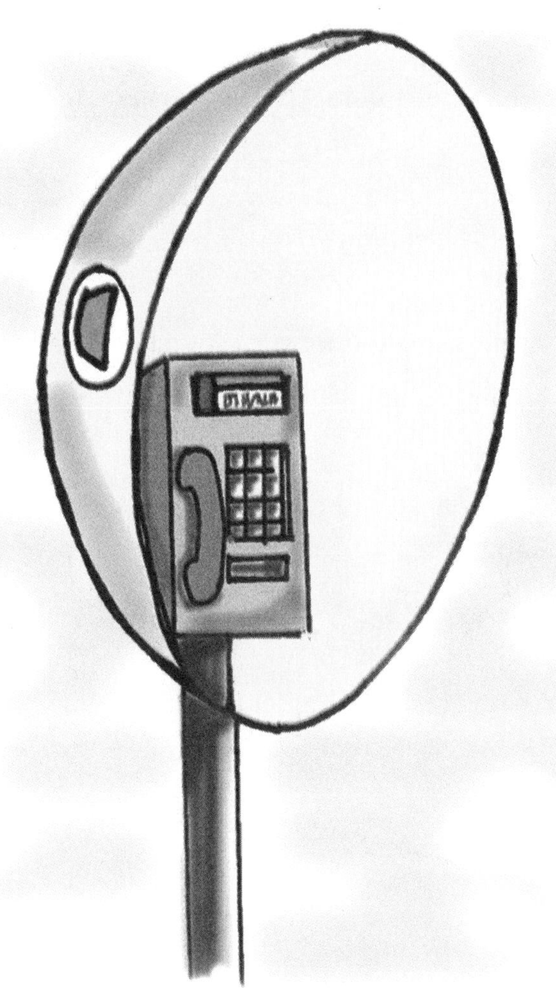

Você pode encontrar find **uma cabine** (kah-bee-nee) booth **telefônica,** fondly called **"o orelhão"** (oh-rel-yown) big ear because of its shape, just about everywhere. **Você pode comprar cartões** (kar-toynsh) phone cards **de telefone nos barzinhos** (bar-zeen-yoosh) local street bars **e jornaleiros** (zhor-nah-lay-roosh) newsstands**.**

So, let's learn how to operate **o telefone.**

As instruções (een-stroo-soynsh) instructions can look **complicadas,** (kohm-plee-kah-dahs) complicated but remember, some of these **palavras você** should be able to recognize already. Ready? Well, before you turn the page it would be a good idea to go back **e** review all your numbers one more time.

To dial from the United States to most other countries **você** need that country's international area code. Your **lista** (lees-tah) telephone book **telefônica** at home should have a listing of international area codes.

Aqui are some **muito** useful words built around the word, **"telefone."**

- ❒ **a telefonista** *(teh-leh-foh-nees-tah)* .... operator ______________
- ❒ **a cabine telefônica** *(kah-bee-nee)(teh-leh-foh-nee-kah)* ..... telephone booth ______________
- ❒ **a lista telefônica** *(lees-tah)(teh-leh-foh-nee-kah)* .... telephone book ______________
- ❒ **a conversação telefônica** *(kohn-vair-sah-soun)(teh-leh-foh-nee-kah)* telephone conversation ______________

When **você** leave your contact numbers with friends, family **ou** business colleagues, **você** should include your destination country's area code **e** city code whenever possible. For example,

Country Codes		**City Codes**	
Brazil	55	São Paulo	11
		Rio	21
		Brasília	61
		Salvador	71
Portugal	351	Lisboa	1

To call from one city to another city while abroad, **você** may need to call **a** *(teh-leh-foh-nees-tah)* **telefonista** (operator) in your hotel. Tell **a telefonista, "Eu** *(gohs-tah-ree-ah)* **gostaria** (would like) **de telefonar para** *(heh-see-fee)* **Recife,"** ou **"Gostaria de telefonar para Salvador."**

Now you try it: ______________________________ (I would like to call to Belem.)

When answering **o telefone,** pick up the receiver **e** say, "*(ah-loh)* **Alô?**" The person calling will probably say, **"Alô.** *(kame)* **Quem fala?"** Be ready to respond with, **"Aqui é** ______________ (your name)."

Com números de telefone the number **seis** (6) is replaced with **"***(may-ah)* **meia."** *(may-ah)* **Meia** stands for *(may-ah-doo-zee-ah)* **meia-dúzia** (half-dozen). So if your **número de telefone** is 246-6205, **você** would say **"dois-quatro-meia-meia-dois-zero-cinco."** Now **você** say it.

When saying good-bye, say "*(ah-teh)* **até** (until) *(loh-goo)* **logo**," (then) or "**até** (until) **amanhã**," (tomorrow) or simply "*(chow)* **tchau**." (good-bye)

Your turn —

______________________________ (Hello. Here is . . .)

______________________________ (good-bye) ______________________________ (until tomorrow)

Do not forget that **você pode** *(pair-goon-tar)* **perguntar** (ask) . . .

Quanto custa uma chamada (call) **para os Estados Unidos?** ______________________________

Quanto custa uma chamada para a Inglaterra? ______________________________

Here are some countries **você** may wish to call.

- ❒ **a Argentina** *(ar-zhehn-chee-nah)*. . . . . Argentina ______________
- ❒ **a Bolívia** *(boh-lee-vee-ah)* . . . . Bolivia ______________
- ❒ **o Chile** *(shee-lee)*. . . . . Chile ______________
- ❒ **a Colômbia** *(koh-lohm-bee-ah)*. . . . . Colombia ______________

Aqui estão some sample telephone phrases. Write them in the blanks **abaixo.**

Eu gostaria (gohs-tah-ree-ah) would like **de telefonar** (teh-leh-foh-nar) **para Miami.** ____________________

Gostaria de telefonar para a Varig (vah-reeg) **no aeroporto** (ah-air-oh-por-too)**.** ____________________

Gostaria de chamar call (as in summon) **um médico** (meh-jee-koo) doctor**.** ____________________

Meu (meh-oo) my **número é 526-05-29.** ____________________

Qual what **é o seu** (seh-oo) your **número?** ____________________

Qual é o número do of the **hotel?** ____________________

Marília: **Bom dia. Aqui é Marília Menezes. Gostaria de falar com o Senhor Torres.**

____

Secretária: **Um momento. Desculpe, o telefone está ocupado** (oh-koo-pah-doo) busy/occupied**.**

____

Marília: **Pode** (poh-jee) can you **repetir** (heh-peh-cheer) **por favor?**

____

Secretária: **Desculpe, o telefone está ocupado.**

____

Marília: **Está bem. Obrigada.**

____

Agora você are ready to use any **telefone**, anywhere. Just take it slowly **e** speak clearly.

- ❒ **a Cuba** *(koo-bah)* .... Cuba
- ❒ **o Equador** *(eh-kwah-dor)* .... Ecuador ____________
- ❒ **a Espanha** *(es-pahn-yah)* .... Spain ____________
- ❒ **o México** *(meh-shee-koo)* .... Mexico ____________
- ❒ **o Moçambique** *(moh-sahm-bee-kee)* .... Mozambique ____________

O Metrô

(meh-troh) subway

(meh-troh)
"O metrô" é o nome português para "the subway." **Há um metrô no Rio e em São Paulo. Ônibus** are also **muito** popular **e** let you see the sights as well, but they can be very full at certain times of the day.

o metrô (meh-troh) subway

o ônibus (ow-nee-boos) bus

a estação de metrô (es-tah-sown) (meh-troh) station

o ponto de táxi (pohn-too) stop

o ponto de ônibus (ow-nee-boos)

Maps displaying the various **linhas** (leen-yahs) lines **e paradas** (pah-rah-dahs) stops are generally posted inside every **estação** (es-tah-sown) station **de metrô. As linhas** are generally color-coded to facilitate reading just like your example on the next page. How do **você** use **o metrô?** Check **o nome** of the last **parada** on **a linha** (leen-yah) which **você** want to take **e** catch **o metrô** traveling in that direction.

- ❒ **o Panamá** *(pah-nah-mah)*.................................... Panama ________
- ❒ **o Paraguai** *(pah-rah-gwhy)* .... Paraguay ________
- ❒ **o Peru** *(peh-roo)* .... Peru ________
- ❒ **o Uruguai** *(oo-roo-gwhy)*...................................... Uruguay ________
- ❒ **a Venezuela** *(veh-neh-zoo-eh-lah)* .... Venezuela ________

Agora, locate your destination, select the correct line on your practice **metrô e** hop on board.

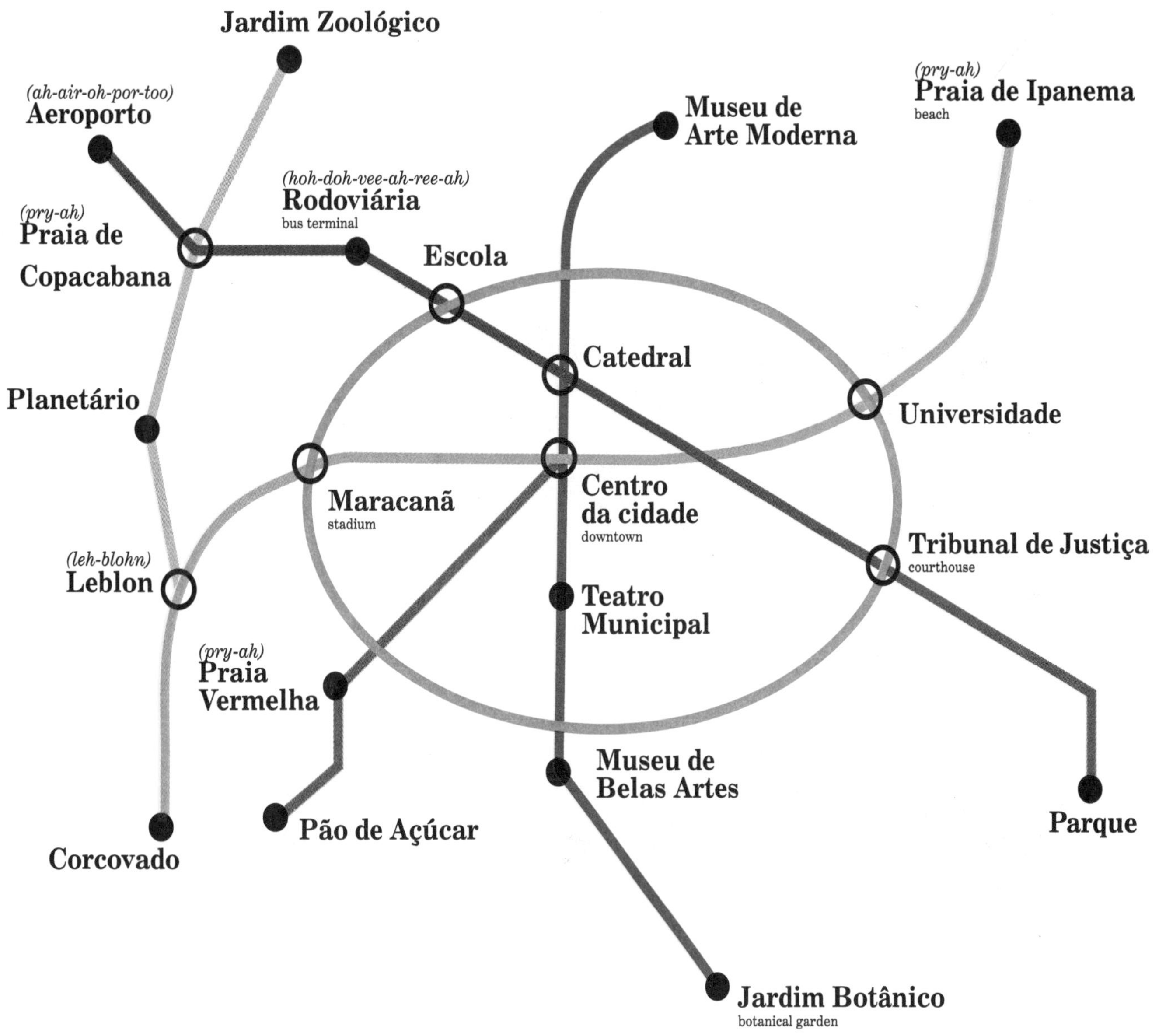

Jardim Zoológico

(ah-air-oh-por-too)
Aeroporto

(pry-ah)
Praia de Ipanema
beach

Museu de Arte Moderna

(hoh-doh-vee-ah-ree-ah)
Rodoviária
bus terminal

(pry-ah)
Praia de Copacabana

Escola

Catedral

Planetário

Universidade

Maracanã
stadium

Centro da cidade
downtown

(leh-blohn)
Leblon

Tribunal de Justiça
courthouse

Teatro Municipal

(pry-ah)
Praia Vermelha

Museu de Belas Artes

Pão de Açúcar

Parque

Corcovado

Jardim Botânico
botanical garden

Say these questions aloud many times and don't forget your **passagem de metrô**!

Onde é a estação de metrô? *(es-tah-sown)*

Onde é o ponto de ônibus?

Onde é o ponto de táxi?

Aqui are a few holidays **e** greetings which **você** might experience during your visit.

- ❒ **véspera de ano novo** *(vehs-peh-rah)(jee)(ah-noo)(noh-voo)* .... New Year's Eve (Dec. 31)
- ❒ **dia de ano novo** *(jee-ah)(jee)(ah-noo)(noh-voo)*.............................. New Year's Day (Jan. 1)
  –**Feliz Ano Novo!** *(feh-lees)(ah-noo)(noh-voo)* .... Happy New Year!
- ❒ **Feliz aniversário!** *(feh-lees)(ah-nee-vair-sah-ree-oo)* .... Happy Birthday!

Practice the following basic *(pair-goon-tahs)* **perguntas** (questions) out loud **e** then write them in the blanks below.

1. **Com que** (how often) *(freh-kwane-see-ah)* **freqüência vem** (comes) **o metrô?** ______________________

   Com que freqüência vem o ônibus? ______________________

   Com que freqüência vem o trem? ______________________

2. **A que horas vem o metrô?** ______________________

   A que horas vem o ônibus? A que horas vem o ônibus?

   A que horas vem o trem? ______________________

3. **Quanto custa uma passagem de metrô?** ______________________

   Quanto custa uma passagem de ônibus? ______________________

   Quanto custa uma passagem de avião? ______________________

4. **Onde posso** (can (I)) **comprar** (buy) **uma passagem de metrô?** ______________________

   Onde posso comprar uma passagem de ônibus? ______________________

   Onde posso comprar uma passagem de avião? ______________________

Let's change directions **e** learn **três** new verbs. **Você** know the basic "plug-in" formula, so write out your own sentences using these new verbs.

(lah-var)
lavar ______________________
to wash

(pair-dair)
perder ______________________
to lose

(toh-mar)
tomar ______________________
to take

- ❒ **Páscoa** *(pahs-koh-ah)* .... Easter
  - –**Feliz Páscoa!** *(feh-lees)(pahs-koh-ah)* .... Happy Easter!
- ❒ **véspera de Natal** *(vehs-peh-rah)(jeh)(nah-tahl)* .... Christmas Eve (Dec. 24)
- ❒ **Natal** *(nah-tahl)* .... Christmas (Dec. 25)
  - – **Feliz Natal!** *(feh-lees)(nah-tahl)* .... Merry Christmas!

(vehn-dair) **Vender** e (kohm-prar) **Comprar**

to sell / to buy

Shopping abroad is exciting. The simple everyday task of buying **um** (lee-troo) **litro** (liter) **de** (lay-chee) **leite** (milk) **ou uma** (mah-sah) **maçã** (apple) becomes a challenge that **você** should **agora** be able to meet quickly **e** easily. Of course, **você** will purchase (lame-brahn-sahs) **lembranças,** (souvenirs) (seh-loosh) **selos e** (kar-toynsh) **cartões** (pohs-tiesh) **postais** but do not forget those many other items ranging from shoelaces to (ahs-pee-ree-nah) **aspirina** (aspirin) that **você** might need unexpectedly. Locate your store, draw a line to it **e,** as always, write your new words in the blanks provided.

(mah-gah-zee-nee) **o magazine** (department store (Brazil)) / (grahn-jee) (ar-mah-zame) **o grande armazém** (department store (Portugal)) ________________

(see-neh-mah) **o cinema** (cinema) ________________

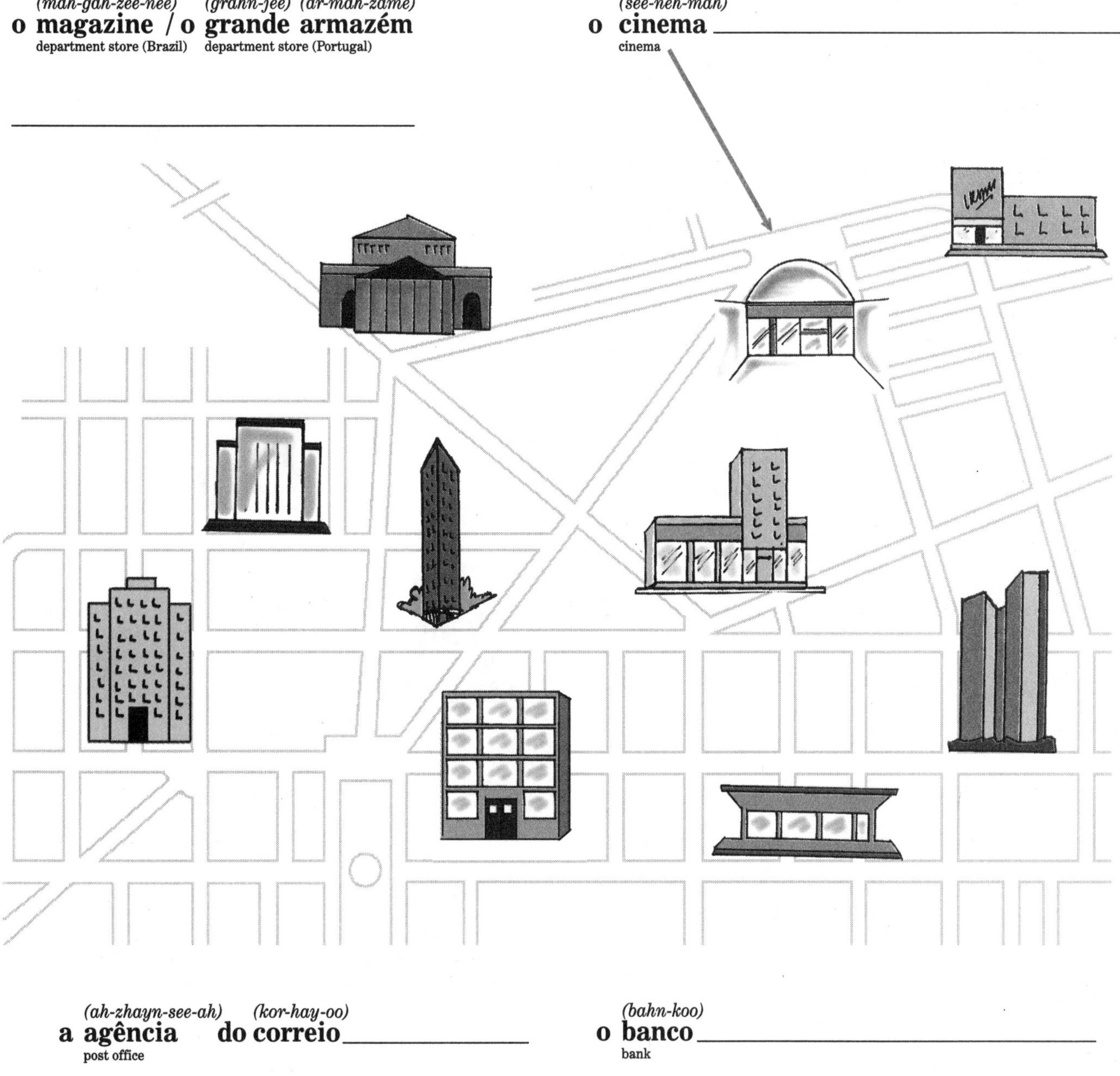

(ah-zhayn-see-ah) (kor-hay-oo) **a agência do correio** (post office) ________________

(bahn-koo) **o banco** (bank) ________________

(oh-tel) **o hotel** (hotel) / (poh-zah-dah) **a pousada** (inn) ________________

(pohs-too) (jee) (gah-zoh-lee-nah) **o posto de gasolina** (service station) ________________

As lojas (loh-zhahs) stores **estão** generally **abertas** (ah-bair-tahs) open from 8:00 or 8:30 until 19:00.

a **tinturaria** (cheen-too-rah-ree-ah) dry cleaner's ______

a **livraria** (lee-vrah-ree-ah) bookstore ______

______ o **açougue** (ah-soh-gee) butcher shop (Brazil) / o **talho** (tahl-yoo) butcher shop (Portugal)

______ o **mercado** (mair-kah-doo) **de frutas** (froo-tahs) **e legumes** (leh-goo-meesh) greengrocer

______ a **farmácia** (far-mah-see-ah) pharmacy, drugstore

______ o **estacionamento** (es-tah-see-oh-nah-mehn-too) parking lot

______ o **jornaleiro** (zhor-nah-lay-roo) newsstand

______ a **agência** (ah-zhayn-see-ah) **de viagens** (vee-ah-zhehns) travel agency

______ a **delegacia** (deh-leh-gah-see-ah) **de polícia** (poh-lee-see-ah) police station

Sábados stores **estão** usually **abertas** open until **meio-dia.** (may-oh-jee-ah) noon **Elas** are **fechadas** closed **aos domingos.** Shopping malls tend to be **abertas** on both **sábados e domingos.**

a **delicatessen** (deh-lee-kah-tehs-sen) delicatessen ______

a **charutaria** (shah-roo-tah-ree-ah) tobacco shop ______

(bar-zeen-yoo)
o **barzinho**
beverage bar with snacks

(floh-ree-kool-too-rah)
a **floricultura**
florist shop

(pay-shah-ree-ah)
a **peixaria** ______________________
fish store

(loh-zhah) (mah-teh-ree-ahl)(foh-toh-grah-fee-koo)
a **loja de material fotográfico** ______________
camera store

(mair-kah-doo)
o **mercado** ______________________
market

(soo-pair-mair-kah-doo)
o **supermercado** ______________________
supermarket

(heh-loh-zhoh-ah-ree-ah)
a **relojoaria** ______________________
watchmaker's shop

(pah-dah-ree-ah)
a **padaria** a padaria, a padaria
bakery

(loh-zhah) (doh-seesh)
a **loja de doces** ______________________
pastry shop

(lah-vahn-deh-ree-ah)
a **lavanderia** ______________________
laundry

(pah-peh-lah-ree-ah)
a **papelaria**
stationery store

(kah-beh-lay-ray-roo)
o **cabeleireiro**
hairdresser

Nos Estados Unidos, the ground floor **e** the first floor are one and the same. **No Brasil** the ground floor is called **o térreo** *(tair-heh-oo)* **(T)**. The **primeiro** *(pree-may-roo)* (first) **piso** *(pee-zoo)* (floor) **(1° piso) é** the next floor up **e** so on.

O Magazine
(mah-gah-zee-nee) department store

At this point, **você** should just about be ready for your **viagem. Você** have gone shopping for those last-minute odds 'n ends. Most likely, the store directory at your local **magazine** (mah-gah-zee-nee) department store did not look like the one **abaixo!** (ah-by-shoo) **"Criança"** (kree-ahn-sah) is Portuguese for "child" so if **você precisa de** (need) something for a child, **você** would probably look on **terçeiro** (tair-say-roo) **piso, não é?**

4º PISO	**iluminação** **artigos para bebês** **seção de perdidos**	**serviços ao cliente** **cerâmicas** **porcelana**	**móveis** **antiguidades** **acessórios para carros**
3º PISO	**vestuário feminino** **tudo para crianças**	**vestuário masculino** **artigos esportivos** **brinquedos**	**artigos para presente** **roupa de cama** **quadros**
2º PISO	**alimentação** **doces** **charutaria** **café**	**bebidas** **jornais e revistas** **discos**	**móveis de escritório** **artigos de cozinha**
1º PISO	**ternos masculinos** **sapatos de homem** **instrumentos musicais**	**bolsas e malas** **eletrônicos** **artigos de informática**	**livros** **jóias e bijuterias** **papelaria**
T	**máquina fotográfica** **guarda-chuvas** **relógios**	**vídeos** **perucas** **artigos de praia** **chapéus femininos**	**roupas íntimas** **perfumaria** **sapatos femininos**

Let's start a checklist **para a sua** (your) **viagem** (vee-ah-zhame). Besides **roupas** (hoh-pahs) (clothing), **o que você precisa?** As you learn these **palavras,** assemble these items **em um canto** (kahn-too) (corner) of your **casa.** Check **e** make sure that they **estão limpas** (leem-pahs) (clean) **e** ready **para a sua viagem.** Be sure to do the same **com** the rest of **as coisas** (koy-zahs) that **você** pack. On the next pages, match each item to its picture, draw a line to it and write out the word many times. As **você** organize these things, check them off on this list. Do not forget to take the next group of sticky labels and label these **coisas** (koy-zahs) **hoje** (today).

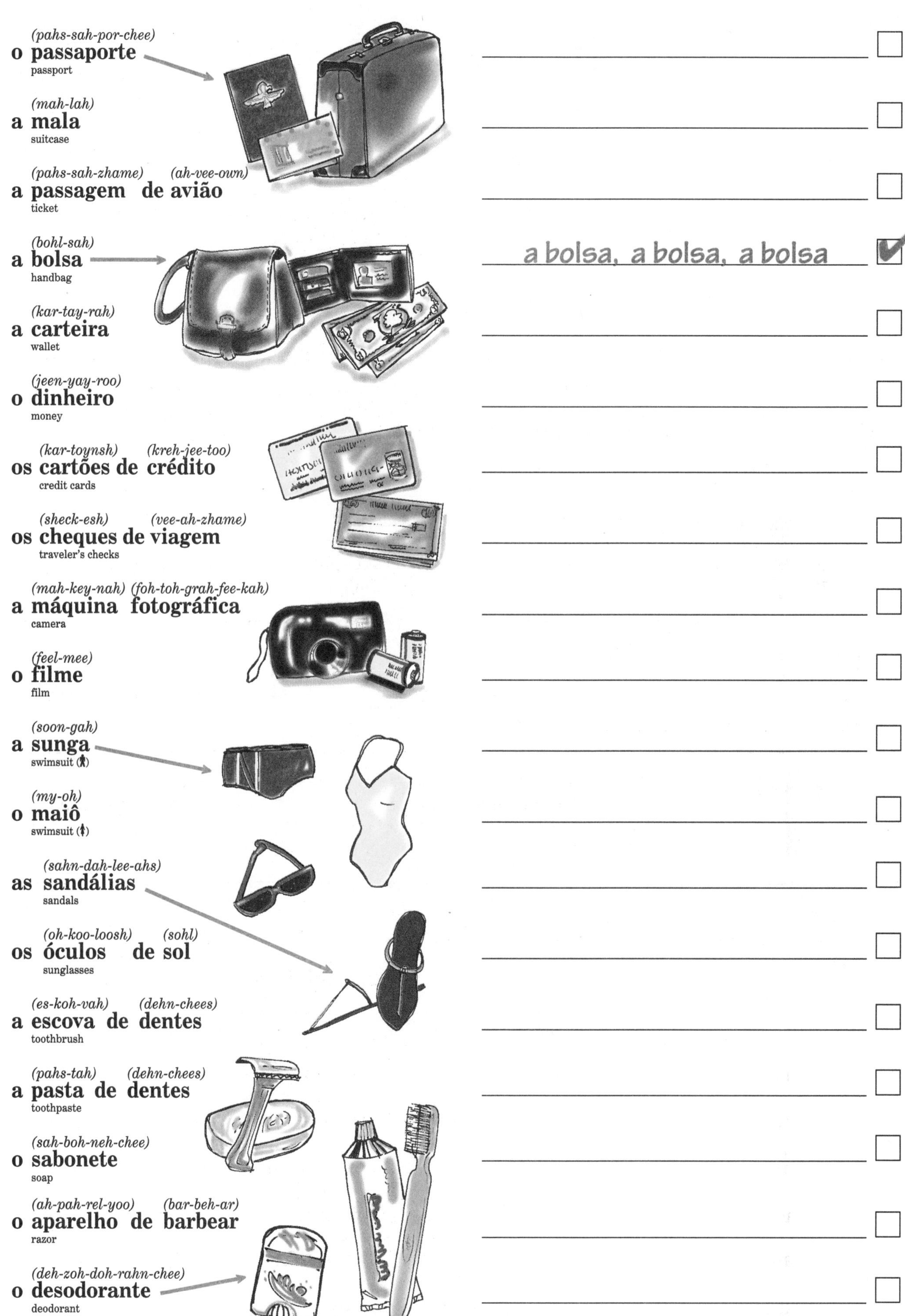

(pahs-sah-por-chee)
o passaporte
passport

(mah-lah)
a mala
suitcase

(pahs-sah-zhame) (ah-vee-own)
a passagem de avião
ticket

(bohl-sah)
a bolsa
handbag

a bolsa, a bolsa, a bolsa

(kar-tay-rah)
a carteira
wallet

(jeen-yay-roo)
o dinheiro
money

(kar-toynsh) (kreh-jee-too)
os cartões de crédito
credit cards

(sheck-esh) (vee-ah-zhame)
os cheques de viagem
traveler's checks

(mah-key-nah) (foh-toh-grah-fee-kah)
a máquina fotográfica
camera

(feel-mee)
o filme
film

(soon-gah)
a sunga
swimsuit (♂)

(my-oh)
o maiô
swimsuit (♀)

(sahn-dah-lee-ahs)
as sandálias
sandals

(oh-koo-loosh) (sohl)
os óculos de sol
sunglasses

(es-koh-vah) (dehn-chees)
a escova de dentes
toothbrush

(pahs-tah) (dehn-chees)
a pasta de dentes
toothpaste

(sah-boh-neh-chee)
o sabonete
soap

(ah-pah-rel-yoo) (bar-beh-ar)
o aparelho de barbear
razor

(deh-zoh-doh-rahn-chee)
o desodorante
deodorant

(pehn-chee)
o **pente**
comb

o pente, o pente, o pente

(kah-zah-koo)
o **casaco**
coat

(gwahr-dah-shoo-vah)
o **guarda-chuva**
umbrella

(kah-pah) (shoo-vah)
a **capa de chuva**
raincoat

(loo-vahs)
as **luvas**
gloves

(vee-zay-rah)
a **viseira**
visor

(shah-peh-oo) (pry-ah)
o **chapéu de praia**
beach hat

(boh-tahs)
as **botas**
boots

(sah-pah-toosh)
os **sapatos**
shoes

(tay-nees)
os **tênis**
tennis shoes

(tair-noo)
o **terno**
suit

(grah-vah-tah)
a **gravata**
tie

(kah-mee-zah)
a **camisa**
shirt

(lehn-soo)
o **lenço**
handkerchief

(zhah-kay-tah)
a **jaqueta**
jacket, blazer

(kahl-sah)
a **calça**
trousers

(jeansh)
o **jeans**
jeans

(shorch)
o **short**
shorts

(kah-mee-zeh-tah)
a **camiseta**
T-shirt

(koo-eh-kah)
a cueca
underpants

(kah-mee-zeh-tah)
a camiseta
undershirt

(vehs-chee-doo)
o vestido
dress

(bloo-zah)
a blusa
blouse

(sy-ah)
a saia — a saia, a saia, a saia, a saia
skirt

(soo-eh-tair)
a suéter
sweater

(kohm-bee-nah-sown)
a combinação
slip

(soo-chee-own)
o sutiã
bra

(kahl-seen-yah)
a calcinha
underpants

(may-ahs)
as meias
socks

(may-ah-kahl-sah)
a meia-calça
pantyhose

(pee-zhah-mah)
o pijama
pajamas

(kah-mee-zoh-lah)
a camisola
nightshirt

(hoh-pown) (bahn-yoo)
o roupão de banho
bathrobe

(shee-neh-loosh)
os chinelos
slippers

From now on, **você tem** (sah-boh-neh-chee) **"sabonete" e não** "soap." Having assembled these (koy-zahs) **coisas** (things), **você** are ready **para viajar.** Let's add these important shopping phrases to your basic repertoire.

(kay) (tah-mahn-yoo)
Que tamanho?
what size

(es-chee) (vehs-chee) (sair-vee)
Este veste bem. / Este serve bem.
this fits well fits

(vehs-chee)
Este não veste bem. / Este não serve bem.
does not fit

Treat yourself to a final review. **Você sabe** the names for **lojas** *(loh-zhahs)* **em português,** so let's practice shopping. Just remember your key question **palavras** that you learned in Step 2. Whether **você** need to buy **bolsas ou livros** the necessary **palavras** are the same.

1. First step — **onde?**

Onde é a padaria? **Onde é o banco?** **Onde é o jornaleiro?** *(zhor-nah-lay-roo)*

____
(Where is the department store?)

____
(Where is the market?)

____
(Where is the supermarket?)

2. Second step — tell them what **você** are looking for, **precisa ou quer!**

Eu preciso de . . . *(preh-see-zoo) (dee)* need

Eu quero . . . want

Você tem . . . ? do you have

____
(Do you have postcards?)

____
(I want four stamps.)

____
(I need toothpaste.)

____
(I want to buy film.)

____
(Do you have coffee?)

Go through the glossary at the end of this **livro e** select (veen-chee) **vinte** **palavras.** Drill the above patterns **com** these twenty **palavras.** Don't cheat. Drill them **hoje. Agora,** take **vinte** more **palavras do** (from) your glossary **e** do the same.

3. Third step — find out **quanto** (koos-tah) **custa a** (koy-zah) **coisa.**

Quanto custa isso? **Quanto custa um litro** (liter) **de** (lay-chee) **leite** (milk)**?** **Quanto custa um selo?**

____
(How much does the toothpaste cost?)

____
(How much does the soap cost?)

____
(How much does a cup of tea cost?)

4. Fourth step — success! I found it!

Once **você** find what **você** would like, (jee-gah) **diga,** (say)

(es-chee)
Quero este, (this one) **por favor.** ____

or

Me dá (give me) **este, por favor.** _____ Me dá este, por favor. _____

Ou if **você** would not like it, (jee-gah) **diga,**

Não quero este, obrigado. ____

or

Eu não (gohs-too) **gosto.** (I do not like it) ____

Congratulations! You have finished. By now you should have stuck your labels, flashed your cards, cut out your menu guide and packed your (mah-lahs) **malas** (suitcases)**. Você** should be very pleased with your accomplishment. You have learned what it sometimes takes others years to achieve and **você** hopefully had fun doing it. **Boa viagem!**

Glossary

This glossary contains words used in this book only. It is not meant to be a dictionary. Consider purchasing a dictionary which best suits your needs - small for traveling, large for reference, or specialized for specific vocabulary needs.

Remember that Portuguese words can change their endings depending upon how they are used. Not all variations are given here, but in many cases you will see "o/a" at the end of a word. This should help you to remember that this word can change its ending. Learn to look for the core of the word.

A

a *(ah)* .... the
à cobrar *(ah)(koh-brar)* .... collect (telephone call)
à milanesa *(ah)(mee-lah-neh-zah)* .... cooked in a batter
A que horas? *(ah)(kay)(oh-rahs)* .... At what time?
abaixo *(ah-by-shoo)* .... below
abajur, o *(ah-bah-zhoor)* .... lamp
aberto/a *(ah-bair-too)* .... open
abra *(ah-brah)* .... open!
abre *(ah-bree)* .... opens
abril *(ah-breel)* .... April
abrir *(ah-breer)* .... to open
absoluto/a *(ahb-soh-loo-too)* .... absolute
absurdo/a *(ahb-soor-doo)* .... absurd
acessórios para carros, os *(ah-sehs-soh-ree-oosh)(pah-rah)(kar-hoosh)* .... automobile accessories
acidente, o *(ah-see-dehn-chee)* .... accident
açougue, o *(ah-soh-gee)* .... butcher shop
açúcar, o *(ah-soo-kar)* .... sugar
adeus *(ah-deh-oos)* .... good-bye
aeroporto, o *(ah-air-oh-por-too)* .... airport
África do Sul, a *(ah-free-kah)(doo)(sool)* .... South Africa
agência de câmbio, a *(ah-zhayn-see-ah)(jeh)(kahm-bee-oo)* .... money-exchange office
agência de viagens, a *(ah-zhayn-see-ah)(jeh)(vee-ah-zhehns)* .... travel agency
agência do correio, a *(ah-zhayn-see-ah)(doh)(kor-hay-oo)* .... post office
agora *(ah-goh-rah)* .... now
agosto *(ah-gohs-too)* .... August
agrião, o *(ah-gree-own)* .... watercress
água, a *(ah-gwah)* .... water
água com gás, a *(ah-gwah)(kohm)(gahz)* .... sparkling water
água mineral, a *(ah-gwah)(mee-neh-rahl)* .... mineral water
água tônica, a *(ah-gwah)(toh-nee-kah)* .... tonic water
álcool, o *(ahl-kohl)* .... alcohol
Alemanha, a *(ah-leh-mahn-yah)* .... Germany
alemão/a *(ah-leh-mown)* .... German
alfândega, a *(ahl-fane-deh-gah)* .... customs
ali *(ah-lee)* .... there
alimentação, a *(ah-lee-mehn-tah-sown)* .... food
almoço, o *(ahl-moh-soo)* .... lunch
alô *(ah-loh)* .... hello
alto/a *(ahl-too)* .... tall, high
aluguél de carros, o *(ah-loo-gehl)(jee)(kar-hoosh)* .... car-rental agency
amanhã *(ah-mahn-yahn)* .... tomorrow
amarelo/a *(ah-mah-reh-loo)* .... yellow
América, a *(ah-meh-ree-kah)* .... America
América do Norte, a *(ah-meh-ree-kah)(doo)(nor-chee)* .... North America
América do Sul, a *(ah-meh-ree-kah)(doo)(sool)* .... South America
americana, a *(ah-meh-ree-kah-nah)* .... American (♀)
americano, o *(ah-meh-ree-kah-noo)* .... American (♂)
amigo, o *(ah-mee-goo)* .... friend (male)
andar *(ahn-dar)* .... to walk
animal, o *(ah-nee-mahl)* .... animal
ano, o *(ah-noo)* .... year
antiguidades, as *(ahn-chee-gwee-dah-jeesh)* .... antiques
anual *(ah-noo-ahl)* .... annual
ao *(ah-oh)* .... to the
ao forno *(ah-oh)(for-noo)* .... baked
aos *(ah-ohs)* .... on the
aparelho de barbear, o *(ah-pah-rel-yoo)(deh)(bar-beh-ar)* .... razor
apartamento, o *(ah-par-tah-mehn-too)* .... hotel room
aplicação, a *(ah-plee-kah-sown)* .... application
aprender *(ah-prehn-dair)* .... to learn
aproximadamente *(ah-proh-see-mah-dah-mehn-chee)* .... approximately
aqui *(ah-key)* .... here
Argentina, a *(ar-zhehn-chee-nah)* .... Argentina
armário, o *(ar-mah-ree-oo)* .... cupboard, wardrobe
arte, a *(ar-chee)* .... art
artesanato, o *(ar-teh-zah-nah-too)* .... crafts
artigos, os *(ar-chee-goosh)* .... goods, appliances
artigos de informática, os *(ar-chee-goosh)(jee)(een-for-mah-chee-kah)* .... computer goods
artista, a/o *(ar-chees-tah)* .... artist
as *(ahs)* .... the (plural, feminine)
às *(ahs)* .... at
aspirina, a *(ahs-pee-ree-nah)* .... aspirin
assado/a *(ahs-sah-doo)* .... roasted
assento, o *(ahs-sehn-too)* .... seat
assinatura, a *(ahs-see-nah-too-rah)* .... signature
até amanhã *(ah-teh)(ah-mahn-yahn)* .... until tomorrow
até logo *(ah-teh)(loh-goo)* .... until then
atenção, a *(ah-tehn-sown)* .... attention
ativo *(ah-chee-voo)* .... active
atlântico/a *(aht-lahn-chee-koo)* .... Atlantic
ato, o *(ah-too)* .... act (of a play)
atrás *(ah-trahs)* .... behind
atum, o *(ah-toom)* .... tuna
Austrália, a *(ows-trah-lee-ah)* .... Australia
auto-estrada, a *(ow-too-es-trah-dah)* .... freeway
ave, a *(ah-vee)* .... bird
avenida, a *(ah-veh-nee-dah)* .... avenue
aves, as *(ah-veesh)* .... poultry
avião, o *(ah-vee-own)* .... airplane
avó, a *(ah-voh)* .... grandmother
avô, o *(ah-voh)* .... grandfather
azul *(ah-zool)* .... blue
azulejos pintados à mão, os *(ah-zoo-leh-zhoosh)(peen-tah-doosh)(ah)(mown)* .... hand-painted tiles

B

baixo/a *(by-shoo)* .... short, low
balão, o *(bah-lown)* .... balloon
balcão, o *(bahl-kown)* .... balcony, counter
balé, o *(bah-lay)* .... ballet
banco, o *(bahn-koo)* .... bank
banheiro, o *(bahn-yay-roo)* .... restroom, bathroom
barato/a *(bah-rah-too)* .... inexpensive
barco, o *(bar-koo)* .... boat
barzinho, o *(bar-zeen-yoo)* .... street bar with snacks
básico/a *(bah-zee-koo)* .... basic
batata, a *(bah-tah-tah)* .... potato
bebê, o *(beh-bay)* .... baby

beber *(beh-bair)* . . . . to drink
bebida, a *(beh-bee-dah)* . . . . beverage
belas artes, as *(beh-lahs)(ar-chees)* . . . . fine arts
Bélgica, a *(bel-zhee-kah)* . . . . Belgium
bem *(bame)* . . . . well, good
bicicleta, a *(bee-see-kleh-tah)* . . . . bicycle
bife, o *(bee-fee)* . . . . beefsteak
bijuteria, a *(bee-zhoo-teh-ree-ah)* . . . . jewelry
biscoito, o *(bees-koy-too)* . . . . cookie
blusa, a *(bloo-zah)* . . . . blouse
boa noite *(boh-ah)(noy-chee)* . . . . good night
boa sorte *(boh-ah)(sor-chee)* . . . . good luck
boa tarde *(boh-ah)(tar-jee)* . . . . good afternoon
Boa viagem! *(boh-ah)(vee-ah-zhame)* . . . . Have a good trip!
Bolívia, a *(boh-lee-vee-ah)* . . . . Bolivia
bolo, o *(boh-loo)* . . . . cake
bolsa, a *(bohl-sah)* . . . . handbag
bom *(bohm)* . . . . good
Bom apetite! *(bohm)(ah-peh-chee-chee)* . . Enjoy your meal!
bom dia *(bohm)(jee-ah)* . . . . . . good morning, good day, hello
botas, as *(boh-tahs)* . . . . boots
branco *(brahn-koo)* . . . . white
Brasil, o *(brah-zeel)* . . . . Brazil
brasileiro/a *(brah-zee-lay-roo)* . . . . Brazilian
brinquedos, os *(breen-kay-doosh)* . . . . toys

C

cabeleireiro, o *(kah-beh-lay-ray-roo)* . . . . hairdresser
cabine telefônica, a *(kah-bee-nee)(teh-leh-foh-nee-kah)* . . . . telephone booth
cachorro, o *(kah-shor-hoo)* . . . . dog
cadeira, a *(kah-day-rah)* . . . . chair
café da manhã, o *(kah-fay)(dah)(mahn-yahn)* . . . breakfast
café, o *(kah-fay)* . . . . coffee, coffee house, coffee shop
cafezinho, o *(kah-fay-zeen-yoo)* . . . . espresso-type coffee
caixa do correio, a *(ky-shah)(doh)(kor-hay-oo)* . . . . mailbox
caixa, o/a *(ky-shah)* . . . . cashier
caju, o *(kah-zhoo)* . . . . cashew fruit
calça, a *(kahl-sah)* . . . . trousers
calcinha, a *(kahl-seen-yah)* . . . . underpants (♀)
calendário, o *(kah-lehn-dah-ree-oo)* . . . . calendar
calma, a *(kahl-mah)* . . . . calm
calor, o *(kah-lor)* . . . . heat
cama, a *(kah-mah)* . . . . bed
camisa, a *(kah-mee-zah)* . . . . shirt
camiseta, a *(kah-mee-zeh-tah)* . . . . T-shirt, undershirt
camisola, a *(kah-mee-zoh-lah)* . . . . nightshirt
Canadá, o *(kah-nah-dah)* . . . . Canada
canadense *(kah-nah-dehn-see)* . . . . Canadian
caneta, a *(kah-neh-tah)* . . . . pen
canto, o *(kahn-too)* . . . . corner
cão, o *(kown)* . . . . dog
capa de chuva, a *(kah-pah)(jeh)(shoo-vah)* . . . . raincoat
capacidade, a *(kah-pah-see-dah-jee)* . . . . capacity
capela, a *(kah-peh-lah)* . . . . chapel
capital, a *(kah-pee-tahl)* . . . . capital
caramelo, o *(kah-rah-meh-loo)* . . . . caramel
caranguejo, o *(kah-rahn-gay-zhoo)* . . . . crab
cardápio, o *(kar-dah-pee-oo)* . . . . menu
Carnaval, o *(kar-nah-vahl)* . . . . carnival
carne, a *(kar-nee)* . . . . meat
carneiro, o *(kar-nay-roo)* . . . . mutton
caro/a *(kah-roo)* . . . . expensive
carregador, o *(kar-heh-gah-dor)* . . . . porter
carro, o *(kar-hoo)* . . . . car
carro alugado, o *(kar-hoo)(ah-loo-gah-doo)* . . . . rental car
carta, a *(kar-tah)* . . . . letter
cartão de telefone, o *(kar-town)(jee)(teh-leh-foh-nee)* . . . . phonecard
cartão postal, o *(kar-town)(pohs-tahl)* . . . . postcard
carteira, a *(kar-tay-rah)* . . . . wallet
cartões de crédito, os *(kar-toynsh)(jeh)(kreh-jee-too)* . . . . credit cards
casa, a *(kah-zah)* . . . . house
casaco, o *(kah-zah-koo)* . . . . coat
catedral, a *(kah-teh-drahl)* . . . . cathedral
católico/a *(kah-toh-lee-koo)* . . . . Catholic
catorze *(kah-tor-zee)* . . . . fourteen
causa, a *(kow-zah)* . . . . cause
cavalheiro, o *(kah-vahl-yay-roo)* . . . . man
cem *(same)* . . . . one hundred
centígrado, o *(sehn-chee-grah-doo)* . . . . Centigrade
centro, o *(sehn-troo)* . . . . center
cerâmica, a *(seh-rah-mee-kah)* . . . . ceramics
cerveja, a *(sair-veh-zhah)* . . . . beer
cesto de papel, o *(sehs-too)(jeh)(pah-pel)* . . wastepaper basket
chá, o *(shah)* . . . . tea
chá mate, o *(shah)(mah-chee)* . . . . Brazilian iced tea
chamada, a *(shah-mah-dah)* . . . . call, telephone call
chamar *(shah-mar)* . . . . to call
champanhe, a/o *(shahm-pahn-yee)* . . . . champagne
chapéu de praia, o *(shah-peh-oo)(jee)(pry-ah)* . . . beach hat
charutaria, a *(shah-roo-tah-ree-ah)* . . . . tobacco shop
chegada, a *(sheh-gah-dah)* . . . . arrival
chegar *(sheh-gar)* . . . . to arrive
cheque, o *(sheck-ee)* . . . . check
cheques de viagem, os *(sheck-esh)(jeh)(vee-ah-zhame)* . . . . traveler's checks
Chile, o *(shee-lee)* . . . . Chile
chinelos, os *(shee-neh-loosh)* . . . . slippers
chinês *(shee-naysh)* . . . . Chinese
chocolate quente, o *(shoh-koh-lah-chee)(kane-chee)* . . . . hot chocolate
chocolate, o *(shoh-koh-lah-chee)* . . . . chocolate
chope, o *(shoh-pee)* . . . . draught beer
chove *(shoh-vee)* . . . . it rains
churrasco, o *(shoor-hahs-koo)* . . . . barbecue
chuveiro, o *(shoo-vay-roo)* . . . . shower
cidade, a *(see-dah-jee)* . . . . city
científico *(see-ehn-chee-fee-koo)* . . . . scientific
cinco *(seen-koo)* . . . . five
cinema, o *(see-neh-mah)* . . . . cinema
cinqüenta *(seen-kwehn-tah)* . . . . fifty
cinza *(seen-zah)* . . . . gray
clássico/a *(klahs-see-koo)* . . . . classical, classic
closet, o *(kloh-zet)* . . . . closet
cobertor, o *(koh-bair-tor)* . . . . blanket
coisa, a *(koy-zah)* . . . . thing
colher, a *(kohl-yair)* . . . . spoon
Colômbia, a *(koh-lohm-bee-ah)* . . . . Colombia
com *(kohm)* . . . . with
com fome *(kohm)(foh-mee)* . . . . with hunger
com licença *(kohm)(lee-sehn-sah)* . . . . excuse me
com sede *(kohm)(seh-jee)* . . . . with thirst
combinação, a *(kohm-bee-nah-sown)* . . . . slip
começar *(koh-meh-sar)* . . . . to begin, to commence
comer *(koh-mair)* . . . . to eat
cômico/a *(koh-mee-koo)* . . . . comical
como *(koh-moo)* . . . . how
Como vai? *(koh-moo)(vy)* . . . . How are you?
companhia, a *(kohm-pahn-yee-ah)* . . . . company
complicado/a *(kohm-plee-kah-doo)* . . . . complicated
comprar *(kohm-prar)* . . . . to buy
computador, o *(kohm-poo-tah-dor)* . . . . computer
concerto, o *(kohn-sair-too)* . . . . concert
conhaque, o *(kohn-yah-kay)* . . . . cognac, brandy
conta, a *(kohn-tah)* . . . . bill
conversação, a *(kohn-vair-sah-sown)* . . . . conversation
conversação telefônica, a *(kohn-vair-sah-sown)(teh-leh-foh-nee-kah)* . . . . telephone conversation
cópia, a *(koh-pee-ah)* . . . . copy
copo de vinho, o *(koh-poo)(jee)(veen-yoo)* . . . . wine glass
copo, o *(koh-poo)* . . . . glass
cor, a *(kor)* . . . . color
Corcovado, o *(kor-koh-vah-doo)* . . . . mountain in Rio
cordeiro, o *(kor-day-roo)* . . . . lamb
corredor, o *(kor-heh-dor)* . . . . aisle
correio, o *(koh-hay-oo)* . . . . mail, post office

correspondência, a *(kor-hehs-pohn-dane-see-ah)* ...... mail
correto/a *(kor-heh-too)* .... correct
cortina, a *(kor-chee-nah)* .... curtain
costa, a *(kohs-tah)* .... coast
Costa Rica, a *(kohs-tah)(hee-kah)* .... Costa Rica
couro, o *(koh-roo)* .... leather
cozido/a *(koh-zee-doo)* .... cooked
cozido no vapor *(koh-zee-doo)(noh)(vah-por)* ..... steamed
cozinha, a *(koh-zeen-yah)* .... kitchen
creme, o *(kreh-mee)* .... cream
criança, a *(kree-ahn-sah)* .... child
Cristo Redentor *(krees-too)(heh-dehn-tor)* .... Christ, the Redeemer
Cuba, a *(koo-bah)* .... Cuba
cueca, a *(koo-eh-kah)* .... underpants (male)
cultura, a *(kool-too-rah)* .... culture
curto/a *(koor-too)* .... short
custa *(koos-tah)* .... (it) costs
custar *(koos-tar)* .... to cost

D

da (de + a) *(dah)* .... from the, of the
dama, a *(dah-mah)* .... woman
da-me *(dah-mee)* .... give me (Portugal)
de *(deh), (jee), (dee), (jeh)* .... of, from
de ida *(jee)(ee-dah)* .... one way
de ida e volta *(jee)(ee-dah)(eh)(vohl-tah)* .... round trip
de nada *(jee)(nah-dah)* .... you're welcome
decisão, a *(deh-see-sown)* .... decision
declaração, a *(deh-klah-rah-sown)* .... declaration
delegacia de polícia, a *(deh-leh-gah-see-ah)(deh) (poh-lee-see-ah)* .... police station
delicatessen, a *(deh-lee-kah-tehs-sen)* .... delicatessen
delicioso/a *(deh-lee-see-oh-zoo)* .... delicious
desconforto, o *(dehs-kohn-for-too)* .... discomfort
desculpe *(dehs-kool-pee)* ...... excuse me (as in I am sorry)
desodorante, o *(deh-zoh-doh-rahn-chee)* .... deodorant
despertador, o *(dehs-pair-tah-dor)* .... alarm clock
desvio, o *(dehs-vee-oo)* .... detour
devagar *(deh-vah-gar)* .... slow
dez *(dehsh)* .... ten
dezembro *(deh-zem-broo)* .... December
dezenove *(deh-zeh-noh-vee)* .... nineteen
dezesseis *(deh-zehs-saysh)* .... sixteen
dezessete *(deh-zehs-seh-chee)* .... seventeen
dezoito *(deh-zoy-too)* .... eighteen
dia, o *(jee-ah)* .... day
dia de ano novo, o *(jee-ah)(jee)(ah-noo)(noh-voo)* .... New Year's Day
dicionário, o *(jee-see-oh-nah-ree-oo)* .... dictionary
diferença, a *(jee-feh-rehn-sah)* .... difference
diferente *(jee-feh-rehn-chee)* .... different
difícil *(jee-fee-seel)* .... difficult
diga *(jee-gah)* .... say!
dinheiro, o *(jeen-yay-roo)* .... money
direção, a *(jee-reh-sown)* .... direction
direita *(jee-ray-tah)* .... right
disco, o *(jees-koo)* .... disc, record, CD
discreto *(jees-kreh-too)* .... discreet
distância, a *(jees-tahn-see-ah)* .... distance
divisão, a *(jee-vee-sown)* .... division
dizer *(jee-zair)* .... to say
do (de + o) *(doo), (doh)* .... from the, of the
do lado de *(doo)(lah-doo)(dee)* .... next to
doce, o *(doh-see)* .... pastry
documento, o *(doh-koo-mehn-too)* .... document
doente *(doh-ehn-chee)* .... sick
dois *(doysh)* .... two
dólar, o *(doh-lar)* .... dollar
doméstico/a *(doh-mehs-chee-koo)* .... domestic
domingo, o *(doh-meen-goo)* .... Sunday
dona, a *(doh-nah)* .... lady, housewife (term of respect)
dormir *(dor-meer)* .... to sleep
dos *(dohs)* .... from the
doutor, o *(doh-tor)* .... doctor (title)
doze *(doh-zee)* .... twelve
duas *(doo-ahs)* .... two

E

é *(eh)* .... is, (it) is
e *(eh)* .... and
e meia *(eh)(may-ah)* .... half past
E para beber? *(eh)(pah-rah)(beh-bair)* .... and to drink?
economia, a *(eh-koh-noh-mee-ah)* .... economy
Ecuador, o *(eh-kwah-dor)* .... Ecuador
ela *(eh-lah)* .... she
elas *(eh-lahs)* .... they (♀)
ele *(eh-lee)* .... he
eles *(eh-leesh)* .... they (♂ or mixed)
elétrico/a *(eh-leh-tree-koo)* .... electric
eletrônicos, os *(eh-leh-troh-nee-koosh)* .... electronic goods
em *(ehm)* .... in, into
em cima *(ehm)(see-mah)* .... upstairs, on top
em frente *(ehm)(frehn-chee)* .... straight ahead
em frente de *(ehm)(frehn-chee)(dee)* .... in front of
e-mail, o *(ee-may-oo)* .... e-mail
embaixo *(ehm-by shoo)* .... downstairs
embaixo de *(ehm-by-shoo)(dee)* .... under
empurre *(ehm-poor-hee)* .... push! (doors)
encomenda, a *(ehn-koh-mehn-dah)* .... order
encontrar *(ehn-kohn-trar)* .... to find, to meet
endereço, o *(ehn-deh-reh-soo)* .... address
enorme *(eh-nor-mee)* .... enormous
entender *(ehn-tehn-dair)* .... to understand
entrada, a *(ehn-trah-dah)* .... entrance, main course
entrar *(ehn-trar)* .... to enter
entre *(ehn-tree)* .... between
erro, o *(air-hoo)* .... error
escola, a *(es-koh-lah)* .... school
escova de dentes, a *(es-koh-vah)(jee)(dehn-chees)* .. toothbrush
escreva *(es-kreh-vah)* .... write!, write out!
escrever *(es-kreh-vair)* .... to write
escritório, o *(es-kree-toh-ree-oo)* .... office
espaço, o *(es-pah-soo)* .... space
Espanha, a *(es-pahn-yah)* .... Spain
espanhol *(es-pahn-yohl)* .... Spanish
especial do dia, o *(es-peh-see-ahl)(doo)(jee-ah)* .. daily special
espelho, o *(es-pel-yoo)* .... mirror
esplêndido *(es-plehn-jee-doo)* .... splendid
esporte, o *(es-por-chee)* .... sport
esquerda *(es-kair-dah)* .... left
está *(es-tah)* .... is
estabilidade, a *(es-tah-bee-lee-dah-jee)* .... stability
estação, a *(es-tah-sown)* .... station
estação de metrô, a *(es-tah-sown)(jee)(meh-troh)* .... subway station
estação de trem, a *(es-tah-sown)(jee)(trame)* .. train station
estacionamento, o *(es-tah-see-oh-nah-mehn-too)* .. parking lot
estacionar *(es-tah-see-oh-nar)* .... to park
estado, o *(es-tah-doo)* .... state
Estados Unidos, os *(es-tah-doosh)(oo-nee-doosh)* .... the United States
estão *(es-town)* .... (they) are
estas *(es-tahs)* .... these
estátua, a *(es-tah-too-ah)* .... statue
estava *(es-tah-vah)* .... (it) was
este *(es-chee)* .... this, this one
estou *(es-toh)* .... (I) am
estrada, a *(es-trah-dah)* .... road
estudante, a/o *(es-too-dahn-chee)* .... student
eu *(eh-oo)* I
eu estou *(eh-oo)(es-toh)* .... I am
eu quero *(eh-oo)(kair-oo)* .... I want
eu sou *(eh-oo)(soh)* .... I am
eu tenho *(eh-oo)(tehn-yoo)* .... I have
Europa, a *(eh-oo-roh-pah)* .... Europe
exato/a *(eh-zah-too)* .... exact
excelente *(eh-seh-lehn-chee)* .... excellent

exemplo, o *(eh-zame-ploo)* .... example
experiência, a *(es-peh-ree-ayn-see-ah)* .... experience
expressão, a *(es-prehs-sown)* .... expression
extremo,o *(es-treh-moo)* .... extreme

F

faca, a *(fah-kah)* .... knife
fahrenheit *(fah-rehn-heit)* .... Fahrenheit
falar *(fah-lar)* .... to speak
fama, a *(fah-mah)* .... fame
família, a *(fah-mee-lee-ah)* .... family
famoso/a *(fah-moh-zoo)* .... famous
farmácia, a *(far-mah-see-ah)* .... pharmacy, drugstore
favor, o *(fah-vor)* .... favor
fax, o *(fahks)* .... fax
faz *(fahs)* .... it makes
fazer *(fah-zair)* .... to make, to do
fazer a mala *(fah-zair)(ah)(mah-lah)* .... to pack
fechado/a *(feh-shah-doo)* .... closed
fechar *(feh-shar)* .... to close
feira, a *(fay-rah)* .... market
feito/a *(fay-too)* .... finished, ready
Feliz Aniversário! *(feh-lees)(ah-nee-vair-sah-ree-oo)* .... Happy Birthday
Feliz Ano Novo! *(feh-lees)(ah-noo)(noh-voo)* .. Happy New Year
Feliz Natal! *(feh-lees)(nah-tahl)* .... Merry Christmas
Feliz Páscoa! *(feh-lees)(pahs-koh-ah)* .... Happy Easter
festival, o *(fehs-chee-vahl)* .... festival
fevereiro *(feh-veh-ray-roo)* .... February
figura, a *(fee-goo-rah)* .... figure
filé, o *(fee-lay)* .... filet
filha, a *(feel-yah)* .... daughter
filho, o *(feel-yoo)* .... son
filhos, os *(feel-yoosh)* .... children
filme, o *(feel-mee)* .... film
final, o *(fee-nahl)* .... final
flor, a *(flor)* .... flower
floricultura, a *(floh-ree-kool-too-rah)* .... florist shop
fogão, o *(foh-gown)* .... stove
foi *(foy)* .... was
folclore, o *(fohl-kloh-ree)* .... folklore
fome, a *(foh-mee)* .... hunger
forma, a *(for-mah)* .... form, shape
formulário, o *(for-moo-lah-ree-oo)* .... form
fortuna, a *(for-too-nah)* .... fortune
fotografia, a *(foh-toh-grah-fee-ah)* .... photograph
França, a *(frahn-sah)* .... France
francês *(frahn-saysh)* .... French
frango, o *(frahn-goo)* .... chicken
frase, a *(frah-zee)* .... sentence, phrase
freqüência, a *(freh-kwane-see-ah)* .... frequency
freqüente *(freh-kwehn-chee)* .... frequent
frio *(free-oo)* .... cold
frito/a *(free-too)* .... fried
fruta, a *(froo-tah)* .... fruit
frutos do mar, os *(froo-toosh)(doh)(mar)* .... seafood
futebol, o *(foo-cheh-bohl)* .... soccer, football
futuro, o *(foo-too-roo)* .... future

G

galáxia, a *(gah-lahk-see-ah)* .... galaxy
galeria, a *(gah-leh-ree-ah)* .... gallery
garagem, a *(gah-rah-zhame)* .... garage
garçom, o *(gar-sohm)* .... waiter
garçonete, a *(gar-soh-neh-chee)* .... waitress
garfo, o *(gar-foo)* .... fork
garrafa, a *(gar-hah-fah)* .... bottle
gato, o *(gah-too)* .... cat
geladeira, a *(zheh-lah-day-rah)* .... refrigerator
geléia, a *(zheh-lay-ah)* .... jam, jelly
gelo, o *(zheh-loo)* .... ice
glória, a *(gloh-ree-ah)* .... glory
gorjeta, a *(gor-zheh-tah)* .... tip
gostaria de *(gohs-tah-ree-ah)(deh)* .... (I) would like
grande *(grahn-jee)* .... large, big
grande armazém, o *(grahn-jee)(ar-mah-zame)* .. department store
gratinado/a *(grah-chee-nah-doo)* .... grated
graus, os *(grouse)* .... degrees
gravata, a *(grah-vah-tah)* .... tie
grave *(grah-vee)* .... grave, serious
grelhado/a *(grehl-yah-doo)* .... grilled
grupo, o *(groo-poo)* .... group
guarda-chuva, o *(gwahr-dah-shoo-vah)* .... umbrella
guardanapo, o *(gwahr-dah-nah-poo)* .... napkin

H

há *(ah)* .... there is, there are
habitual *(ah-bee-too-ahl)* .... habitual
história, a *(ees-toh-ree-ah)* .... history
hoje *(oh-zhee)* .... today
homem, o *(oh-mehn)* .... man
Honduras, a *(ohn-doo-rahs)* .... Honduras
honesto *(oh-nehs-too)* .... honest
honra, a *(ohn-hah)* .... honor
hora, a *(oh-rah)* .... hour, time
horário, o *(oh-rah-ree-oo)* .... timetable
hotel, o *(oh-tel)* .... hotel
humor, o *(oo-mor)* .... humor

I

idéia, a *(ee-day-ah)* .... idea
igreja, a *(ee-greh-zhah)* .... church
ilegal *(ee-leh-gahl)* .... illegal
iluminação, a *(ee-loo-mee-nah-sown)* .... lights
imaginação, a *(ee-mah-zhee-nah-sown)* .... imagination
importância, a *(eem-por-tahn-see-ah)* .... importance
importante *(eem-por-tahn-chee)* .... important
impossível *(eem-pohs-see-vel)* .... impossible
incêndio, o *(een-sane-jee-oo)* .... fire
incluído/a *(een-kloo-ee-doo)* .... included
incorreto/a *(een-kor-heh-too)* .... incorrect
influência, a *(een-floo-ayn-see-ah)* .... influence
informação, a *(een-for-mah-sown)* .... information
Inglaterra, a *(een-glah-tair-hah)* .... England
inglês *(een-glaysh)* .... English
ingresso, o *(een-grehs-soo)* .... ticket
instrução, a *(een-stroo-sown)* .... instruction
instrumento, o *(een-stroo-mehn-too)* .... instrument
inteligência, a *(een-teh-lee-zhayn-see-ah)* ..... intelligence
intenção, a *(een-tehn-sown)* .... intention
interessante *(een-teh-rehs-sahn-chee)* .... interesting
interior, o *(een-teh-ree-or)* .... interior
internacional *(een-tair-nah-see-oh-nahl)* ..... international
inverno, o *(een-vair-noo)* .... winter
ir *(eer)* .... to go
ir de avião *(eer)(jee)(ah-vee-own)* ..... to go by plane, to fly
ir de carro *(eer)(jee)(kar-hoo)* .... to go by car, to drive
Irlanda do Norte, a *(eer-lahn-dah)(doo)(nor-chee)* .... Northern Ireland
irmã, a *(eer-mahn)* .... sister
irmão, o *(eer-mown)* .... brother
isso *(ees-soo)* .... that
Itália, a *(ee-tah-lee-ah)* .... Italy

J

janeiro *(zhah-nay-roo)* .... January
janela, a *(zhah-neh-lah)* .... window
jantar, o *(zhahn-tar)* .... dinner
japonês *(zhah-poh-naysh)* .... Japanese
jaqueta, a *(zhah-kay-tah)* .... jacket
jardim, o *(zhar-deem)* .... garden
jardim botânico, o *(zhar-deem)(boh-tah-nee-koo)* .... botanical garden
jardim zoológico, o *(zhar-deem)(zoh-oh-loh-zhee-koo)* .. zoo
jeans, o *(jeansh)* .... jeans
jogo, o *(zhoh-goo)* .... game
jóias, as *(zhoy-ahs)* .... gemstones
jornal, o *(zhor-nahl)* .... newspaper

jornaleiro, o *(zhor-nah-lay-roo)* .... newsstand
jornalista, a/o *(zhor-nah-lees-tah)* .... journalist
jovem *(zhoh-vame)* .... young
judeu *(zhoo-deh-oo)* .... Jewish (♂)
judia *(zhoo-jee-ah)* .... Jewish (♀)
julho *(zhool-yoo)* .... July
junho *(zhoon-yoo)* .... June
justiça, a *(zhoos-chee-sah)* .... justice

L

lanchonete, a *(lahn-shoh-neh-chee)* .... informal restaurant
lápis, o *(lah-peesh)* .... pencil
laranja *(lah-rahn-zhah)* .... orange (color)
laranja, a *(lah-rahn-zhah)* .... orange (fruit)
lavanderia, a *(lah-vahn-deh-ree-ah)* .... laundry
lavar *(lah-var)* .... to wash
Leblon *(leh-blohn)* .... area of Rio
legal *(leh-gahl)* .... legal, cool
legume, o *(leh-goo-mee)* .... vegetable
leia *(lay-ah)* .... read!
leite, o *(lay-chee)* .... milk
lembrança, a *(lame-brahn-sah)* .... souvenir
lenço, o *(lehn-soo)* .... handkerchief
ler *(lair)* .... to read
leste *(lehs-chee)* .... east
lição, a *(lee-sown)* .... lesson
licor, o *(lee-kor)* .... liquor
limão, o *(lee-mown)* .... lime
limonada, a *(lee-moh-nah-dah)* .... lemonade
limpo/a *(leem-poo)* .... clean
linha, a *(leen-yah)* .... line
lista, a *(lees-tah)* .... list
lista telefônica, a *(lees-tah)(teh-leh-foh-nee-kah)* .... telephone book
litro, o *(lee-troo)* .... liter
livraria, a *(lee-vrah-ree-ah)* .... bookstore
livre *(lee-vree)* .... free, available
livro, o *(lee-vroo)* .... book
local *(loh-kahl)* .... local
loja, a *(loh-zhah)* .... store
loja de material fotográfico, a *(loh-zhah)(jeh)(mah-teh-ree-ahl)(foh-toh-grah-fee-koo)* .... camera store
longo/a *(lohn-goo)* .... long
luvas, as *(loo-vahs)* .... gloves

M

maçã, a *(mah-sah)* .... apple
mãe, a *(mah-een)* .... mother
magazine, o *(mah-gah-zee-nee)* .. department store (Brazil)
maio *(my-oo)* .... May
maiô, o *(my-oh)* .... swimsuit (♀)
mais *(mysh)* .... more
mal *(mahl)* .... badly
mala, a *(mah-lah)* .... suitcase
mandar *(mahn-dar)* .... to send
manhã, a *(mahn-yahn)* .... morning
manteiga, a *(mahn-tay-gah)* .... butter
mapa, o *(mah-pah)* .... map
máquina, a *(mah-kee-nah)* .... machine
máquina fotográfica, a *(mah-kee-nah)(foh-toh-grah-fee-kah)* .... camera
maracujá, a *(mah-rah-koo-zhah)* .... passion fruit
março *(mar-soo)* .... March
marrom *(mar-hohm)* .... brown
masculino *(mahs-koo-lee-noo)* .... masculine
matemática, a *(mah-teh-mah-chee-kah)* ...... mathematics
matrimônio, o *(mah-tree-moh-nee-oo)* .... matrimony
mau *(mow)* .... bad
máximo/a *(mah-see-moo)* .... maximum
me dá *(mee)(dah)* .... give me!
mecânico, o *(meh-kah-nee-koo)* .... mechanic
medicina, a *(meh-jee-see-nah)* .... medicine
médico, o *(meh-jee-koo)* .... doctor
mediterrâneo, o *(meh-jee-tair-hah-neh-oo)* ... Mediterranean

meia, a *(may-ah)* .... sock
meia *(may-ah)* .... six (when saying telephone numbers)
meia-calça, a *(may-ah-kahl-sah)* .... pantyhose
meia-dúzia, a *(may-ah-doo-zee-ah)* .... half-dozen
meia-noite, a *(may-ah-noy-chee)* .... midnight
meio/a *(may-oo)* .... half
meio-dia, o *(may-oo-jee-ah)* .... noon
melodia, a *(meh-loh-jee-ah)* .... melody
menina, a *(meh-nee-nah)* .... girl
menino, o *(meh-nee-noo)* .... boy
menu, o *(meh-noo)* .... menu
mercado, o *(mair-kah-doo)* .... market
mês, o *(maysh)* .... month
mesa, a *(meh-zah)* .... table, desk
metro, o *(meh-troo)* .... meter
metrô, o *(meh-troh)* .... metro, subway
metropolitano/a *(meh-troh-poh-lee-tah-noo)* .. metropolitan
meu *(meh-oo)* .... my
México, o *(meh-shee-koo)* .... Mexico
mil *(meel)* .... thousand
mínimo/a *(mee-nee-moo)* .... minimum
ministro, o *(mee-nees-troo)* .... minister (government)
minuto, o *(mee-noo-too)* .... minute
misto/a *(mees-too)* .... mixed
Moçambique, o *(moh-sahm-bee-kee)* .... Mozambique
moderno/a *(moh-dair-noo)* .... modern
modo, o *(moh-doo)* .... means, way
moeda, a *(moh-eh-dah)* .... coin
momento, o *(moh-mehn-too)* .... moment
monastério, o *(moh-nahs-teh-ree-oo)* .... monastery
montanha, a *(mohn-tahn-yah)* .... mountain
morango, o *(moh-rahn-goo)* .... strawberry
motocicleta, a *(moh-toh-see-kleh-tah)* .... motorcycle
mousse, a *(mohs-see)* .... mousse
móveis, os *(moh-vaysh)* .... furniture
muito/a *(mwee-too)* .... very, a lot
mulher, a *(mool-yair)* .... woman
multicolorido/a *(mool-chee-koh-loh-ree-doo)* .. multi-colored
municipal *(moo-nee-see-pahl)* .... municipal
museu, o *(moo-zeh-oo)* .... museum
música, a *(moo-zee-kah)* .... music
musical *(moo-zee-kahl)* .... musical

N

na (em + a) *(nah)* .... in the, into the
nada *(nah-dah)* .... nothing
não *(nown)* .... no
não ... nada *(nown) ... (nah-dah)* .... nothing
não é? *(nown)(eh)* .... isn't it?
não gosto *(nown)(gohs-too)* .... (I) do not like it
Natal, o *(nah-tahl)* .... Christmas
natural *(nah-too-rahl)* .... natural
naturalmente *(nah-too-rahl-mehn-chee)* .... naturally
náutico/a *(now-chee-koo)* .... nautical
necessário/a *(neh-sehs-sah-ree-oo)* .... necessary
neva *(neh-vah)* .... it snows
névoa, a *(neh-voh-ah)* .... fog
no (em + o) *(noh)* .... in, in the, into the
noite, a *(noy-chee)* .... evening, night
nome, o *(noh-mee)* .... name
normal *(nor-mahl)* .... normal
norte *(nor-chee)* .... north
nós *(noys)* .... we
nos *(nohs)* .... in the
nota, a *(noh-tah)* .... bill (currency)
nove *(noh-vee)* .... nine
novembro *(noh-vem-broo)* .... November
noventa *(noh-vehn-tah)* .... ninety
novo/a *(noh-voo)* .... new
número, o *(noo-meh-roo)* .... number

O

o *(oh)* .... the
o que *(oh)(kay)* .... what

objeto, o *(ohb-zheh-too)* ... object
obrigada *(oh-bree-gah-dah)* ... thank you (♀)
obrigado *(oh-bree-gah-doo)* ... thank you (♂)
ocasião, a *(oh-kah-zee-own)* ... occasion
oceano, o *(oh-seh-ah-noo)* ... ocean
ocidente, o *(oh-see-dehn-chee)* ... occident, west
óculos, os *(oh-koo-loosh)* ... eyeglasses
óculos de sol, os *(oh-koo-loosh)(jee)(sohl)* ... sunglasses
ocupado/a *(oh-koo-pah-doo)* ... occupied, busy
oeste *(oh-ehs-chee)* ... west
oi *(oy)* ... hi, hello
oitenta *(oy-tehn-tah)* ... eighty
oito *(oy-too)* ... eight
olá *(oh-lah)* ... hi, hello
onde *(ohn-jee)* ... where
ônibus, o *(ow-nee-boos)* ... bus
ontem *(ohn-tame)* ... yesterday
onze *(ohn-zee)* ... eleven
opção, a *(ohp-sown)* ... option
ópera, a *(oh-peh-rah)* ... opera
operação, a *(oh-peh-rah-sown)* ... operation
oportunidade, a *(oh-por-too-nee-dah-jee)* ... opportunity
oposição, a *(oh-poh-zee-sown)* ... opposition
ordinário/a *(or-jee-nah-ree-oo)* ... ordinary
orelhão, o *(oh-rel-yown)* ... nickname for telephone booth
oriental *(oh-ree-ehn-tahl)* ... oriental
original *(oh-ree-zhee-nahl)* ... original
os *(ohs)* ... the (plural)
ostra, a *(ohs-trah)* ... oyster
ou *(oh)* ... or
outono, o *(oh-toh-noo)* ... autumn
outubro *(oh-too-broo)* ... October
oval *(oh-vahl)* ... oval
ovo, o *(oh-voo)* ... egg

P

pacote, o *(pah-koh-chee)* ... package
padaria, a *(pah-dah-ree-ah)* ... bakery
pagar *(pah-gar)* ... to pay, to pay for
página, a *(pah-zhee-nah)* ... page
pai, o *(pie)* ... father
pais, os *(piesh)* ... parents
palácio, o *(pah-lah-see-oo)* ... palace
palavra, a *(pah-lah-vrah)* ... word
palavras cruzadas, as *(pah-lah-vrahs)(kroo-zah-dahs)* ... crossword puzzle
palma, a *(pahl-mah)* ... palm
Panamá, o *(pah-nah-mah)* ... Panama
pânico, o *(pah-nee-koo)* ... panic
pão, o *(pown)* ... bread
Pão de Açúcar, o *(pown)(jeh)(ah-soo-kar)* ... Sugar Loaf (in Rio)
papel, o *(pah-pel)* ... paper
papelaria, a *(pah-peh-lah-ree-ah)* ... stationery store
para *(pah-rah)* ... to, for
parada, a *(pah-rah-dah)* ... stop
Paraguai, o *(pah-rah-gwhy)* ... Paraguay
pare *(pah-ree)* ... stop!
parentes, os *(pah-rehn-cheesh)* ... relatives
partida, a *(par-chee-dah)* ... departure
partir *(par-cheer)* ... to depart
Páscoa, a *(pahs-koh-ah)* ... Easter
passagem, a *(pahs-sah-zhame)* ... ticket
passaporte, o *(pahs-sah-por-chee)* ... passport
pasta de dentes, a *(pahs-tah)(jeh)(dehn-chees)* ... toothpaste
pausa, a *(pow-zah)* ... pause
pedir *(peh-jeer)* ... to order, to request
peixaria, a *(pay-shah-ree-ah)* ... fish store
peixe, o *(pay-shee)* ... fish
pente, o *(pehn-chee)* ... comb
pequeno almoço, o *(peh-kay-noo)(ahl-moh-soo)* ... breakfast
pequeno/a *(peh-kay-noo)* ... small
pêra, a *(pair-ah)* ... pear
perder *(pair-dair)* ... to lose
perfeito/a *(pair-fay-too)* ... perfect
perfume, o *(pair-foo-mee)* ... perfume
pergunta, a *(pair-goon-tah)* ... question
perguntar *(pair-goon-tar)* ... to question
Peru, o *(peh-roo)* ... Peru
perucas, as *(peh-roo-kahs)* ... wigs
pia, a *(pee-ah)* ... washstand, sink
pianista, o/a *(pee-ah-nees-tah)* ... pianist
piano, o *(pee-ah-noo)* ... piano
pijama, o *(pee-zhah-mah)* ... pijamas
piloto, o *(pee-loh-too)* ... pilot
pimenta, a *(pee-mehn-tah)* ... pepper
piso, o *(pee-zoo)* ... floor
planetário, o *(plah-neh-tah-ree-oo)* ... planetarium
plataforma, a *(plah-tah-for-mah)* ... platform
pobre *(poh-bree)* ... poor
pode *(poh-jee)* ... (you) can
poder *(poh-dair)* ... to be able to, can
pois não *(poysh)(nown)* ... of course
polícia, a *(poh-lee-see-ah)* ... police
política, a *(poh-lee-chee-kah)* ... politics
Pólo Norte, o *(poh-loo)(nor-chee)* ... North Pole
Pólo Sul, o *(poh-loo)(sool)* ... South Pole
ponto, o *(pohn-too)* ... point
ponto de ônibus, o *(pohn-too)(jee)(ow-nee-boos)* ... bus stop
ponto de táxi, o *(pohn-too)(jee)(tahk-see)* ... taxi stand
ponto de vista, o *(pohn-too)(jeh)(vees-tah)* ... viewpoint
por favor *(por)(fah-vor)* ... please, excuse me (to catch attention)
por que *(por)(kay)* ... why
porão, o *(poh-rown)* ... basement
porcelana, a *(por-seh-lah-nah)* ... porcelain
porco, o *(por-koo)* ... pork
porta, a *(por-tah)* ... door
portão, o *(por-town)* ... gate
porto, o *(por-too)* ... port wine
Portugal, o *(por-too-gahl)* ... Portugal
português *(por-too-gaysh)* ... Portuguese
possível *(pohs-see-vel)* ... possible
posso *(pohs-soo)* ... (I) can
posto de gasolina, o *(pohs-too)(jee)(gah-zoh-lee-nah)* ... service station, gas station
pouco/a *(poh-koo)* ... a little
pousada, a *(poh-zah-dah)* ... small hotel, inn
praia, a *(pry-ah)* ... beach
prática, a *(prah-chee-kah)* ... practice
prato, o *(prah-too)* ... plate
prato feito, o *(prah-too)(fay-too)* ... reasonably priced meal
precioso/a *(preh-see-oh-zoo)* ... precious
precisar de *(preh-see-zar)(dee)* ... to need, to have need of
preciso/a *(preh-see-zoo)* ... precise
preço, o *(preh-soo)* ... price
preparo, o *(preh-pah-roo)* ... preparation
presente, o *(preh-zehn-chee)* ... present, gift
presunto, o *(preh-zoon-too)* ... ham
preto *(preh-too)* ... black
primavera, a *(pree-mah-veh-rah)* ... spring
primeiro/a *(pree-may-roo)* ... first
principal *(preen-see-pahl)* ... principal, main
problema, o *(proh-bleh-mah)* ... problem
produto, o *(proh-doo-too)* ... product
professor, o *(proh-fehs-sor)* ... professor
programa, o *(proh-grah-mah)* ... program
proibido/a *(proh-ee-bee-doo)* ... prohibited
promessa, a *(proh-mehs-sah)* ... promise
pronúncia, a *(proh-noon-see-ah)* ... pronunciation
protestante *(proh-tehs-tahn-chee)* ... Protestant
público, o *(poo-blee-koo)* ... public
purê de batatas, o *(poo-ray)(jee)(bah-tah-tahs)* ... mashed potatoes
púrpura *(poor-poo-rah)* ... purple
puxe *(poo-shee)* ... pull! (doors)

Q

quadro, o *(kwah-droo)* ... picture
qual *(kwahl)* ... which, what

quando *(kwahn-doo)* ... when
quanto *(kwahn-too)* ... how much
Quanto custa isso? *(kwahn-too)(koos-tah)(ees-soo)* ... how much does that cost
quantos/quantas *(kwahn-toosh)/(kwahn-tahs)* ... how many
quarenta *(kwah-rehn-tah)* ... forty
quarta-feira, a *(kwahr-tah-fay-rah)* ... Wednesday
quarto, o *(kwahr-too)* ... bedroom
quatorze *(kwah-tor-zee)* ... fourteen
quatro *(kwah-troo)* ... four
que *(kay)* ... what
Que horas são? *(kay)(oh-rahs)(sown)* ... What time is it?
queijo, o *(kay-zhoo)* ... cheese
quem *(kame)* ... who
quente *(kane-chee)* ... hot
querer *(kair-air)* ... to want
quero *(kair-oo)* ... (I) want
quinhentos *(keen-yehn-toosh)* ... five hundred
quinta-feira, a *(keen-tah-fay-rah)* ... Thursday
quinze *(keen-zee)* ... fifteen, quarter (time)

R

R$ ... abbreviation for real (Brazilian currency)
raça, a *(hah-sah)* ... race
rádio, o *(hah-joo)* ... radio
raio, o *(hi-oo)* ... ray
rápido/a *(hah-pee-doo)* ... rapid
reação, a *(heh-ah-sown)* ... reaction
reais, os *(heh-eyes)* ... reals
real, o *(heh-ahl)* ... real (unit of Brazilian currency)
rebelião, a *(heh-beh-lee-own)* ... rebellion
receber *(heh-seh-bair)* ... to receive
recebimento de bagagem, o *(heh-seh-bee-mehn-too)(jee)(bah-gah-zhame)* ... baggage claim
refeição, a *(heh-fay-sown)* ... meal
refrigerante, o *(heh-free-zheh-rahn-chee)* ... soft drink
regular *(heh-goo-lar)* ... regular
relação, a *(heh-lah-sown)* ... relation
relaxado/a *(heh-lah-shah-doo)* ... relaxed
religião, a *(heh-lee-zhee-own)* ... religion
relógio, o *(heh-loh-zhee-oo)* ... clock, watch
relojoaria, a *(heh-loh-zhoh-ah-ree-ah)* ... watchmaker's shop
repetir *(heh-peh-cheer)* ... to repeat
repita por favor *(heh-pee-tah)(por)(fah-vor)* ... please repeat!
república, a *(heh-poo-blee-kah)* ... republic
reserva, a *(heh-zair-vah)* ... reservation
reservar *(heh-zair-var)* ... to reserve
resposta, a *(hehs-pohs-tah)* ... answer
restaurante, o *(hehs-tow-rahn-chee)* ... restaurant
revista, a *(heh-vees-tah)* ... magazine
revolução, a *(heh-voh-loo-sown)* ... revolution
rico/a *(hee-koo)* ... rich
rodoviária, a *(hoh-doh-vee-ah-ree-ah)* ... bus station
romano/a *(hoh-mah-noo)* ... Roman
romântico/a *(hoh-mahn-chee-koo)* ... romantic
rosa *(hoh-zah)* ... pink
roupa, a *(hoh-pah)* ... clothing
roupa de cama, a *(hoh-pah)(jee)(kah-mah)* ... bedding
roupão de banho, o *(hoh-pown)(jeh)(bahn-yoo)* ... bathrobe
roupas íntimas, as *(hoh-pahs)(een-chee-mahs)* ... lingerie
rua, a *(hoo-ah)* ... street
rubi, o *(hoo-bee)* ... ruby
russo *(hoos-soo)* ... Russian

S

sábado, o *(sah-bah-doo)* ... Saturday
saber *(sah-bair)* ... to know (a fact), to know (how to)
sabonete, o *(sah-boh-neh-chee)* ... soap
saia, a *(sy-ah)* ... skirt
saída de emergência, a *(sah-ee-dah)(jeh)(eh-mair-zhayn-see-ah)* ... emergency exit
saída, a *(sah-ee-dah)* ... exit
sal, o *(sahl)* ... salt
sala de espera, a *(sah-lah)(jeh)(es-peh-rah)* ... waiting room
sala de jantar, a *(sah-lah)(deh)(zhahn-tar)* ... dining room
sala, a *(sah-lah)* ... living room
salada, a *(sah-lah-dah)* ... salad
salário, o *(sah-lah-ree-oo)* ... salary
salmão, o *(sahl-mown)* ... salmon
sandálias, as *(sahn-dah-lee-ahs)* ... sandals
sanduíche, o *(sahn-doo-ee-shee)* ... sandwich
santo, o *(sahn-too)* ... saint
são *(sown)* ... are
sapatos, os *(sah-pah-toosh)* ... shoes
sardinha, a *(sar-jeen-yah)* ... sardine
saudável *(sow-dah-vel)* ... healthy
se diz *(seh)(jeesh)* ... one says
seção de não fumantes, a *(seh-sown)(jee)(nown)(foo-mahn-chees)* ... non-smoking section
seção de perdidos e achados, a *(seh-sown)(jeh)(pair-jee-doosh)(eh)(ah-shah-doosh)* ... lost-and-found office
secretária, a *(seh-kreh-tah-ree-ah)* ... secretary (♀)
secretário, o *(seh-kreh-tah-ree-oo)* ... secretary (♂)
sede, a *(seh-jee)* ... thirst
seguinte *(seh-geen-chee)* ... following
segunda *(seh-goon-dah)* ... second
segunda-feira, a *(seh-goon-dah-fay-rah)* ... Monday
segundo, o *(seh-goon-doo)* ... second (time)
seis *(saysh)* ... six
seleção, a *(seh-leh-sown)* ... selection
selo, o *(seh-loo)* ... stamp
sem *(same)* ... without
semana, a *(seh-mah-nah)* ... week
senhor, o *(sehn-yor)* ... Mr., sir
senhora, a *(sehn-yoh-rah)* ... Mrs, Ms.
senhorita, a *(sehn-yoh-ree-tah)* ... Miss
sensação, a *(sehn-sah-sown)* ... sensation
sentado *(sehn-tah-doo)* ... seated
serviço, o *(sair-vee-soo)* ... service
serviços ao cliente, os *(sair-vee-soosh)(ah-oh)(klee-ehn-chee)* ... customer service
servir *(sair-veer)* ... to fit (clothing), to serve
sessenta *(sehs-sehn-tah)* ... sixty
sete *(seh-chee)* ... seven
setembro *(seh-tem-broo)* ... September
setenta *(seh-tehn-tah)* ... seventy
seu *(seh-oo)* ... your, his, her, its
severo/a *(seh-veh-roo)* ... severe
sexta-feira, a *(saysh-tah-fay-rah)* ... Friday
short, o *(shorch)* ... shorts
sidra, a *(see-drah)* ... cider
siga *(see-gah)* ... continue!
silêncio, o *(see-lane-see-oo)* ... silence
sim *(seem)* ... yes
simples *(seem-pleesh)* ... simple
simultâneo/a *(see-mool-tah-neh-oo)* ... simultaneous
sinfonia, a *(seen-foh-nee-ah)* ... symphony
sistema, o *(sees-teh-mah)* ... system
sobre *(soh-bree)* ... on top of, over, on
sobremesa, a *(soh-breh-meh-zah)* ... dessert
social *(soh-see-ahl)* ... social
sofá, o *(soh-fah)* ... sofa
sólido/a *(soh-lee-doo)* ... solid
sopa, a *(soh-pah)* ... soup
sorvete, o *(sor-veh-chee)* ... ice cream
sou *(soh)* ... (I) am
sua *(soo-ah)* ... your
suco, o *(soo-koo)* ... juice
suéter, a *(soo-eh-tair)* ... sweater
Suíça, a *(swee-sah)* ... Switzerland
sul *(sool)* ... south
sunga, a *(soon-gah)* ... swimsuit (♂)
supermercado, o *(soo-pair-mair-kah-doo)* ... supermarket
sutiã, o *(soo-chee-own)* ... bra

T

tabaco, o *(tah-bah-koo)* ... tobacco
talho, o *(tahl-yoo)* ... butcher shop (Portugal)
tamanho, o *(tah-mahn-yoo)* ... size

também *(tahm-bame)* ... also

tapete, o *(tah-peh-chee)* ... carpet

tarde, a *(tar-jee)* ... afternoon

tarifa, a *(tah-ree-fah)* ... tariff, fare

táxi, o *(tahk-see)* ... taxi

tchau *(chow)* ... good-bye, bye

teatro, o *(teh-ah-troo)* ... theater

técnico/a *(tek-nee-koo)* ... technical

telefonar *(teh-leh-foh-nar)* ... to telephone, to call

telefone, o *(teh-leh-foh-nee)* ... telephone

telefonista, a *(teh-leh-foh-nees-tah)* ... operator

telegrama, o *(teh-leh-grah-mah)* ... telegram

televisão, a *(teh-leh-vee-zown)* ... television

tem *(tame)* ... (you) have

temperatura, a *(tame-peh-rah-too-rah)* ... temperature

tempo, o *(tame-poo)* ... weather

tenho *(tehn-yoo)* ... (I) have

tênis, os *(tay-nees)* ... tennis shoes

ter *(tair)* ... to have

ter que *(tair)(kay)* ... to have to, must

terça-feira, a *(tair-sah-fay-rah)* ... Tuesday

terçeiro/a *(tair-say-roo)* ... third

terminal, o *(tair-mee-nahl)* ... terminal

termômetro, o *(tair-moh-meh-troo)* ... thermometer

terno, o *(tair-noo)* ... suit

térreo, o *(tair-heh-oo)* ... ground floor

tia, a *(chee-ah)* ... aunt

tinturaria, a *(cheen-too-rah-ree-ah)* ... dry cleaner's

tio, o *(chee-oo)* ... uncle

típico/a *(chee-pee-koo)* ... typical

tira-gosto, o *(chee-rah-gohs-too)* ... appetizer

toalha, a *(toh-ahl-yah)* ... towel

tomar *(toh-mar)* ... to take

tomate, o *(toh-mah-chee)* ... tomato

torta, a *(tor-tah)* ... pie

total, o *(toh-tahl)* ... total

tráfego, o *(trah-feh-goo)* ... traffic

trágico/a *(trah-zhee-koo)* ... tragic

tranqüilo/a *(trahn-kwee-loo)* ... tranquil, quiet

transparente *(trahns-pah-rehn-chee)* ... transparent

transportar *(trahns-por-tar)* ... to transport

travesseiro, o *(trah-vehs-say-roo)* ... pillow

trem, o *(trame)* ... train

três *(traysh)* ... three

treze *(treh-zee)* ... thirteen

trezentos *(treh-zehn-toosh)* ... three hundred

triângulo, o *(tree-ahn-goo-loo)* ... triangle

tribunal de justiça, o *(tree-boo-nahl)(deh)(zhoos-chee-sah)* ... courthouse, Court of Justice

trinta *(treen-tah)* ... thirty

triunfante *(tree-oon-fahn-chee)* ... triumphant

trivial *(tree-vee-ahl)* ... trivial

trocar *(troh-kar)* ... to transfer (vehicles), to change (money)

troco, o *(troh-koo)* ... change (money)

trompeta, a *(trohm-peh-tah)* ... trumpet

tropical *(troh-pee-kahl)* ... tropical

tu *(too)* ... you (familiar)

tudo *(too-doo)* ... everything

Tudo bem? *(too-doo)(bame)* ... How's it going?

tumulto, o *(too-mool-too)* ... tumult

túnel, o *(too-nel)* ... tunnel

turismo, o *(too-rees-moo)* ... tourism

turista, o/a *(too-rees-tah)* ... tourist

tutor, o *(too-tor)* ... tutor

U

último/a *(ool-chee-moo)* ... ultimate, last

ultrapassar *(ool-trah-pahs-sar)* ... to pass (vehicles)

um *(oom)* ... a, an (♂, singular)

uma *(oo-mah)* ... a, an (♀, singular)

união, a *(oo-nee-own)* ... union

uniforme, o *(oo-nee-for-mee)* ... uniform

universidade, a *(oo-nee-vair-see-dah-jee)* ... university

urgência, a *(oor-zhayn-see-ah)* ... urgency

urgente *(oor-zhehn-chee)* ... urgent

Uruguai, o *(oo-roo-gwhy)* ... Uruguay

usado/a *(oo-zah-doo)* ... used

usar *(oo-zar)* ... to use

usual *(oo-zoo-ahl)* ... usual

utensílio, o *(oo-tehn-see-lee-oo)* ... utensil

utilidade, a *(oo-chee-lee-dah-jee)* ... utility

V

vaca, a *(vah-kah)* ... beef

vacina, a *(vah-see-nah)* ... vaccine

vaga, a *(vah-gah)* ... vacancy

vagão, o *(vah-gown)* ... wagon, compartment

vai *(vy)* ... go!

vaidade, a *(vy-dah-jee)* ... vanity

vale, o *(vah-lee)* ... valley

válido/a *(vah-lee-doo)* ... valid

variedade, a *(vah-ree-eh-dah-jee)* ... variety

vários/as *(vah-ree-oosh)* ... various

vaso sanitário, o *(vah-zoo)(sah-nee-tah-ree-oo)* ... toilet

vaso, o *(vah-zoo)* ... vase

Vaticano, o *(vah-chee-kah-noo)* ... the Vatican

vegetariano, o *(veh-zheh-tah-ree-ah-noo)* ... vegetarian

veículo, o *(veh-ee-koo-loo)* ... vehicle

velho/a *(vel-yoo)* ... old

velocidade, a *(veh-loh-see-dah-jee)* ... velocity, speed

vem *(vame)* ... comes

vender *(vehn-dair)* ... to sell

Venezuela, a *(veh-neh-zoo-eh-lah)* ... Venezuela

venta *(vehn-tah)* ... it is windy

ver *(vair)* ... to see

verão, o *(veh-rown)* ... summer

verbo, o *(vair-boo)* ... verb

vermelho/a *(vair-mel-yoo)* ... red

véspera de ano novo, a *(vehs-peh-rah)(jee)(ah-noo)(noh-voo)* ... New Year's Eve

véspera de Natal, a *(vehs-peh-rah)(jeh)(nah-tahl)* ... Christmas Eve

vestido, o *(vehs-chee-doo)* ... dress

vestir *(vehs-cheer)* ... to fit (clothing), to wear

vestuário, o *(vehs-too-ah-ree-oo)* ... clothing

via aérea *(vee-ah)(ah-air-ee-ah)* ... by airmail

viagem, a *(vee-ah-zhame)* ... trip

viajante, o/a *(vee-ah-zhahn-chee)* ... traveler

viajar *(vee-ah-zhar)* ... to travel

vídeos, os *(vee-joosh)* ... videos

vinagre, o *(vee-nah-gree)* ... vinegar

vinho, o *(veen-yoo)* ... wine

vinho tinto, o *(veen-yoo)(cheen-too)* ... red wine

vinte *(veen-chee)* ... twenty

violeta *(vee-oh-leh-tah)* ... violet

violino, o *(vee-oh-lee-noo)* ... violin

vir *(veer)* ... to come

virar *(vee-rar)* ... to turn

vire *(vee-ree)* ... turn!

visa, a *(vee-zah)* ... visa

viseira, a *(vee-zay-rah)* ... visor

visita, a *(vee-zee-tah)* ... visit

visitar *(vee-zee-tar)* ... to visit

vista, a *(vees-tah)* ... view

vitamina, a *(vee-tah-mee-nah)* ... milk blended with fruit

vitela, a *(vee-teh-lah)* ... veal

viver *(vee-vair)* ... to live

você *(voh-say)* ... you

vocês *(voh-saysh)* ... you (plural)

X

xícara, a *(shee-kah-rah)* ... cup

Z

zero *(zeh-roo)* ... zero

zodíaco, o *(zoh-jee-ah-koo)* ... zodiac

zona, a *(zoh-nah)* ... zone

zoologia, a *(zoh-oh-loh-zhee-ah)* ... zoology

25 Beverage and Menu Guides

This beverage guide is intended to explain the variety of beverages available to you while **em Brasil ou** any other Portuguese-speaking country. It is by no means complete. Some of the experimenting has been left up to you, but this should get you started.

BEBIDAS QUENTES (hot drinks)

café/cafezinho .... coffee
café com leite .... coffee with milk
espresso .... espresso
capuccino .... capuccino
chocolate quente .... hot chocolate

chá .... tea
chá com limão .... tea with lemon
chá com leite .... tea with milk

BEBIDAS FRIAS (cold drinks)

leite .... milk
milk-shake .... milkshake
vitamina .... milk and fruit drink
suco .... juice
suco de laranja ..... orange juice
suco de tomate ..... tomato juice
água .... water
água mineral .... mineral water
água com gás .... sparkling water
água tônica .... tonic water
sidra .... cider
chá mate .... Brazilian iced tea
refrigerante .... soft drink
guaraná .... soft drink made from Amazonian berries
gelo .... ice

VINHOS (wine)

There are four main types of **vinho**, but quality levels vary drastically. **Vinho** can be purchased by the **garrafa** (bottle) or by the **copo** (glass).

vinho tinto .... red wine
vinho branco ...... white wine
vinho rosé .... rosé wine
vinho tinto suave .. light red wine

vinho de mesa ..... ordinary table wine
vinho doce .... sweet wine
vinho seco .... dry wine
champanhe .... champagne
vinho do porto ..... port wine
sangria .... wine drink made with fruits, brandy, lemonade and ice

CERVEJAS (beer)

There are many brands of beer. **Cerveja** is generally purchased by the **garrafa** (bottle) or **chope** (draught).

BEBIDAS ALCOÓLICAS (alcohol)

vodca .... vodka
uísque .... whiskey, bourbon
uísque escocês ... scotch
gim .... gin
rum .... rum
cachaça .... liquor distilled directly from the unrefined sugar cane, fermented, then boiled down to a concentrate. The national drink of Brazil which retains the scent of sugar cane.
conhaque .... cognac
licor .... liqueur
batida .... cocktail of **cachaça** blended with fruit and condensed milk
caipirinha .... cocktail of **cachaça**, lime and sugar

CUT ALONG DOTTED LINE, FOLD AND TAKE WITH YOU

Pão e Massa (bread and pasta)

pão	bread
bisnaga	baguette
pão integral	whole wheat bread
pão de milho	corn bread
pão de batata	potato bread
pão francês	French bread
torrada	toast
espagueti	spaghetti

Legumes (vegetables)

agrião	watercress
alcachofra	artichokes
alface	lettuce
aspargos	asparagus
batata doce	sweet potatoes
beringela	eggplant
beterrabas	beets
cebola	onions
cenoura	carrots
cogumelos	mushrooms
couve-flor	cauliflower
ervilhas	peas
espinafre	spinach
feijão	black beans
feijão roxo	kidney beans
lentilha	lentils
milho	corn
rabanete	radishes

Batatas (potatoes)

batatas assadas	baked potatoes
batatas cozidas	boiled potatoes
batatas fritas	French fried potatoes
batatas recheadas	stuffed potatoes
purê de batatas	mashed potatoes
salada de batatas	potato salad

Lingüiças (sausages)

salaminho	salami
lingüiça de porco	pork sausage
toucinho	bacon
presunto	ham

FOLD HERE

Fruta (fruit)

abacate	avocado
abacaxi	pineapple
ameixa	plum
banana	banana
cajú	cashew fruit
cereja	cherry
côco	coconut
coquetel de frutas	fruit cocktail
damasco	apricot
figo	fig
frambueza	raspberries
fruta-de conde	sweetsop
goiaba	guava
jaca	jackfruit
laranja	orange
limão	lime
maçã	apple
mamão	papaya
manga	mango
maracujá	passion fruit
melancia	watermelon
melão	melon
morango	strawberries
pêra	pear
pêssego	peach
uvas	grapes

Bebidas (beverages)

refrigerantes	soft drinks
cerveja	beer
leite	milk
café	coffee
suco de . . .	juice of . . .
limonada	lemonade
água mineral	mineral water

(bohm) *(ah-peh-chee-chee)*
Bom apetite!
enjoy your meal

FOLD HERE

O Cardápio

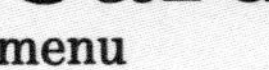

menu

Modo de Preparo

à milanesa	in batter
ao forno	baked
assado	roasted
cozido	cooked, broiled
crú	raw
frito	fried
gratinado	grated, au gratin
grelhado	grilled
no vapor	steamed
picante	spicy
sauté	sautéed
mal passado	rare
ao ponto	medium
bem passado	well-done

Diversos (general)

alho	garlic
azeite	olive oil
geléia	jam
mel	honey
molho	sauce
mostarda	mustard
pimenta	pepper
queijo	cheese
sal	salt
vinagre	vinegar
bolo	cake
doce	pastry
sorvete	ice cream
creme chantilly	whipped cream

Tira-gostos (appetizers)

bolinho de bacalhau	codfish cake
bolinho de caranguejo	crab cake
coxinha de galinha	chicken croquettes
aipim frito	deep fried cassava
provolone à milanesa	provolone cheese balls breaded and fried
ostras	oysters
espeto de camarão	barbecued shrimp usually brought to you on the beach
caviar	caviar
porções variadas	assorted appetizers
frios	cold cuts
presunto defumado	smoked ham

Sopas (soups)

feijoada	stew of black beans, sausage, pork, dried beef, onions, garlic and tomato served with boiled rice and orange slices
canja de galinha	chicken soup
tutu	mush of beans, bacon, beef, sausage, manioc flour and onion
xinxim de galinha	spicy chicken and shrimp stew, served with rice

Ovos (eggs)

bem cozidos	hard-boiled eggs
mal cozidos	soft-boiled eggs
fritos	fried eggs
mexidos	scrambled eggs
poché	poached eggs
omelete de . . .	omelette with . . .
suflê	soufflé

Carne (meat)

churrasco	portions of barbecued meat

FOLD HERE

Vaca (beef)

almôndegas	meat balls
fígado	liver
filé	filet, steak
língua	tongue
rosbife	roast beef

Porco (pork)

costeleta de porco	pork chops
lombo	pork loin
lombo recheado	stuffed pork loin
porco assado	roast pork
presunto	ham

Cordeiro (lamb)

cordeiro assado	roast lamb
costeleta de cordeiro	lamb chops

Aves (poultry and game)

codorna	quail
coelho	rabbit
faisão	pheasant
frango	young chicken
galheto	grilled young chicken
galinha	chicken
pato	duck
pato ao tucupi	roast duck with a manioc juice
perdiz	partridge
peru	turkey

Sobremesas (desserts)

mousse de chocolate	chocolate mousse
mousse de maracujá	passion fruit mousse
pudim de leite	caramel flan
quindim	flan of egg yolk, coconut and sugar
Romeu e Julieta	guava paste and cheese with cream
sorvete de fruta	fruit ice cream
torta de morango	strawberry pie

FOLD HERE

Peixe e Frutos do Mar (fish and seafood)

acarajé	large fritter of black-eyed beans and shrimp
atum	tuna
bacalhau	cod
badejo	bass
camarão	prawns, shrimp
caranguejo	crab
lagosta	lobster
linguado	sole
lula	squid
mexilhão	mussels
moqueca	seafood stew
moqueca de camarão	shrimp stew
moqueca de peixe	halibut stew
siri	stuffed crab
sururu	mussel dish
truta	trout
vatapá	shrimp, coconut milk, nuts and spices served with rice
zarzuela de mariscos	thick seafood stew

Saladas (salads)

salada de alface	lettuce salad
salada de batata	potato salad
salada da casa	seasonal salad
salada de frutas	fruit salad
salada de legumes	vegetable salad
salada de mista	mixed salad
salada de pepino	cucumber salad
salada de tomate	tomato salad
salpicão de galinha	chicken salad

Acompanhamentos ou Guarnições (side dishes)

couve	collard greens
arroz	rice
farofa	manioc flour mixture
feijão	black beans
fubá	corn meal

(eh-oo)
eu

(noys)
nós

(eh-lee)
ele

(voh-say)
você

(eh-lah)
ela

(eh-leesh) (eh-lahs)
eles/elas

(fah-lar)
falar
(eh-oo) (fah-loo)
eu falo

(kair-air)
querer
(eh-oo) (kair-oo)
eu quero

(kohm-prar)
comprar
(eh-oo) (kohm-proo)
eu compro

(tair)
ter
(eh-oo) (tehn-yoo)
eu tenho

(ahn-dar)
andar
(eh-oo) (ahn-doo)
eu ando

(veer)
vir
(eh-oo) (vehn-yoo)
eu venho

we	I
you	he
they (♂) / they (♀)	she
to want I want	to speak I speak
to have I have	to buy I buy
to come I come	to walk I walk

(ehn-trar) **entrar** *(eh-oo)* *(ehn-troo)* **eu entro**	*(vee-vair)* **viver** *(eh-oo)* *(vee-voo)* **eu vivo**
(preh-see-zar) *(dee)* **precisar de** *(eh-oo)* *(preh-see-zoo)* *(dee)* **eu preciso de**	*(vehn-dair)* **vender** *(eh-oo)* *(vehn-doo)* **eu vendo**
(ah-prehn-dair) **aprender** *(eh-oo)* *(ah-prehn-doo)* **eu aprendo**	*(heh-peh-cheer)* **repetir** *(eh-oo)* *(heh-pee-too)* **eu repito**
(koh-mair) **comer** *(eh-oo)* *(koh-moo)* **eu como**	*(beh-bair)* **beber** *(eh-oo)* *(beh-boo)* **eu bebo**
(ehn-kohn-trar) **encontrar** *(eh-oo)* *(ehn-kohn-troo)* **eu encontro**	*(eh-tehn-dair)* **entender** *(eh-oo)* *(ehn-tehn-doo)* **eu entendo**
(mahn-dar) **mandar** *(eh-oo)* *(mahn-doo)* **eu mando**	*(es-kreh-vair)* **escrever** *(eh-oo)* *(es-kreh-voo)* **eu escrevo**

to live

I live

to enter

I enter

to sell

I sell

to need

I need

to repeat

I repeat

to learn

I learn

to drink

I drink

to eat

I eat

to understand

I understand

to find/meet

I find/meet

to write

I write

to send

I send

(teh-leh-foh-nar)
telefonar
(eh-oo) *(teh-leh-foh-noo)*
eu telefono

(pah-gar)
pagar
(eh-oo) *(pah-goo)*
eu pago

(dor-meer)
dormir
(eh-oo) *(dur-moo)*
eu durmo

(mee) *(dah)* *(por)* *(fah-vor)*
Me dá . . . por favor.

(fah-zair)
fazer
(eh-oo) *(fah-soo)*
eu faço

(jee-zair)
dizer
(eh-oo) *(jee-goo)*
eu digo

(vair)
ver
(eh-oo) *(veh-zhoo)*
eu vejo

(eer)
ir
(eh-oo) *(voh)*
eu vou

(lair)
ler
(eh-oo) *(lay-oo)*
eu leio

(poh-dair)
poder
(eh-oo) *(pohs-soo)*
eu posso

(tair) *(kay)*
ter que
(eh-oo) *(tehn-yoo)* *(kay)*
eu tenho que

(sah-bair)
saber
(eh-oo) *(say)*
eu sei

to pay

I pay

to telephone

I telephone

Give me . . . please.

to sleep

I sleep

to say

I say

to make/do

I make/do

to go

I go

to see

I see

to be able to/can

I am able to/can

to read

I read

to know (fact)/(how to)

I know

to have to/must

I have to/must

(peh-jeer) **pedir** *(eh-oo) (peh-soo)* **eu peço**	*(eer) (jee) (ah-vee-own)* **ir de avião** *(eh-oo) (voh) (jee) (ah-vee-own)* **eu vou de avião**
(vee-ah-zhar) **viajar** *(eh-oo) (vee-ah-zhoo)* **eu viajo**	*(pair-dair)* **perder** *(eh-oo) (pair-koo)* **eu perco**
(sheh-gar) **chegar** *(eh-oo) (sheh-goo)* **eu chego**	*(troh-kar)* **trocar** *(eh-oo) (troh-koo)* **eu troco**
(fah-zair) (ah) (mah-lah) **fazer a mala** *(eh-oo) (fah-soo) (ah) (mah-lah)* **eu faço a mala**	*(eer) (jee) (kar-hoo)* **ir de carro** *(eh-oo) (voh) (jee) (kar-hoo)* **eu vou de carro**
(ah) **há**	*(voh-say) (tame)* **Você tem . . . ?**
(par-cheer) **partir** *(eh-oo) (par-too)* **eu parto**	*(toh-mar)* **tomar** *(eh-oo) (toh-moo)* **eu tomo**

to fly/go by airplane

I fly/go by airplane

to order/request

I order/request

to lose

I lose

to travel

I travel

to transfer/change

I transfer/change

to arrive

I arrive

to drive/go by car

I drive/go by car

to pack

I pack

Do you have . . .

there is/there are

to take

I take

to depart

I depart

(oh-zhee) **hoje**	*(koh-moo) (vy)* **Como vai?**
(ohn-tame) **ontem**	*(por) (fah-vor)* **por favor**
(ah-mahn-yahn) **amanhã**	*(oh-bree-gah-doo) (oh-bree-gah-dah)* **obrigado / obrigada**
(kohm) (lee-sehn-sah) **com licença**	*(dehs-kool-pee)* **desculpe**
(chow) (ah-deh-oos) **tchau / adeus**	*(kwahn-too) (koos-tah) (ees-soo)* **Quanto custa isso?**
(grahn-jee) (peh-kay-noo) **grande - pequeno**	*(ah-bair-too) (feh-shah-doo)* **aberto - fechado**

How are you?

today

please

yesterday

thank you (♂)/
thank you (♀)

tomorrow

excuse me
(I'm sorry)

excuse me
(when interrupting)

How much does
this cost?

good-bye

open - closed

large - small

(doh-ehn-chee) *(sow-dah-vel)* **doente - saudável**	*(bohm)* *(mow)* **bom - mau**
(kane-chee) *(free-oo)* **quente - frio**	*(koor-too)* *(lohn-goo)* **curto - longo**
(ahl-too) *(by-shoo)* **alto - baixo**	*(ehm)* *(see-mah)* *(ehm-by-shoo)* **em cima - embaixo**
(es-kair-dah) *(jee-ray-tah)* **esquerda - direita**	*(hah-pee-doo)* *(deh-vah-gar)* **rápido - devagar**
(vel-yoo) *(zhoh-vame)* **velho - jovem**	*(bah-rah-too)* *(kah-roo)* **barato - caro**
(poh-bree) *(hee-koo)* **pobre - rico**	*(mwee-too)* *(poh-koo)* **muito - pouco**

good - bad

ill - healthy

short - long

hot - cold

upstairs - downstairs

tall - short

fast - slow

left - right

inexpensive - expensive

old - young

a lot - a little

poor - rich

Now that you've finished...

You've done it!

You've completed all the Steps, stuck your labels, flashed your cards and cut out your menu guide. Do you realize how far you've come and how much you've learned?

You can now confidently

- ask questions,
- understand directions,
- make reservations,
- order food and
- shop anywhere.

And you can do it all in a foreign language! You can now go anywhere — from a large cosmopolitan restaurant to a small, out-of-the-way village where no one speaks English. Your experiences will be much more enjoyable and worry-free now that you speak the language.

Yes, learning a foreign language can be fun.

Kristine Kershul

Send us this order form with your check, money order or credit card details. If paying by credit card, you may fax your order to **(206) 284-3660** or call us toll-free at **(800) 488-5068**. All prices are in US dollars and are subject to change without notice.

* What about shipping costs?

STANDARD DELIVERY per address

If your items total	please add
up to $ 20.00	$5.00
$20.01 - $ 40.00	$6.00
$40.01 - $ 60.00	$7.00
$60.01 - $ 80.00	$8.00
$80.01 - $ 100.00	$9.00

If over $100, please call for charges.

For shipping outside the U.S., please call, fax or e-mail us at info@bbks.com for the best-possible shipping rates.

Formulário de Encomenda

order form

10 minutes a day® Series	QTY.	PRICE	TOTAL
ARABIC *in 10 minutes a day*®		$19.95	
CHINESE *in 10 minutes a day*®		$19.95	
FRENCH *in 10 minutes a day*®		$19.95	
GERMAN *in 10 minutes a day*®		$19.95	
HEBREW *in 10 minutes a day*®		$19.95	
INGLÉS *en 10 minutos al día*®		$19.95	
ITALIAN *in 10 minutes a day*®		$19.95	
JAPANESE *in 10 minutes a day*®		$19.95	
NORWEGIAN *in 10 minutes a day*®		$19.95	
PORTUGUESE *in 10 minutes a day*®		$18.95	
RUSSIAN *in 10 minutes a day*®		$19.95	
SPANISH *in 10 minutes a day*®		$18.95	
***10 minutes a day*® AUDIO**	**QTY.**	**PRICE**	**TOTAL**
FRENCH *in 10 minutes a day*® AUDIO		$59.95	
FRENCH AUDIO CDs only *(no book)*		$42.95	
ITALIAN *in 10 minutes a day*® AUDIO		$59.95	
ITALIAN AUDIO CDs only *(no book)*		$42.95	
SPANISH *in 10 minutes a day*® AUDIO		$59.95	
SPANISH AUDIO CDs only *(no book)*		$42.95	
***Language Map*® Series**	**QTY.**	**PRICE**	**TOTAL**
ARABIC *a language map*®		$7.95	
CHINESE *a language map*®		$7.95	
FRENCH *a language map*®		$7.95	
GERMAN *a language map*®		$7.95	
GREEK *a language map*®		$7.95	
HAWAIIAN *a language map*®		$7.95	
HEBREW *a language map*®		$7.95	
INGLÉS *un mapa del lenguaje*®		$7.95	
ITALIAN *a language map*®		$7.95	
JAPANESE *a language map*®		$7.95	
NORWEGIAN *a language map*®		$7.95	
POLISH *a language map*®		$7.95	
PORTUGUESE *a language map*®		$7.95	
RUSSIAN *a language map*®		$7.95	
SPANISH *a language map*®		$7.95	
VIETNAMESE *a language map*®		$7.95	

† For delivery to individuals in Washington State, you must add 8.8% sales tax on the item total and the shipping costs combined. If your order is being delivered outside Washington State, you do not need to add sales tax.

Item Total	
* Shipping	+
Total	
† Sales Tax	+
ORDER TOTAL	

Name ____________________

Address ____________________

____

City ____________ State ______ Zip ______

Day Phone (________)____________________

❑ My check or money order for $____________ is enclosed.
Please make checks and money orders payable to Bilingual Books, Inc.

❑ Bill my credit card ❑ VISA ❑ MC ❑ AMEX
No. ____________________ Exp. date ____/____
Signature ____________________

Bilingual Books, Inc. • 1719 West Nickerson Street
Seattle, WA 98119 USA

10 minutes a day® AUDIO CD Series

by Kristine K. Kershul

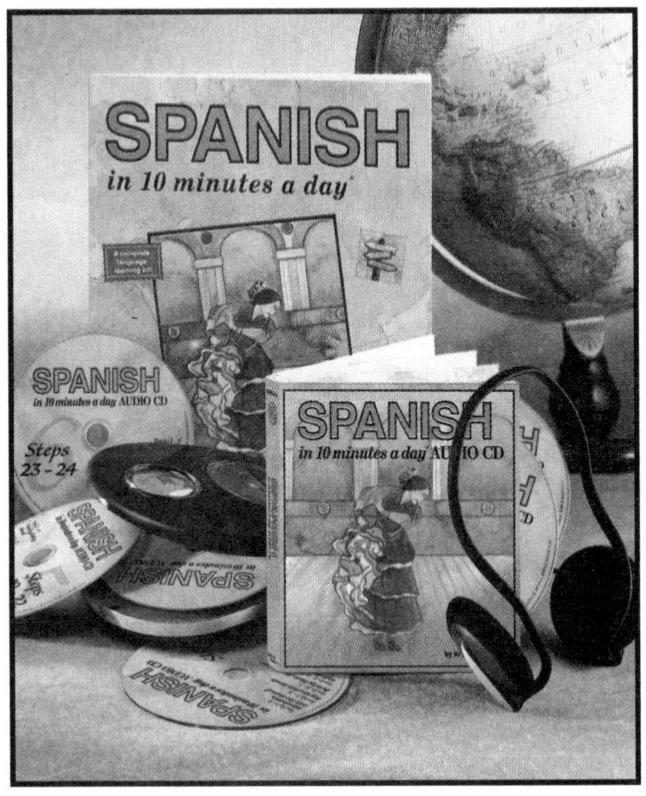

The ***10 minutes a day*® AUDIO CD Series** is based on the immensely successful ***10 minutes a day*®** Series. Millions of people around the world have used the ***10 minutes a day*®** Series for over two decades.

- Eight hours of personal instruction on six CDs.
- Use the CDs in combination with the companion book, and maximize your progress as you see AND hear the language.
- Listen to native speakers and practice right along with them.
- Suitable for the classroom, the homeschooler, as well as business and leisure travelers.
- The CDs in the ***10 minutes a day*® AUDIO CD Series** may also be purchased separately from the ***10 minutes a day*®** books.

Language Map® Series

by Kristine K. Kershul

These handy ***Language Maps*®** provide the essential words and phrases to cover the basics for any trip.

- Over 1,000 essential words and phrases divided into convenient categories.
- Laminated , folding design allows for quicker reference while resisting spills, tearing, and damage from frequent use.
- Durable, to hold up to being sat on, dropped, and stuffed into backpacks, pockets, and purses.
- An absolute must for anyone traveling abroad or studying at home.

For a list of available languages and ordering information, please see the order form on the previous page.

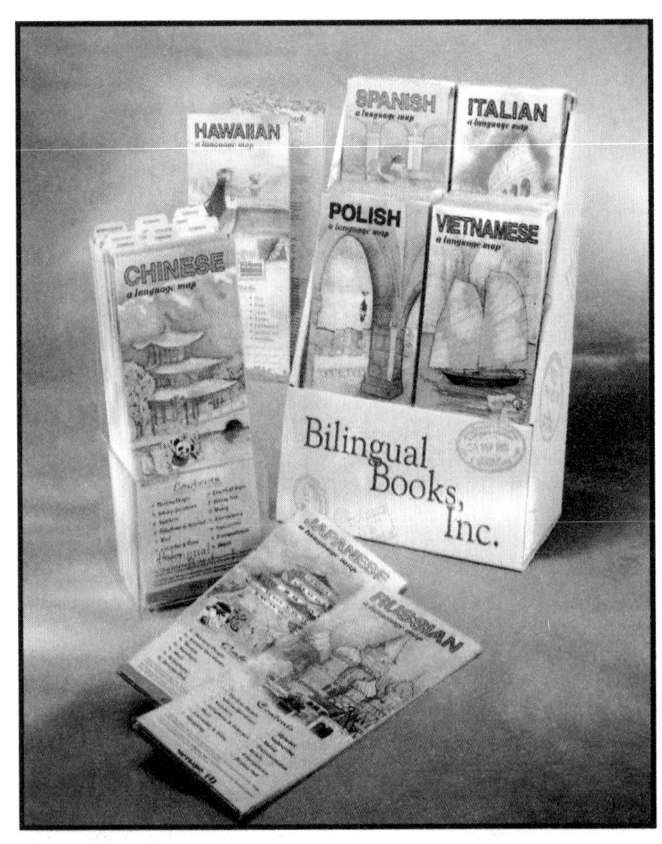